Christianity for

C000063306

Christianity for the Twenty-First Century

The Life and Work of Alexander Men

edited by
Elizabeth Roberts and Ann Shukman

SCM PRESS LTD

0 334 02613 X

Royalties on this book will be donated to the
Alexander Men Foundation
c/o SS Cosma & Damian
Stoleshnikov pereulok 2, Moscow 103009

First published 1996
by SCM Press Ltd
9–17 St Albans Place, London N1 0NX

Typeset at The Spartan Press Ltd,
Lymington, Hampshire
Printed in Great Britain by
Biddles Ltd, Guildford and King's Lynn

Dedicated to the Memory of
John and Irina Findlow

Contents

About this Book   ix

Editors' Notes   x

Foreword *by Rt Revd Richard Harries, Bishop of Oxford*   xi

Introduction *by Ann Shukman*   1

Part I: The Christian Life Today

1   Why be a Christian?   29

2   Religion, Knowledge of God, and the Problem
    of Evil   39

3   Faith and its Enemies   54

4   A Credo for Today's Christian   68

5   Christianity: The Universal Vision   75

Part II: The Russian Experience

6   Religion, the 'Cult of Personality', and the Secular State 107

7   Russia in Crisis   139

8   Two Understandings of Christianity   151

9   The Russian Orthodox Church Today   164

Contents

Part III: Epilogue

10 The Christian Hope: 'Karabakh' or Bethlehem?   173

11 Christianity for the Twenty-First Century   179

Afterword *by Cardinal Jean-Marie Lustiger*   193

Notes   197

Select Bibliography   213

Index   215

About this Book

Many people have helped this anthology reach publication. Elizabeth Roberts' personal contact with Fr Alexander Men during his lifetime led her immediately after his death in 1990 to initiate the translation of his work. In 1992, at her instigation, the Bowerdean Press published a short collection of his sermons from Lent to Pentecost under the title *Awake to Life!* Her contribution to the present book was to initiate the idea of a more comprehensive selection. She liased from the start with Fr Alexander's family and friends in Moscow and Paris, gathered the team of volunteer translators, and invited Ann Shukman to be the text editor. Ann Shukman is responsible for the book in its final form.

Thanks are due first of all to those of Fr Alexander's followers in Russia who made the selection, who have given every encouragement to this English anthology, and who have supplied many explanations. Among them are Abbot Ignaty Krekshin, Natalya Fedorovna Men, Ekaterina Genieva, and Aleksandr Gurevich.

The translators include: David E. Burke, Xenia Dennen, Terry and Grace Garrett, Donald Henderson, Richard Kindersley, Suzanne Pattle, Elizabeth Roberts, and Ann Shukman. Particular thanks are due to Richard Kindersley for much painstaking work on the annotations. Fr Sergei Hackel read the typescript.

Help with the oriental names and references was supplied by Anita Singh and Steve Tsang, both of St Antony's College, Oxford.

To all these, and to the many others who responded to telephone enquiries, grateful thanks.

Editors' Notes

Names and transliteration

The simplest form of transliteration from Cyrillic has been adopted, and names well-known in other spellings have been retained in their familiar forms.

Fr Alexander Men is referred to throughout in this English form, but in bibliographical references in transliterated form, *Aleksandr Men'*.

It is the practice for the higher Russian clergy to be given Slavonic forms of names which differ from the Russian. Thus metropolitan Sergi (instead of Sergei), etc.

For Chinese names and transliteration the Pinyin system has been adopted. Thus Beijing instead of Peking, Daoism instead of Taoism etc.

Editorial and translators' notes

Editorial and translators' notes are enclosed in square brackets.

Quotations

As far as has been possible all passages quoted from English books in the Russian texts have been given in the original English. In one or two cases it has not been possible to locate the original English work and the quotation has been translated from the Russian. Where this is so it has been indicated in the notes.

Biblical quotations are from the Revised Standard Version.

Foreword

Alexander Men is gradually being recognized as one of the outstanding Christians of the twentieth century. For thirty years he was a priest in an atheistic country, where the church was tightly constrained and persecuted. But millions of other believers were also in that position. He was an outstanding parish priest, drawing people into his congregation from miles around and sometimes baptizing as many as sixty adults at a time. But there have been other faithful priests who have also had flourishing ministries. He had a profound intelligence, reading Kant and other major works from the age of thirteen. At the end of a busy day in the parish he would write learned, thoughtful books into the small hours. But the church has had other intellectuals.

What makes Fr Alexander Men outstanding is the combination of all these qualities in a lively, warm, humorous and unified personality. His vast intellectual gifts were used in the service of Christ. His ambition was nothing less than fundamentally to shift the whole atheistic ideology of the Soviet intelligentsia. But it was not speculative truth in which he was interested. It was truth refined in the fires of adversity and persecution, truth which drew the simple and sophisticated alike because it was above all a truth that was to be lived and which brought true life.

Alexander Men is of particular importance to us in the West because he reveals the distortion of our own church life, split as it is between those who are increasingly conservative and those who are increasingly liberal. He himself was nothing if not Christ-centred and Christ-committed. But the God-man in whom he believed was one who had touched and who seeks to transform the whole of human life. His faith, instead of leading him to withdraw from the maelstrom of human existence, made him more open – more open to other people and their concerns, more open to the truth in other religions and more open to God speaking in and through all things. In the West liberals can sometimes so affirm the world that they lose contact with its Christ centre. Conservative forces can so cling to the centre that they are afraid to be truly open and affirming to what is outside. Alexander Men, by contrast, firmly orthodox in his beliefs, was wonderfully world-affirming and embracing, even though he knew the depth of depravity and evil under the Soviet system.

I know that many, like me, will be grateful, first of all, to Elizabeth Roberts for initiating this project to introduce the life and work of Alexander Men to English-speaking readers. Then, to Ann Shukman, both for her fascinating account of Alexander Men's life, showing as it does that the influence of one single person upon another is in the end more powerful than any ideology, and for her supervision of the readable translations of some of Fr Alexander's works. A short collection of his sermons from Lent to Pentecost was published under the title *Awake to Life!* by the Bowerdean Press in 1992, but here Ann Shukman and her co-editor Elizabeth Roberts, together with their team of translators and advisors, have given us a comprehensive selection, showing the width of Fr Alexander's interests and his passion to communicate the Christian faith in the extraordinary society of his time. These are writings which are of enormous interest in their own right. They also set forth the persuasive power of Christian truth in our time and will firm up the discipleship of many Christians in our own society.

Richard Oxon
August 1995

Introduction

The Anthology

This anthology brings together a selection of writings by Fr Alexander Men. The passages chosen vary very considerably in style and content. Four, for instance, are intended for readers concerned with the historical and philosophical dimensions of Christianity in the world today. (These are: 'Religion, Knowledge of God, and the Problem of Evil', 'Faith and its Enemies', 'Christianity: the Universal Vision', and 'Religion, "the Cult of Personality", and the Secular State'). Two are the texts of lectures given to a non-specialist but educated audience. ('Two Understandings of Christianity' and 'Christianity for the Twenty-First Century'). And three are interviews for the public at large ('Why be a Christian?', 'Russia in Crisis', and 'The Russian Orthodox Church Today').

Fr Alexander's literary output is immense (his chief works are listed in the bibliography), and the present anthology is a sample of the diversity of his styles and concerns. All his writing, however, whether popular or scholarly, had one purpose: to make the Christian faith real and accessible to those who had been deprived of all religion under Soviet rule. He wrote to answer the needs of his readers who were hungry for knowledge of the Gospels and of the traditions of Christianity, especially the traditions of their own country, so long denied them. He wrote to open people's eyes to the riches of Western Christian thinking, and to the spiritual inheritance of the rest of the world. He wrote to emphasize time and again that human beings, made in God's image, are creatures of spirit as well as flesh, and that creeds which deny the spirit are the source of misery and cruelty in human societies.

But all this literary output, given the circumstances of religious oppression which lasted in the Soviet Union until the middle of 1988, was deprived of a normal critical reception. 'I write blindly,' he said of himself, 'receiving no critical comments or press notices.' His works were circulated by *samizdat*, in typescript copies passed from hand to hand, or printed abroad and smuggled back into Russia.

These are factors which need to be borne in mind. Fr Alexander was not, and could not be, a participant in the common discourse of European theologians and religious writers – though the range of his reading is still extraordinary. He was an educator in the widest sense of the word, presenting the Christian faith to those who were learning from scratch. But more than that he was a visionary who looked to the future seeing the tremendous potential of Christianity for saving the world and bringing human beings to fulfil their potential.

Five years have passed since Fr Alexander's death and the number and influence of his followers continue to grow. His books are now freely available in Russia. A university has been founded in his name in Moscow. An annual international commemorative conference draws people from many walks of life who have come to share his understanding of a Christianity open to all the multitude of the gifts of the spirit in human life, deeply ecumenical, a Christianity of hope and energy.

The writings included in this anthology have been chosen by Ignaty Krekshin, abbot of the Bobrinev monastery near Moscow and one of Fr Alexander's followers, in association with Fr Alexander's widow, Natalya Fedorovna Men. It is their hope that the selection will bring something of his ideas and his vision to the English-speaking world.

Alexander Men: A Biography In Context

22 January 1935 – 9 September 1990

Childhood and youth

By 1935 when Alexander Men was born in Moscow, the public

existence of the Russian Orthodox Church had virtually come to an end. More than 95% of all churches had been closed under Stalin's aggressively anti-religious campaign, as had all monasteries and seminaries. Countless numbers of Christians – priests and lay people – had been killed or were lingering in the camps of the Gulag.

To the physical annihilation of the church had been added the intellectual losses and spiritual dismemberment inflicted by the Soviet regime since the October revolution of 1917. The group of outstanding Christian thinkers, among them Nicolas Berdyaev, S. L. Frank, and Fr Sergi Bulgakov, all former Marxists, who contributed to the Russian religious renaissance of the first decades of this century, had been exiled by the Soviet government in 1922, and for many decades their writings were proscribed.

The Russian Orthodox Church had enjoyed a brief time of renewal and reform after the fall of the monarchy in February 1917: the patriarchate had been restored thus ending the two-hundred-year 'synodal period' when the church had been administered by a government department under a lay procurator-general. But the anti-church legislation brought in by the new Bolshevik government, together with the confiscations of church property, the start of the civil war and mass emigrations, soon put paid to these hopes. An *émigré*, largely right-wing monarchist group formed a break-away church (the 'Karlovci synod', nowadays known as the Russian Orthodox Church Abroad), which further undermined the authority of the new patriarch, Tikhon.

Another schism had been deliberately fostered by the Soviet authorities: patriarch Tikhon had been arrested in 1922, and during his absence a government-sponsored 'Renovationist' movement had been started. The Renovationists stood for quite extreme reforms and active public support of the regime: for instance they declared capitalism to be a sin and the revolution to be the realization of the principles of the Gospels. Though Tikhon was released from prison, he died in 1925 before being able to restore unity. But the Renovationist movement never achieved wide support and it, like all other forms of religious life, was not spared when the Stalinist anti-religious campaign began in the late twenties, at the time of the first five-year plan and the beginning of the collectivization of the peasantry.

Before his death, Tikhon had named three possible successors, but none had been at liberty. One of them in turn nominated metropolitan Sergi (Sergei Stragorodsky), who became *de facto* head of the church. Sergi in turn was arrested and then released, and under pressures which can only be imagined had issued in 1927 a declaration of loyalty to the Soviet regime. But this too did not help the church. In 1929 the remaining bishops and priests were arrested, and this, together with the physical assault on church buildings, icons and libraries, ushered in a period which has been described as the worst persecution of Christians since the time of Diocletian.

Metropolitan Sergi's declaration of loyalty to the regime had caused consternation among the faithful. Many believed that it was a betrayal, and that anyway being merely 'the replacement of a replacement' he had no right to act in the name of the church. This was the moment when several leading clergy 'went under-ground' and had formed what became known as the 'catacomb church'. These people lived for the most part isolated from one another, sustaining the small number of laity who were able, or who dared, to keep contact with them. Few survived beyond the end of the war.

In an extraordinary way, however, the gift of faith never depends wholly on social factors or church structures. One such person in whom the gift of faith was strong was Elena Semenovna Zupersein who was to be the mother of Alexander Men. She was born in 1908 into a Jewish family in Kharkov but early on, to her parents' disapproval, felt drawn to Christianity. As a young woman she moved to Moscow to live with her cousin Vera Yakovlevna Vasilevskaya who was at that time also feeling her way towards Christianity. In 1934 Elena married a young engineer, also Jewish, called Vladimir Grigorevich Men. Their first son, Alexander (Alik) was born in January 1935, and a second son, Pavel, followed in December 1938. Vera, who worked as a child psychologist, had a close friend at work who was a committed Orthodox Christian and the 'spiritual child' of a catacomb priest, Fr Serafim (Sergei Batyukov).

This remarkable man, ordained at the age of thirty-nine in 1919, had been priest of the church of St Kir and St Ioann, one of the most active parishes in Moscow. He had not accepted Sergi's declaration of loyalty and had gone into hiding, eventually settling in the little town of Zagorsk (today known again by its pre-revolutionary name of Sergiev Posad), the site of the great monastery of the Trinity, founded by St Sergius of Radonezh in the fourteenth century. Here he was looked after by two former nuns from the Diveevo convent, founded by St Serafim of Sarov, and here his former parishioners, and those from another famous Moscow parish, St Nicholas on Maroseika street, used to come in secret to visit him.

This was the catacomb priest to whom Vera's friend brought Elena and her baby son in September 1935, and mother and child were secretly baptized. Vera herself was baptized a little later and for the rest of her life devoted herself to the care of her cousin and the two little boys. The two cousins and the two little boys became Fr Serafim's 'spiritual children', making occasional clandestine visits to him for confession, communion and counsel. Vera Vasilevskaya left an account of her spiritual journey and of Fr Serafim's spiritual direction, which appears to have been quite directive and authoritarian, though personally adapted to her particular needs.[1]

When the war came and the German army invaded the Soviet Union in June 1941 Vladimir was far away in Sverdlovsk (Ekaterinburg) and he urged his family to leave Moscow and join him in safety as so many others were doing. But Fr Serafim advised them to stay, and indeed to move out of Moscow to Zagorsk, assuring them that they would be safe under the protection of St Sergius. In spite of the proximity of the front, and the danger to them as Jews, the family survived the war.

Fr Serafim died early in 1942 having heard Alik's first confession, and telling Vera and Elena that he would grow up to be a great man. Before he died, he entrusted the spiritual care of the family to two other catacomb priests, but they were soon arrested. There remained, however, in Zagorsk, a tiny clandestine community of nuns, led by Mother Mariya, who

was to become Alik's spiritual guide over the next few years.
Later Fr Alexander was to remember her:

> She lived an ascetic and prayerful life, completely free of
> hypocrisy, bigotry, and narrowness . . . She was always filled
> with paschal joy, a deep dedication to the will of God, and a
> feeling of closeness to the spiritual world.[2]

She, like Fr Serafim, represented a particularly vital strand in
Russian Orthodoxy, the tradition of the spiritual guides, the
startsy, of the monastery of Optina Pustyn (also known simply as
Optino).

Towards the middle of the last century, this obscure
monastery, situated near Kozelsk some 300 kilometres south-
west of Moscow, suddenly started to attract crowds of pilgrims.
In the Orthodox monastic tradition, older monks had always
been the spiritual guides to the younger monks, but what
happened at Optino was that the older monks, the *startsy*, began
to offer spiritual counsel to lay people as well. The *startsy*
received people all day, they were open to all, rich and poor, the
nobility and the peasants. Tolstoy and Dostoevsky came here, as
did Vladimir Solovyev, and many other well-known writers and
thinkers. In this way Optino built a bridge over the divide which
separated the church from the social and cultural life of the
country.[3]

Fr Serafim had been a disciple of the last Optino *starets*,
Nektary, and Mother Mariya came from the same tradition,
being 'open to people, to their problems, their longings, open to
the world'. Until it was closed by the Soviet authorities in the
twenties, it was Optino, Fr Alexander was to write later, which
after a long rupture did in fact renew the dialogue between the
church and society:

> It was an undertaking of great, exceptional importance despite
> the distrust and opposition of the authorities. In Father
> Seraphim and Mother Maria I saw a living extension of that

dialogue. This idea of dialogue with the world has stuck with me all my life . . .[4]

In this way, in spite of the outward ruin of the church, the young Alik, brought up by his deeply religious mother and aunt, came at an early age under the influence of two people who embodied one of the most vital strands in contemporary Russian Orthodoxy. That was perhaps the first miracle of his life: the second was to come in the post-war years.

In 1943, Stalin decided to re-create the church. He summoned metropolitan Sergi and two other bishops and ordered them to call a convocation of bishops (most of whom were in the camps) and elect Sergi as patriarch. Sergi died in 1945 and he was succeeded by Alexi I (Sergei Simansky). The election of Alexi was considered valid by the remaining clergy of the catacomb church, and what was left of the church began gradually and tentatively to renew its public existence. The harsh legislation of 1929 was very slightly liberalized, the authorities made special efforts to recruit clergy from abroad, and the churches and monasteries which had been reopened during the German occupation of western Russia and the Ukraine were not closed down again as the Red Army recaptured these areas. But all church life was controlled by the new Council for the Affairs of the Orthodox Church (in 1965 to become the Council for Religious Affairs), which had its officials in every diocese and district.

Nonetheless the Moscow where the young Alik Men spent his teenage years had at least the vestiges of church life. By the age of twelve his vocation to the priesthood had become clear to him, and he was blessed in this by Mother Mariya. As a teenager he became server and choir member at the church of the Nativity of John the Baptist. Meanwhile his official and unofficial education proceeded apace. At school he showed outstanding intellectual gifts but always remained a popular and sociable lad. Natural science became a passion:

From my early childhood, the contemplation of nature has been my *theologia prima*. I used to go into a forest or a museum of palaeontology in the same way I went into a church. And even now, a branch with its leaves or a bird in full flight has for me more meaning than a hundred icons . . . God has given us two books, the Bible and nature.[5]

But at the same time he was pursuing another, unofficial education. Through Fr Serafim, Elena and Vera had become acquainted with some of the former parishioners of St Nicholas on Maroseika Street. This famous church had been served by two notable priests, Fr Aleksei Mechev, and after him by his son, Fr Sergei Mechev. The parish had been outstanding in Moscow for its active laity, among whom were many intellectuals. Among these 'Maroseikans' was a former priest of the catacomb church, the historian and ethnographer, Boris Aleksandrovich Vasilev, who had spent many years in the camps. In the immediate post-war years he and his wife were for a time the centre of a small circle of thinking Christians, which included Elena and Vera, and the intellectually precocious Alik. Boris Vasilev seems to have taken a personal interest in him and encouraged him in his ambition to find a reconciliation between science and theology.

Alik, like most Muscovites of that time, lived with his family in one room in a communal flat. The family consisted of himself, his parents, his little brother, and his aunt Vera. But every evening he would retire to bed behind a screen, where he could read oblivious to the life of the family going on around him. And early in the morning he awoke before the others to continue these private studies. By thirteen he was reading Kant. Soon after, by chance or providence, he came across the works of the exiled Russian religious philosophers, and at the age of fifteen he found a copy of a book by Vladimir Solovyev in the flea market and began a life-long admiration for that visionary thinker.

From another acquaintance, Nikolai Evgrafovich Pestov, a professor of chemistry, who was also a theologian and the author of a multi-volume study of contemporary Orthodox piety, Alik borrowed books on Catholicism and Western Christianity. At the same time he was reading the Church Fathers, and studying biblical criticism and the history of the classical world and of the East. Before he was eighteen he was following the study course for the seminary on his own. Mother Mariya continued to

encourage him in his biblical studies. Anatoly Vedernikov, then
director of studies at the seminary, and later editorial secretary
of the *Journal of the Moscow Patriarchate*, encouraged him in
his vocation.[6]

The story of how, in Stalinist Russia, this boy could acquire
such a quantity of prohibited literature is yet to be told. Much
later a close friend was to say of him:

> Animals loved him, and plants, and things, and of course
> books. He used to say that books found their own way to
> him when they were needed, just like friends and relatives
> coming to a birthday party.[7]

But books have owners, and there is no doubt that the young
Alik earned the trust and admiration of those he came in
contact with. Still, this all-encompassing unofficial education in
philosophy and theology is like the second miracle in his life.

The death of Stalin in 1953 and the wave of antisemitism
that followed it coincided with the end of Alexander's school
course. University was denied him on racial grounds and
instead he enrolled as a student in the Institute of Fur at
Moscow which enabled him to continue his studies in biology.
In his own time he now followed the course of reading for the
theological academy, and also began to read another proscribed author, Fr Pavel Florensky. At this time he chose as his
'spiritual father' Fr Nikolai Golubtsov, also a 'Maroseikan',
and then priest at a church near the Donskaya monastery in
Moscow. Fr Nikolai embodied the same principles of openness
as Fr Serafim.[8]

In 1955 the Institute was transferred to Irkutsk in Siberia,
where Alexander was to stay for three years. Here he shared a
room with Gleb Yakunin, also to become a priest and later a
fearless critic of the church establishment. Alexander soon
made links with the cathedral which was situated opposite the
Institute, doing jobs for the bishop, reading in the library, but
somehow avoiding too much comment from the authorities or
his fellow students.

In 1956, at the age of twenty-one, Alexander married a fellow student, Natalya Grigorenko. This was the year of the Twentieth Party Congress and Khrushchev's speech denouncing the crimes of Stalin; it was the beginning of a short-lived thaw. Many church people, both clergy and lay, were released from the camps. But as far as the church was concerned the thaw did not last, for in 1958 a new and violent anti-religious campaign was launched.

The Khrushchev campaign against religion lasted until 1964. By then more than half of all churches had been closed, along with many monasteries and five seminaries. Many cruelties were perpetrated by the authorities. The country was deluged with atheist propaganda and a new journal, *Science and Religion*, was launched to disprove the claims of faith. Khrushchev announced that communism would be achieved in twenty years, and in 1961 Gagarin, making the first manned space flight, declared he had proved God did not exist because he hadn't met him up there.

In 1958 Alexander Men was just about to sit his final exams. He looked forward to three years working in his specialist field and then to entering the seminary to train as a priest. But the authorities heard of his contacts with the cathedral: he was refused permission to sit his exams, and abruptly returned to Moscow with Natalya. Here Fr Nikolai Golubtsov arranged for him to be ordained deacon on 1 July 1958, and he was appointed to a parish in the village of Akulovo, south-west of Moscow. He, Natalya and their baby daughter Irina moved into a cold delapidated house, Alexander to work with an elderly and irascible priest.

On 1 September 1960 he was ordained priest in the Donskaya monastery in Moscow by metropolitan Stefany, another 'Maroseikan', and was posted to Alabino, a hundred kilometres south-west of Moscow.

Parish priest and evangelist

Alexander was now twenty-five years old, mature beyond his years, with a quite extraordinary intellectual and spiritual training behind him. He was already writing his books. To his intellectual and spiritual gifts was added another, particularly important one for the life of a parish priest in times of persecution, a gift of getting on with all kinds of people. During the Khrushchev anti-religious campaign priests were forbidden to officiate anywhere outside their church buildings without official permission from the local authorities: any infringement, whether baptizing at home, conducting funerals, or giving the last rites, could be used as a means of inculpating and arresting them. Fr Alexander, however, knew how to talk to the local officials and continued to carry out all these normal functions of a priest, time and again.[9]

Fr Alexander had the ability to win trust among all kinds of people, whether the village *babushki,* or the average Soviet official, or the educated and despiritualized intelligentsia. Sergei Averintsev, the prominent Christian philosopher, was to say of him later that he was 'the man sent from God to be missionary to the wild tribe of the Soviet intelligentsia'[10] and it was in the remote village of Alabino that this ministry began.

The parish at Alabino soon became a kind of haven at that time of persecutions. As people were drawn to him, a little community nicknamed 'the abbey' soon formed. But it was not to last long. The scandals caused by the indiscretions of a drunken lay reader brought the attention of the security forces: the Mens' house was searched, Fr Alexander interrogated and accused of dealing in stolen goods. The case went to the prosecutor-general himself who even planned to stage a show trial of this too successful priest. But it was the summer of 1964, Khrushchev was losing power, the anti-religious campaign subsided and the case, providentially, was dropped.

The Alabino period was marked by another development. At Fr Alexander's initiative, a group of a dozen young clergy of the Moscow region, including Fr Gleb Yakunin, Fr Dmitri Dudko and Fr Nikolai Eshliman, used to meet for discussion and to share experiences. The group was frequently joined by Anatoly Levitin-Krasnov, the author of numerous *samizdat* writings on the church. They were all conscious of the lack of support and lack of protest from the hierarchy of the church in the face of the brutalities and illegalities of the Khrushchev campaign. One of the few bishops who stood firm at the time was metropolitan

Ermogen. Fr Alexander wrote to him in the name of the group to invite him to be their bishop; Ermogen agreed and came to Alabino to visit them. With the help of Levitin and with the approval of Ermogen a letter of protest was drafted to the patriarch. But in October 1964 Khrushchev fell. Ermogen judged the moment to be inopportune, and eventually it was only Yakunin and Eshliman who in late 1965 signed letters to the patriarch and head of government. The eighty-five-year-old patriarch, privately, admitted that they were right, but both priests were dismissed and no changes at all took place in the church hierarchy. The famous Yakunin and Eshliman letter may, however, have been a stimulant to the dissident movement of the following years: Solzhenitsyn, who had become a friend of Fr Alexander's, recalls how on reading the letter in the spring of 1966 he realized that he too had to do something.[11]

Why did Fr Alexander not associate himself with the letter? He probably genuinely agreed with his bishop and thought the moment inopportune. He had also just suffered the first serious assault from the authorities in the form of house-searches and interrogations. But probably, more importantly, the whole thrust of his ministry lay in another direction. He said later of Yakunin, 'He is our army, but I'm just a partisan detachment.'[12] The partisan activity consisted in responding to the spiritual needs of those he encountered, in evangelizing, and in doing pastoral work in his parish. Indeed 1966 saw the first of what he called the 'demographic explosions' when people started to seek him out in large numbers. Besides he was intensely engaged in writing.

By this time Fr Alexander had been moved to another parish, Tarasovka, to the north of Moscow. The church there was the third one to which he was appointed with a dedication to the Protection of the Mother of God.

The Brezhnev years (1964–82) saw little let-up in the oppressive nature of the regime. Andropov became head of the KGB: there were a series of political trials; for the first time psychiatric hospitals were used as places of detention. Prague was invaded in 1968, Afghanistan in 1979. Solzhenitsyn was hounded and eventually expelled in 1974, and Andrei Sakharov, the outspoken defender of human rights, was exiled to Gorky in 1980.

But the Brezhnev years were also a time when an interest in spiritual matters awoke in the general public: people became keen on icons, took to placing crosses on their parents' graves, took up yoga, or astrology, or studied the paranormal. Among them were young people who came to Christianity after passing through a period of involvement in Eastern religious practices. This was a time when young intellectuals, often brought up in a wholly atheistic milieu, suddenly became converted and felt the reality of God. The problem was then how to find a priest they could talk to. In Fr Alexander they found just such a person who fully understood their intellectual and spiritual difficulties.

It was during the Tarasovka period that there occurred a meeting which was to have the greatest implications for the development of Fr Alexander's 'missionary work', a meeting which was another of those providential – or miraculous – events of his life.

Assia Douroff was a French woman of Russian origin who worked at the French embassy in Moscow between 1964 and 1979. Through a mutual acquaintance she met Fr Alexander in 1966 and he spoke to her of the urgent need for religious books for the growing number of new converts. Through Assia Fr Alexander was put in touch with the Foyer Oriental Chrétien in Brussels. This was a charity, founded by another Frenchwoman of Russian origin, Irène Posnoff, with the aim of supplying orthodox Christians in communist countries with religious literature. The Foyer ran a publishing house called 'La Vie avec Dieu' for this purpose. Through Assia, Fr Alexander sent them the manuscript of his first book, *The Son of Man*; and so began a long association which resulted in the publication in Brussels, under a pseudonym, of all his other main works. *Heaven on Earth*, on the Orthodox liturgy, in 1969; the first five volumes of *In Search of the Way, the Truth and the Life*, in 1970–72; the sixth volume, *On the Threshhold of the New Testament* in 1983; and a short handbook, *How to Read the Bible* in 1981. Assia Douroff also became the channel through which Solzhenitsyn's books reached the West.[13]

Fr Alexander's time in Tarasovka came to an end in 1970 when a jealous superior denounced him and he had to be urgently moved to a new parish. This was the parish of Novaya Derevnya where he was to stay as priest, and later arch-priest, until his death twenty years later. As there was no accommodation at Novaya Derevnya, the family, now with a son and daughter, acquired a wooden *izba* with an extensive garden in the village of Semkhoz. From the house it was a few minutes walk to the station from where the suburban trains ran on the Moscow line towards Pushkino, the station for Novaya Derevnya.

Novaya Derevnya is situated on the old road that led from Moscow to Sergiev Posad (Zagorsk). The church is a simple wooden one, but it had the advantage of a small parish room with a tiny office where Fr Alexander could receive visitors. Many Moscow intellectuals followed Fr Alexander here: among the famous names who were baptized by Fr Alexander were Nadezhda Mandelshtam, widow of the great poet Osip Mandelshtam, and the song-writer Galich.[14] All his skills were needed to help weld the influx of new parishioners into a Christian community with the older village congregation.

> When I became a priest, I tried to unite the parish, to make it one community and not just a group of people who knew very little about each other, whom fortune had thrown together. I wanted all the members to help each other, to pray together, to study the Scriptures together, and to receive communion together.[15]

– mostly activities which, of course, the authorities had they known would have used as an excuse for interference.

As Fr Alexander's reputation grew, more and more people came to Novaya Derevnya. In the summer they rented rooms or dachas from the local people in order to be near the church. In Moscow a network of small groups was set up, which met weekly, if conditions were favourable, for Bible study, prayer and mutual encouragement. Each group, numbering about a dozen people, was slightly different according to the needs of the individuals gathered there. These groups, which were for a time a unique feature of Fr Alexander's ministry, have been compared with Roman Catholic 'base communities'.[16]

His parishioners were encouraged to attend communion once a month, each time preceded by confession as is the practice of the Orthodox Church. Fr Alexander was careful though to distinguish his own ministry as a confessor from that of a *starets*. The task of a parish priest is different. Whereas a *starets* in a monastery could impose discipline on a younger monk, the parish priest must be on his guard against paternalism and authoritarianism: he has to be content to remind his parishioners of the commandments of the church, to give direction to their spiritual lives, and to help them in their interior strivings.[17]

None of this tremendous pastoral and literary activity could pass unnoticed by the KGB. Fr Alexander was under almost constant surveillance and the security forces observed all the comings and goings to the church from a room in a nearby house. There was jealousy too from some of his fellow clergy: the priest of a neighbouring parish even publicly denounced Fr Alexander and warned his parishioners to keep away from him. Anonymous letters, mostly of a crudely antisemitic kind, multiplied. But Fr Alexander understood the mentality of the security services and probably knew some of his minders personally. He sensed when danger was in the air and would warn his flock to keep away from Novaya Derevnya for a time, or to cease their group meetings.

The death of Brezhnev in 1982 and the accession of Andropov brought a new clamp down, more arrests, directives against contacts with foreigners, harsher conditions in the camps. Not all of Fr Alexander's 'spiritual children' could stand the strain and there were one or two who denounced him. There came a time when he was called in for daily interrogations, sometimes by the KGB and sometimes by the Council for Religious Affairs; his home and office were searched several times. The accession of Gorbachev in March 1985 at first made little difference. In April 1986 Fr Alexander was publicly denounced in the journal *Trud* [*Labour*] along with other prominent church people.

But darkness comes before the dawn and at the end of 1986 came a sudden change: Fr Gleb Yakunin was released from prison, Sakharov was summoned back from exile, and a year later preparations were in full swing for the public national celebration of the millennium of the baptism of ancient Russia in

June 1988. Christianity became officially acknowledged as a valued part of Russian heritage. The event which the millennium was to commemorate was the decision by prince Vladimir of Kiev in the year 988 to adopt Christianity for his country, then called 'Rus'. Rus was an area that covered much of what is now the Ukraine and south-west Russia. Vladimir's decision to adopt Christianity linked Rus with Byzantium and with Christianity of the Eastern, Orthodox branch. The baptism of Rus is considered to be not only the beginning of Christianity in Russia and the Ukraine, but also the beginning of Russian culture.

On 29 April 1988 Gorbachev received patriarch Pimen and other hierarchs of the church in the Kremlin, so putting an end to seventy years of persecution. On 11 May Fr Alexander made the first of what were to be many public addresses on the subject of Christianity. That summer brought an explosion of religious life. There were many baptisms, and many radio and television programmes on religious themes. Foreign evangelists, and foreign sects, started to pour in. In fact, though, all the old legislation proscribing church activities remained in force until 1990, and control by the authorities of the church was hardly eased, especially in the provinces. What do you think of *perestroika*? Fr Alexander was asked. He replied, 'It's good when the hunters are hunting each other, for then the rabbits can play at liberty.'[18]

But Fr Alexander for one did not fear the hunters. He and his parishioners began actively to serve Christ in the world: visits previously forbidden began on a regular basis to the Moscow Pediatric hospital, a Sunday school for children was started at Novaya Derevnya. Fr Alexander himself embarked on a round of public appearances. His lectures over the next two years covered the following subjects: the creeds, the ecumenical councils, the Fathers of the Church, the liturgy, Buddhism, Islam, the catechism for children, Christianity and Russian culture, Russian philosophy of the nineteenth and twentieth centuries; in addition he gave nine lectures on the Nicene creed, six lectures on world religions, six lectures on the Bible and Russian literature. In all he gave over two hundred lectures.[19] He spoke to crowded audiences in palaces of culture, in schools, clubs and institutes, often against a backdrop of slogans from the past – 'The works of

Lenin will live for ever !' His delivery was animated, he spoke without notes or a text. He always allowed time at the end for the audience to send up their questions on little slips of paper which he would answer publicly.

Always there was about him a sense of urgency, a sense that time was short. In spite of all the talk about spirituality nowadays, he would say, much of what passed for religion was sentimental and *ersatz*. 'Notice,' said Fr Alexander, 'that no one, not even the bishops whom they produce on television, is preaching Jesus Christ, or God; they don't speak of the essentials of what we believe.' We must 'hurry to give people the authentic message of Christ', because this liberty could come to an end at any time.[20]

Ironically, the new liberty gave rein to the anti-libertarian, narrowly nationalistic views of many of the Russian Orthodox clergy. The dream of a 'radiant past' when the church had lived an imagined life of grandeur and security prevented a sober reassessment of the church's weaknesses in the present and its failures in the past – its part in the calamity of 1917, its divisions, its lack of social engagement, its lack of scholarship. Notions of pluralism and tolerance were alien to this newly liberated church, and the opinion that 'ecumenism is of the Antichrist' could be heard from even educated members of the clergy.[21] With the growth of nationalism came also an upsurge of antisemitism.

At Easter 1990 Fr Alexander baptized sixty adults. He took part in the opening of the Bible Society in Russia, he was involved in starting a new university (which still continues under his name), and a cultural association, 'Cultural Renaissance'. His friends now began to worry about burn-out. Even before *perestroika* he was leading twice an ordinary person's life. His French biographer, Yves Hamant writes:

> How did he manage to do it all: the parish ministry, all the people he received at home and at Novaya Derevnya; all those he went to see in Moscow; the responsibility for the groups; catachesis; domestic chores; the triangular commutes between home, parish and Moscow? . . . He was no doubt blessed with an extraordinary capacity for work, a powerful memory, and a

rare ability to concentrate. From childhood, he had learned not to waste time . . . He always said: 'When you work, work. When you pray, pray. When you play, play. Do nothing, however, in just any old way, in a mediocre manner. Don't remain idle, with nothing to do. Be very careful not to "kill" time, for by "killing" time, you are killing your own life.'[22]

Many have spoken of his prayer life, the sense he had always of the nearness of God and the presence of Christ. He seemed to be on intimate terms with the saints, Western and Eastern. He had the gift of living completely in the present: everyone who spoke to him felt that he was concerned only with them in the whole world. And he had a deep sense of humour and a gaiety that sprang from his faith. Animals can't laugh at themselves, he would say, only humans can and that's God's way of looking at us.[23]

With the liberty granted by *perestroika*, however, he became increasingly to sense that his time was limited and not a moment should be lost. If the oppression of religious life had come to an end, other menaces seemed to be in the air. On 1 September 1990 he celebrated the thirtieth anniversary of his ordination to the priesthood. In a letter to a friend who had urged him to take things more easily he summed up his situation:

It isn't easy to understand someone who for years has been tied up on a leash. I am not complaining for myself, because God has given me the possibility of doing something, even on the end of this leash . . . In fact I have always had regular meetings with people, just like these. It's only the proportion that has changed. Before, there were thirty people, today, three hundred or more. But the basis is the same, however . . . I don't prepare myself in any special way; I let God inspire me . . . I don't spend more time in public now than I did during the period of stagnation [the Brezhnev years]. It's only the number of listeners that has increased . . . I work now as I have always worked: with my face into the wind. This is not as easy as it may sometimes seem. At the present time the wind is obviously stronger, especially from the Black Hundreds.[24] I have to stand solidly on my two feet, legs spread, in order not to be overturned . . . I'm only an instrument that God is using for the moment. Afterwards, things will be as God wants them.[25]

On Sunday 9 September Fr Alexander set out early as usual from the wooden house in Semkhoz to take the train to Novaya Derevnya where a long day awaited him: the liturgy, confessions, baptisms, funerals. Then he was due to go to Moscow to give another lecture. As far as can be reconstructed what happened is as follows: on the path through the open woodland to the station he was evidently stopped by two men, probably people he knew. One most likely showed him something to read, for he took out his glasses (they were later found by the path). As he bent his head to look down, the other man struck him on the back of the head with an axe. The assailants then fled. The wound was not instantly mortal, and Fr Alexander made his way to the station, where he felt faint, became aware of the bleeding and struggled back along the path to his house. At the garden gate he collapsed and died. No one has been charged with the murder.

Author and thinker

The problem Fr Alexander faced as a Christian evangelist was how to bridge the gap between the inquiring, historically aware, scientifically trained minds of the intelligentsia and the message of the gospels. Until very recently Bibles and commentaries were unobtainable. In the liturgy of the church passages from the Gospels were (and still are) read in Church Slavonic, an archaic language which few could understand. Fr Alexander's first book, *The Son of Man* was written as a 'key to the Gospels' for the thinking enquirer. It tells the story of Jesus of Nazareth according to the Gospels, but sets the narrative into a historically researched context of Roman rule and Jewish beliefs and aspirations. Fr Alexander had begun working on the book while still in his teens and some chapters had been published in the *Journal of the Moscow Patriarchate* in 1959–62. Until the Brussels publication of 1968 he used to give out *samizdat* copies to his converts. The book is written from the point of view of a robust and traditional faith. Fr Alexander has no doubts for instance about the empty tomb or the virgin birth: they are accepted as actual historical facts, realities without which the Christian faith shades off into a watered down liberalism and becomes merely one among many of the world's faiths. In its latest 1992 edition, *The Son of Man* is published as the seventh and culminating volume of Fr Alexander's study of world religions, the series *In Search of the Way, the Truth and the Life*, thus making the point that the coming of Christ was an event of world significance for all mankind, and the answer to the searchings of all the great faiths.

Fr Alexander had embarked on this major project to write a history of the religions and beliefs of mankind around 1960, and the volumes were published in Brussels between 1970 and 1983. The idea for the work was inspired by his reading of Vladimir Solovyev who believed that the study of ancient religions was indispensable for an understanding of world history and of Christianity's place in it. Christianity, according to this view, is neither merely one step in the spiritual development of mankind, nor a synthesis of previous belief systems, but a new revelation.

In the same way that white absorbs all the colors of the rainbow, so the Gospel encompasses the faith of the prophets, the thirst for salvation in Buddhism, the dynamism of Zarathustra, and the humanity of Confucius. It consecrates the best in the ethics of the philosophers of Antiquity and the mysticism of the sages of India. In doing this, Christianity is not a new doctrine, but rather the announcement of a real fact, of an event accomplished on two levels, the terrestrial and celestial. Happening in one place and time, it transcends temporal limits. All roads lead to it. It is by its light that the past, present and future are evaluated and judged. Every movement towards the light of communication with God is, even if accomplished unconsciously, movement towards Christ.[26]

Knowledge of other faiths and philosophies is of great relevance today, in Fr Alexander's opinion, because when people reject Christ they nearly always, consciously or unconsciously, fall back on some doctrine or belief from humanity's past: they may turn to the thought forms or beliefs of Buddhism, of Confucianism, of Zarathustra, of Plato or the other Greek philosophers. This is not to be wondered at since the past of mankind stretches back over many millennia, whereas the two thousand years of Christianity are but a short time for humanity to take in the fullness of the gospel message. Christianity, Fr Alexander often said, has only just begun, and the leaven of the gospel has yet to work through the dough.

The first volume of the series, entitled *The Sources of Religion*, published in 1970, from which two extracts are included in this anthology, deals with problems of religion and the spiritual life in general. Fr Alexander argues that human beings are essentially endowed with a spiritual nature. He discusses the nature of religion, the various assaults on faith, and the problems they give rise to. He argues that there is no fundamental incompatibility between science and religion, but that each sheds light on the other.

Magic and Monotheism followed in 1971. In this book Fr Alexander argues that magic beliefs held human consciousness captive in the rituals that were believed to be essential for the functioning of the stars and the seasons, and human creativity was thereby paralysed. The growth out of magism and into monotheism took place during the second millennium BC, the people of Israel being pioneers in the development of faith in the one God.

The following three volumes, which were published in 1971–72, deal with the spiritual revolution which occurred in the middle of the first millennium BC in China, India, Greece and Palestine. This is the period which Karl Jaspers named the 'axial period', a conception which Fr Alexander discusses in 'Christianity: the Universal Vision' in this anthology. This was the time when abstract thinking began, when trust in a creator God developed and when an ethical awareness came to assume greater importance than the ritual round of previous generations.

At the Gates of Silence (1971) is a study of the spirituality of China and India. The Chinese specialist, Evgeniya Zavadskaya, one of Fr Alexander's parishioners, acted as consultant for this book and writes appreciatively of his scholarship and profound understanding in which 'there is not a shade of condescension or partiality'.[27] *Dionysius, Logos and Fate* (1972) is on Greek philosophy, and *The Messengers of the Kingdom* (1972) on the Israelite prophets. The latest, Moscow, edition of the latter work runs to 430 pages, with a bibliography of nearly a thousand titles, including many Western works of the 1960s.

Finally, *On the Threshhold of the New Testament* (1983), which is over 800 pages long, covers the three centuries before the coming of Christ. This was a period when no great spiritual leaders arose, when the great religions were revealing their limits, and when pessimism and scepticism prevailed.

Fr Alexander's scholarly work did not come to an end with the completion of this series, for at the time of his death he had nearly completed a seven-volume dictionary of the Bible. It contained entries on biblical commentators from Philo and the Church Fathers to modern authors, on the principal schools and tendencies in biblical exegesis, on the history of translations and editions. Fr Alexander was something of a lonely pioneer in the introduction of modern biblical studies in Russia, the church and its teaching establishments still being stuck in the fundamentalism of the past. His scholarly studies of the Bible became one more cause for antagonism towards him.

For publication in Brussels he also prepared commentaries on the books of the New Testament which were designed to be included in a new Russian critical edition of the Bible, based on the Jerusalem Bible, still in preparation.

Where did he find time and energy for all this writing and research? He told a friend that when he got home late from the parish, instead of being tired, his mind was racing, he was eager to change gear, and to settle down to his books. But the tiredness came in the morning when he had to rise early to celebrate the liturgy. He was constantly aware of the needs of his people and their hunger to learn:

My readers are waiting impatiently at my back . . . [I write] simply because 'there's nothing to eat': the old books are mostly out of date, and foreign ones are either unobtainable or 'don't work' with our readership.[28]

He never considered himself an academic, but, as he told abbot Ignaty Krekshin, his true calling was 'to preach the word of God to people in their everyday lives'.

The full assessment of Fr Alexander as a scholar and thinker is a task for the future. So too is the question of his intellectual roots and the sources which inspired him: what did he mean, for instance, when he said of Henri Bergson, 'this philosopher is one of the few who has had enormous influence on me'?[29] But to two Russian religious philosophers he felt himself to be particularly indebted.

Vladimir Sergeevich Solovyev (1853–1900), philosopher, theologian, mystic, and poet, was a thinker whose ideas have had immense influence on the Russian religious thinkers of the succeeding generations. The discovery of his writings as a teenager opened Alexander Men's mind to a whole new dimension and perspective on Christianity. He acknowledged this later by dedicating *In Search of the Way, the Truth and the Life* to Solovyev's memory.

For Solovyev, the central event of the whole of human history was the coming of Christ. In Christ the divine principle was united with the created order and Solovyev coined the phrase 'God-man' [*Bogochelovek*] to designate this alliance, or union. The coming of Christ, the incarnation, was an event, in Solovyev's thinking, which affects the whole created order by bringing it into the dynamic process which will lead to the eventual union of nature and humanity with God. The philosopher S. L. Frank said of Solovyev that in his thinking the Chalcedon doctrine of the unity of the two natures, the divine and the human, in Christ, is raised to the level of a philosophical principle embracing the whole of existence.[30] This principle Solovyev termed *Bogochelovestvo*, 'the principle of God united with humanity', which has become known in English by the rather clumsy, and rather misleading, term of 'Godmanhood'. Under this term is subsumed the cosmogonic process by which the whole created order is drawn into the divine: all aspects of life, all religions, all art, science, philosophy are illumined by this fact that the divine is actively at work in the world, drawing all things towards 'divinization', to their intended fulfilment. The terms 'God-man' and 'Godmanhood', and their opposite 'Man-god' to designate humanism which makes humanity the measure of all things and excludes God, became current usage in many succeeding Russian religious thinkers, including Dostoevsky.

Solovyev's great vision of the meaning of the coming of Christ rested on a sense of the unity of all things before God. This was a vision which Fr Alexander shared, and like Solovyev, he understood not only the unity of the human search for God, expressed in the great religions, but also the essential oneness of Christianity and the need to realize that oneness in ecumenism. In selections 5 and 8 of this anthology Fr Alexander discusses some of Solovyev's ideas.

The other philosopher frequently quoted and referred to by Fr Alexander is Nicolas (Nikolai) Aleksandrovich Berdyaev (1874–1948), one of those ex-Marxist turned Christian thinkers who were exiled by the Soviet government in 1922. Berdyaev developed a philosophy of Christian personalism in which the central idea was that of freedom as an ontological principle deriving from the Godhead itself. From this God-given freedom comes the essential value of each individual person, and Berdyaev's understanding of human creativity as the expression of this gift. Berdyaev stood against materialism, determinism, and what he called 'the *embourgeoisement* of the spirit', the trends which deaden and sap human giftedness. Like Solovyev Berdyaev saw in Christianity the culmination of the age-long human search for God. Some of his ideas of this subject are summarized by Fr Alexander, also in selections 5 and 8 of this anthology.[31]

Witness for our times

Fr Alexander stands for Russian Christians as the figure who speaks to them of Christ, who has returned to them their own lost Christian heritage, who has opened their minds to the riches of Western Christianity, and who has given them a global vision of hope for the future. That he achieved this in a society which was accustomed to use violence and sophisticated thought-control to suppress religion is living proof of Berdyaev's view that the spirit is stronger than the determining forces of society.

One of his followers said of him that what he did for the spiritual life of Russia will come to be seen in the future as something similar to what the great Russian poet, Alexander Pushkin, did for Russian literature at the beginning of the last century: he created the language which was to be the standard for the century; he opened Russian eyes to the culture of the world, and he gave Russians a sense of their destiny in the history of mankind.[32] Perhaps Fr Alexander in giving us Christians a language and perspectives for today will be the pioneer for the Christianity of the future. Another of his followers said simply of him that he was the man for the twenty-first century.[33]

Ann Shukman

Part I
The Christian Life Today

I

Why be a Christian?

In this interview which serves as an introduction to the anthology, Fr Alexander summarizes many of his ideas about Christianity which will be more fully developed in other sections of the anthology. First among them is the idea that human beings by their very nature are seekers after God or after some ideal outside themselves. Secondly, that all the great faiths of the world contain something of God's truth in them, while the full revelation came only with Christ. Thirdly, that the presence of evil in the world is to be accounted for by the God-given freedom which human beings enjoy. And lastly, that intellectual differences between Christians, even over doctrinal matters such as the theory of evolution, are of minor importance compared with the faith in Christ which unites them. The interviewer, Mark Makarov, is an American evangelical who runs a regular radio phone-in programme. The text of this interview was published in A. Men', Byt' Khristianinom, Moscow: Anno Domini 1992, pp. 3–17 (2nd ed. 1994). It has been slightly abridged, but the conversational style has been retained. This is the first of three dialogues included in this anthology, which show something of Fr Alexander's lively personality.

MM: Fr Alexander, I should like to put a question to you that I am sometimes asked myself: 'Need one be a Christian, and if so, why?'

AM: There's one single answer to that, I suppose, and it boils down to this: that *people have always looked for God.* It is a normal human condition to be engaged somehow or other with something higher, with an ideal – even when the human mind distorts or diminishes that ideal or changes it into something non-religious.

   Look at the time of Stalinism, Maoism or any other 'isms' and you will see that when people have God forcibly taken from them, they still seek for a pseudo-god. Idolatry takes the place of true faith but the instinctive yearning for God still remains. Though why need one be specifically Christian?

MM: Perhaps because of the Bible?

AM: Every religion has its sacred books, some are outstanding, full of poetry and great spiritual depths. Many of the sacred books of the East, for instance those of India, the *Mahabharata*, the section of it called *Bhagavadgita*, the Buddhist Sutras have a wealth of meaning and are magnificently written. So what else besides the scriptures?

MM: Christian art?

AM: In Russia nowadays people have become enthusiasts for our country's mediaeval art. I'm very fond of it myself, but for me it's part of our total spiritual culture. But if we look at things objectively, impartially, from the side (as I can't), then the art of ancient Greece is also religious, Indian art is spiritual, [. . .] and do not mosques [. . .] have the word of God somehow imprinted on them too? . . . If we take aesthetic criteria, then [. . .] probably the religion of Zeus and Athena is the very best . . . There are many beautiful ancient (and modern) sacred buildings in all religions, and so Christianity cannot say it holds the trump card on this point. So again we have to ask, why Christianity?

MM: Christian morality?

AM: Yes, of course. And I'm delighted that nowadays the moral values of Christianity are being recognized in our society. But we have to admit that it's just not true, it's mere propaganda, to suggest that there are no moral values outside Christianity [. . .]

   This is not the occasion to run through the moral creeds of every society but there is no doubt at all that profound ethical ideas are to be found in the writings of the Stoics and the Buddhists, and of course, in the Old Testament (which though related to Christianity, is really a pre-Christian religion) [. . .] There is a harshness in the Old Testament which some people in Russia say is not to be found in the New. But this idea is an aberration, for our Lord Jesus was never sentimental and he was often severe in his condemnations. You have to read the Gospels with rose-tinted spectacles not to hear him saying: 'Woe to you, scribes and Pharisees!' or: 'Depart from me, you cursed, into the eternal fire!' [Matt. 25.41]. That's not sentimental.

Of course, Christian ethics has its own special features. Yet if some outsider were to come along and make a comparison of Christian ethics with those of, say, the Stoics (let's take, for instance, Epicurus, Epictetus, Seneca and others who were living around Gospel times) that person would find a great deal in common with the Gospels, though the Greek philosophers never read them.

So again then why Christianity? Must we stay ultimately with the notion of religious pluralism? The idea that God reveals himself or can be known in any form of religion? In that case, goodbye to the idea of the uniqueness of Christianity and goodbye to the Christian faith.

But to get back to the point: it seems to me that nothing proves the uniqueness of Christianity, nothing except one thing alone, namely, *Jesus Christ*. For I'm convinced that each of the founders of the world religions speaks truth to us.

Let's remember what they said. Buddha said that he had achieved a state of absolute detachment after prolonged and difficult exercises. Can we believe him? Yes, of course we can. He was a great man and this was his achievement.

The Greek philosophers spoke of the intellectual difficulty of attaining the idea of God and of the spiritual world. This is true.

Or Muhammad, who said that before God he felt himself to be as nothing, that God took him and revealed himself to him and that before God he felt he was nothing more than a gnat. Can we believe him? Of course we can.

But alone among all these teachers is one who speaks in his own person as if for God himself: 'But *I* say to you' [Matt. 5.22 ff.], or as John has it: 'I and the Father are one' [John 10.30]. Not one of the great teachers of the world's religions ever said anything like that. That then is the only occasion in history when God revealed himself through a real person in some absolute fullness. This is the event we have in the Gospels.

Jesus, the preacher of morals – this is a historic myth. They would not have crucified him for just that alone. Jesus, the self-proclaimed Messiah? Why then did they not crucify Bar-Cochba[1] who also called himself messiah? And there were plenty of false messiahs. What was it in Jesus that aroused such love and such hatred? 'I am the door', he said, the door to eternity [John 10.9]. It seems to me that everything that is valuable in Christianity is valuable only because it is from Christ. What is not from Christ could as well belong to Islam or Buddhism.

Every religion is a path towards God, a conjecture about God, a human approach to God. It is a vector pointing upwards from below. But the coming of Christ is the answer, a vector coming from heaven towards us. On the one hand, an event situated in history, on the other hand, something quite outside history. That's why Christianity is unique, because Christ is unique. That's my answer to the question.

MM: Now let us think about those listeners who find themselves right now at a crossroads and may be thinking: 'Very well, but how am I to know that Christ was actually the one he claimed to be? How can I know that the Bible speaks the truth? How can I make sense of the different religions? What will be my answer to my atheist parents or atheist teachers, what shall I say to the Hare Krishna devotees dancing on the square? Why must I come to Christ? Just because Fr Alexander or Mark Makarov, or some other people think that the Bible speaks the truth? How can I tell whether they are right?

AM: Well, firstly, in the case of someone who already has some sense of what religion is, my answer might be what I have just said: all religions can be believed in. If we believe that God revealed himself to Muhammad, why make an exception for the founder of Christianity and reject what he has to say? If we believe that God does reveal himself, then he does so in different ways to all of them. And I believe that God is somehow at work in every great teacher and so there are no grounds whatever for saying; 'but we reject this Jesus Christ'. No, they are all true, and this means that he too is speaking the truth in saying of himself, 'I and the Father are one' [John 10.30].

But in the case of someone without any religious awareness, then I would reply in the words of the Gospel – you remember what the disciples said to Nathaniel – 'Come and see' [John 1.46].

It's something we have to see and feel, something that we must experience. Mathematics cannot prove the beauty of Beethoven's ninth symphony or of a great painting – say Rublev's 'Trinity'.[2] You have first to hear it, see it, make an inward visit to it – and we have to seek Christ out and try to meet him. Without this encounter no system of proofs will ever convince us, the system will remain merely something schematic and lifeless. We believe in Christ not because someone told us to but because those words invite each one of us to 'come and find out'.

Faith comes from hearing the word, said the apostle Paul. Remember what happened to the Samaritans when the woman came to them and said, 'Here is a man who told me all that I ever did.' They were astonished, but when they went themselves and heard Jesus themselves they concluded; 'Now we understand for ourselves, not because "you told us so", but from our own personal experience' [John 4.42].

That's the scientific approach, genuinely scientific. The fact is that science without experience cannot progress far. And in the case of religious belief, experience plays an enormous role. But it is an inner spiritual experience. This is the reality that human beings have to encounter. Say someone wants to pass an opinion about this reality without having tried to meet it, to encounter it, their opinion will be based on insufficient data. We can see Jesus only with the heart. Other things about him can be learned scientifically, by purely outward means as it were: the fact that he actually existed, what milieu he came from, and so on. These are important questions, but for faith they are secondary.

MM: What about those people (and there are quite a few of them) who have so absorbed their atheist education that they listen to us now and are thinking: 'It would be fine if everything were as you say, but of course everyone knows that there is no God.'

AM: I think that, on the contrary, everyone knows precisely the opposite. As I said at the beginning, the sheer numbers of people from whom God was taken away and who turned to idol-worship, demonstrate (something which, incidentally Mao Tse-tung understood) that people cannot exist without God.

God is the starting point of everything. Human beings live in the world only because they have faith in the meaning of this world. Albert Einstein once said that a person who doesn't believe in the meaning of existence is not fit for life at all. So atheists who say they do not believe in the meaning of existence, in fact, in the depths of their souls, in their subconscious, do believe but conceal their beliefs under various other labels.

People thirst for water because it is a necessity – that's an objective fact. They need food – that's an objective fact – like many others, and there is nothing imaginary about them. If people always thirst to find a higher meaning in existence, and to revere it, and to orient their lives on it, then this means that this need is not merely something pathological, but the normal condition of the human race.

When a person looks back in time now, they will see that always, throughout the centuries, God was present in some form or another. I've just thought of the founder of Positivism, Auguste Comte. He was a man who rejected higher values, though not aggressively and he spoke of God as something unknowable about which nothing could be said. He died on his knees before an altar, but this altar was the armchair where the woman he loved (who also had died) used to sit. He lavished respect and veneration on this armchair. He, by the way, was the first to propose the idea of a temple dedicated to humanity – *le grand être* – the great being of mankind which should be venerated. If we look through the history of all pseudo-religions, then we see how ineradicable is this sense of the sublime, how essential it is to humanity.

And there's another point, which involves indirect evidence [. . .] I'll give you a simple example. So today we are seeing the economic disintegration of our country, but this is not the result of any natural disaster but because the government has proved to be incapable and had led the whole system in the wrong direction.

But what do you think: isn't the universe a more complex system than the entire Soviet Union? If the universe continues to evolve and exist, that means that the thinking principle behind it is obviously more effective than our leadership.

MM: The point you are making is either one of the so-called 'proofs of the existence of God' or simply an argument in favour of the existence of a higher reason.

AM: It is evidence. The word 'proof' itself is rather vague and a bit dubious: nothing can be ultimately proved. Real scientists know that in any field, and particularly in the exact sciences, in the final analysis everything comes down to axioms: an unprovable axiom is the starting point, and entire systems are built on it.

MM: [. . .] The next question that listeners often raise is: 'How can a Christian account for the existence of evil [. . .] and the existence of God?' In other words, how do you answer the so-called 'problem of evil'?

AM: The fact of the matter is that there is moral evil and there is the physical imperfection of the world – they are rather different things.

The physical imperfection of the world is a result of the fact that the world is being created, that it is not finalized, not completed. I very much like what the German poet Novalis, who was a romantic and a mystic, said, namely that humanity is the messiah of nature.

Human beings do in fact occupy a special place in nature. We can believe the Bible that we are called to bring about a special spiritual transformation of nature; and that all creation groans in travail, as Paul says, awaiting the revelation of the children of God, that is, of us, people [Rom. 8. 21–22]. We ought to be influencing nature, but instead we are destroying it.

But then why did people defy God's will and so become the carriers of evil? To explain this completely and rationally means explaining the principle of darkness, giving grounds for it rationally, and justifying it.

The urge towards evil is itself an irrational impulse born out of freedom. I can't of course now go into the thinking of the great Russian philosopher, Nicolas Berdyaev, and his idea that freedom is something concealed from us in the divine nature and is eternal. It's something we can't comprehend, but one thing is sure, and that is that if people have been given freedom by God then we have also been given the possibility of opposing God and of taking a different path.

If people had no possibility of choosing their own path, then their freedom would be like Soviet elections as they used to be when they offered you one candidate and called it a choice. If God had given us freedom and said here is your only path and you can't take another, then that would not be freedom. We would be like rigidly programmed robots, androids. Human beings would not then be made in the image and likeness of the Creator, but they would be the Creator's playthings.

Consequently, God sent his likeness into the world to meet whatever might come so that human beings might carry on creating the world and reveal their many gifts in the world. Hence our supreme status as human beings. We have to answer for our actions, and so we can't expect at every moment that someone from on high will give us a tug on the leash. Moses said: 'I lay before you the paths of good and evil, life and death. Choose life.' [Deut. 30. 15]. Choose what is good. This you see is freedom, two paths.

And when people say to me what about the war and was God watching, I answer, my friends, he wasn't 'watching' at all. He warned us long ago what it would all lead to. If people opened their Bible, they would see what happens when human beings are abused, when spirituality is denied, what the results of materialism are. Everything that happened, let us say in Berlin and in Moscow, God had warned us about. When it all happened according to the scriptures (and indeed everything did happen according to the scriptures!), then people say: 'But where was God?' God is just there where God has always been. He has always given us warning.

It's another matter when people reject responsibility . . . But we must not forget that human beings are very tightly bound together. There is a law which we conventionally call the 'law of solidarity'.

How do you pass on to your child your knowledge, your physical features, character traits, your faith? Only thanks to this law of solidarity, by which people are linked together and enabled to pass on these things. But given that the channel exists, we must act responsibly towards it because it can also pass on evil. Someone, say, who is an alcoholic can pass on their pathological genetic structure to their innocent child. This only adds to that person's responsibilities.

We are not in a nursery school, we are in life, life with all its rigours . . .

Dostoevsky gives a frightening example in *The Brothers Karamazov*: when [a landowner's] dogs were let loose on a child . . . One of my friends wrote to me from prison reflecting on this theme: that God was there. He was present when several dozen grown men, baptized Christians, with crosses round their necks, knowing something of God's law, did not try to save the child but set the dogs on him at the impulse, the whim of the landowner.[3]

This happened through human choice, and not because of some mindless force [. . .]

MM: Our conversation is taking place in the last decade of the twentieth century, when many things are changing before our very eyes, when, here in the Soviet Union, the word 'religion' no longer scares anyone but everyone talks about it warmly. There are many changes in the attitude to religion and to believers in particular, and to Christ.

But how are we, believers, to view these changes? Are they evidence of a genuine spiritual mass movement, or a fashion, or what?

AM: Future historians will be better placed to judge. It does not interest me. I am not a historian, I am a man living in history. And for my part, these changes (which, of course, I have long expected) have made our working conditions easier, though there are some new problems and difficulties.

The late Fr Sergei Zheludkov[4] used to say that the day would come when we would be able to speak on the radio and we would not know what to say. So now our responsibility is all the greater.

Besides, there are other temptations – polarization into extreme modernism or extreme conservatism [. . .] It is most difficult for people who are at the centre, like me. It's just the same as in social life.

MM: Is that why you are attacked by both sides?

AM: Quite correct. But that's normal, I regard it as the norm for myself.

MM: In this respect, I suppose, we with our evangelical outlook are probably more to the right than you.

AM: Most likely you are.

MM: Maybe this is the source of some differences between us?

AM: Perhaps.

MM: [. . .] I am not a supporter of the theory of evolution [. . .] I have put forward arguments in favour of scientific creationism. You, I know, accept the theory of evolution.

AM: [. . .] In my view it is more religious, though it is scientific too. But in my view a religious outlook cannot be intellectually justified except somehow on the level of evolution [. . .][5]

MM: At this point I just want to stress that even quite serious differences of outlook between us should not prevent us (especially you and me) from loving each other as Christians.

AM: Yes of course. Good Lord, these differences don't matter at all [. . .] Ultimately, it's God's business and all we can do is investigate whether the world was created in this way or that. Faith in Christ is not altered by such things. Faith is completely independent of whether we hold to evolutionism or creationism or finally something between the two: creative evolution, as [the philosopher] Henri Bergson did who is a connecting link between evolutionism and creationism [. . .] But all this is secondary. How the universe developed is of no consequence for faith, for my relationship with God and with Christ, for my presence in the world. Though for my intellect, it's a fascinating question, full of interest, it's absorbing, and its bound up with my religious ideas.

And for myself, sometimes a cloud, a bird or a tree can mean more than any religious painting. Nature itself is an icon of the first quality for me [. . .].

2

Religion, Knowledge of God, and the Problem of Evil

The following is an extract from Fr Alexander's book, The Sources of Religion, *which is the first volume of Fr Alexander's seven-volume study of the world's faiths. It comes from a chapter entitled 'Humanity before God'. In this extract the author examines the nature of religious belief emphasizing that the human experience of the divine is a world-wide phenomenon; he argues for the essential importance of religious language and religious symbolism in order to communicate that experience. He has some trenchant remarks to make about Western 'demythologizers', which at the time of writing, in the sixties, were in the public eye: his remarks, setting them in the context of the 'apophatic' tradition in Christian theology and other world religions, have relevance today. In the final section the author tackles the problem of evil in the world from the point of view of Indian philosophy, dualist faiths, and Christianity; he affirms his belief in the dynamic struggle of the world towards perfectability.*

The present extract has been taken from Istoki religii, *Moscow 1991, pp. 72-81. Title and subtitles in this translation have been supplied by the editor.*

The nature of religious faith

Faith is not an escape from life nor is it a way of shutting oneself off in some imaginary world. The word 'religion' comes from the Latin verb *religare*, 'to bind'. Religion is a force binding worlds together, a bridge between the spirit of we who are created and the divine Spirit. Strengthened by this bond, human beings can be active participants in the ongoing creation of the world.

Those who see something humiliating in the worship of God are light years away from understanding what genuine religious life is. They allege that faith fosters a slave mentality and makes for passivity: whereas in fact the striving to bring our own will into harmony with the divine will is an act which derives from our *freedom*. God does not enslave us, does not fetter our will, but on the contrary gives us the full freedom to reject him and to seek our own paths.

We can see this everywhere: in the fact that God does not present himself to us in a compellingly obvious way (either through experience, or by proofs), and in the fact that, by definition, no action by God in the world restricts our freedom of choice. In unity with God, a person finds fullness of being and not abject submission. The historian of religion, Otto Pfleiderer, remarked:

> . . . Man is not afraid that, by this free obedience or surrender to God, he will lose his human freedom and dignity; but, on the contrary, he is confident that, in the alliance with God, he will achieve freedom from the limitations and fetters of surrounding nature, and those worse limitations and fetters of nature within us . . . Seneca said at his early day: 'To obey God is to be free.'[1]

To the religious mind, goodness in life lies in service of the highest objective good, beauty in the reflection of the highest beauty, and our perception of truth lies in communion with the perfect truth which embraces all things, including us too.

So life, according to the teachings of religion, is inseparable from the struggle for the triumph of goodness, the struggle for all that is radiant and sublime; life should not be a matter of passively waiting for 'manna from heaven', but rather a fearless confrontation with evil.

When the young pastor, Dietrich Bonhoeffer, was awaiting death in a Nazi prison he wrote to his friend: 'I should like to speak of God not on the boundaries of life, but at the centre, not in weaknesses but in strength.' The church, he said, should not 'stand at the boundaries where human powers give out, but in the middle of the village.'² Was it not from their faith that Fr Maximilian Kolbe and Mother Maria who gave up their lives for others in the hell of the concentration camps, or pastor David Wilkerson, the contemporary 'apostle to the criminal world', drew the strength to accomplish their life's work?³

Religion is the true foundation of a *moral life*. We find no basis for ethical principles in nature. The biologist Thomas Huxley wittily remarked that the criminal and the honest man both follow nature, though the former does so more closely. We may object that morality is dictated by social duty, but in fact consciousness of this duty in its turn is nothing other than a moral conviction; while it is precisely the denial of meaning to life, and the denial of God, that opens the way to the triumph of limitless egoism and internecine conflict.⁴

The question arises then why it is that some people have irreproachable morals but remain unbelievers. Those who put such questions forget that these 'virtuous atheists' did not appear in a vacuum. From childhood, they were brought up in a milieu that had *always* been in contact with religious culture. All the 'moral codes' of our day, however much this is denied, are based on principles of religious morality.

Dobrolyubov, Chernyshevsky, the revolutionaries of the last century or the heroes of the Resistance were people of out-standing purity and selflessness, but we must not lose sight of the fact that the majority of them came from Christian families or even the families of priests where they received a leavening of morality.

Religious language and religious symbolism

So religion is the *bond* between humanity and the very source of being, a bond which gives human life abundant meaning, which inspires people to serve, which permeates their whole existence with light, and which determines their moral outlook.

Many will object: 'It would be wonderful if religion were reduced just to this, its spiritual kernel. But religion presents us on top of that with all these formulae and dogmas, it breeds theoretical theological constructs as well. Wouldn't it be better to reject all that and keep only pure religion? By all means let's admit the actual existence of some mysterious beneficial force which affects and inspires people. Let's accept this with gratitude and gladness. But why do we need words? Surely they are a hindrance rather than a help.'

Faust's famous confession to Gretchen reflects just such an attitude:

Who dares to claim
That he believes in God?
And whose heart is so dead
That he has ever boldly said:
No, I do not believe?
Embracing all things,
Holding all things in being,
Does He not hold and keep
You, me, even Himself?
Is not the heavens' great vault up there on high,
And here below, does not the earth stand fast?
Do everlasting stars, gleaming with love,
Not rise above us through the sky?
Are we not here and gazing eye to eye?
Does all this not besiege
Your mind and heart,
And weave in unseen visibility
All round you its eternal mystery?
Oh, fill your heart right up with all of this
And when you're brimming over with the bliss
Of such a feeling, call it what you like!
Call it joy, or your heart, or love, or God!
I have no name for it. The feeling's all there is:
The name's more noise and smoke – what does it do
But cloud the heavenly radiance?[5]

*

Religious feeling is indeed an experience surpassing human language and concepts and attempts to express it always impoverish its content. This is true of any deep inner experience, for example of the experience of beauty. 'A thought spoken aloud is a lie,' said the poet Tyutchev. And yet in life we are not put off by this, and although our words cannot adequately express our feelings we continue to use them. When a man says to a woman, 'I love you', he is repeating a conventional formula, although for each individual something unique is lying behind these words. The word is a *symbol* behind which is hidden something immeasurably more profound. And this symbol is a bridge between souls.

It may be that at the higher levels of the human spirit or at moments of special inner elevation, words are superfluous. But as a rule, we cannot manage without words, without concepts or without thinking.

We may readily understand why the theologian William Hamilton or the mystic Jiddu Krishnamurti resisted all definitions of God and even the very word 'God' itself on the grounds that words tend to become fetishized. But on the other hand, their attempt to rise above words was destined to failure. People are not only creatures who contemplate and experience, but beings who think and speak. To reject concepts and words is to go against human nature, against the human need to give meaning to life and experience.

If faith remains a matter of indeterminate inner states, it is in danger of becoming a 'refuge' unrelated to our actions. The voice of God is a voice calling us to work, to overcome and to serve. None of this is possible without words, concepts and symbols. Besides, the *forms* (myths, symbols, icons) in which we clothe our religious experience are essential if people are to share them with one another. So the endeavours of theologians like Rudolf Bultmann to 'demythologize' Christianity are as fruitless as Krishnamurti's were.[6]

In rejecting the idea of God 'up in heaven', another contemporary theologian, Paul Tillich, has suggested that we speak about God as 'inexhaustible depth'.[7] In so doing he failed to see that 'depth' is the same kind of conventional spatial concept as 'heaven'. Besides, the image of 'heaven' with its majesty and immensity is such an excellent symbol of the divine that it has not lost signficance in any epoch. People who favour 'demythologizing' lose sight of the broad scope, the many levels and multifaceted meaning of religious symbols.[8] If ancient people to some extent identified 'heaven' with the space above the earth, in modern times it has acquired a purely spiritual meaning (a meaning which incidentally many ancients already attached to it).

The whole force of an image or myth lies precisely in its organic and synthesizing nature. Image and myth enable us to give concrete signification to things that analytic language is unable to express. That is why the proposal by some theologians to remove the very concepts of 'God' and 'religion' from spiritual life is a mistaken one.[9] Words, for all their limitations, are not simple nor are they things of secondary importance.

Symbols and myths are not invented but grow naturally from an inner understanding. People will always have a need for these signs which reflects both the different facets of earthly being and the higher reality.

Religion could not have a social role unless people had first learned somehow to communicate their inner experiences to one another. If we renounce all ways of religious intercourse and of attempts at mutual understanding then religion will not unite souls but separate them.

According to Christian doctrine God joined himself to humanity in Christ, but are these words really just abstractions? Don't they rather raise humanity to incomparably new heights? Christ prayed that his disciples should be one [John 17.21] as the Persons of the Godhead are one. Are not these words an indication for us of the deepest essential meaning of the doctrine of the Trinity? Doesn't the teaching about the kingdom of God to come give purpose and meaning to the whole march of history? Krishnamurti is right that we need reminding of the limitation of words. Even the apostle Paul said, 'The letter kills but the spirit gives life [II Cor. 3.6] Nonetheless, he preached in words and wrote the epistles.

The apophatic way and human reason

Without noticing it, the opponents of traditional religious symbolism keep using the very ancient language of pantheism, familiar to pre-Christian beliefs. In doing so, the proponents of pseudo-modern theology claim that their purpose is to purify the concept of God from layers of anthropomorphism. Yet if they had taken the trouble seriously to study the theology of the Church Fathers or at least Indian or Platonic religious thought, they would have found that what they call innovation are things that are long since familiar.[10]

Even in antiquity, the spiritual experience of the mystics and the speculations of philosophers had led to the conviction that it was impossible to treat the Godhead as one of the objects of existence. Even the very category of 'existence' seemed inapplicable to God, for, in essence God surpasses all that is created or conditioned.

For several centuries before Christ these ideas formed the basis for the development of 'apophatic' (i.e. *negative*) theology, according to which, with regard to the Godhead, only negative concepts about what God is *not* are allowable.

The *Upanishads* affirm that God is 'not this and not that'. 'He surpasses being itself', says Plato. The Old Testament, although it abounds in anthropomorphic expressions, constantly emphasizes that God is 'holy', which in scriptural language means that in the profundity of his being, God has a nature that is wholly beyond the imagination and thoughts of humanity. Christianity adopted this teaching in its totality, and patristic theology developed it. 'He is higher than anything conceivable' taught Origen. In the words of Pseudo-Dionysius, God is 'not one of the things that are'; that is, no concepts and no kind of being can fathom the depths of God. 'God', according to St Maximus the Confessor, 'encloses in himself the whole of being . . . he is himself well beyond being itself'. Cardinal Nicolas de Cusa said that only the person who understands that God is unknowable can approach him.[11]

However, people cannot be restricted to this 'negative' theology. God manifests himself in life so actively, so powerfully, so vitally and so concretely that simple negation is not enough. Religious life and thought need words of affirmation as well. They may need to be constantly accompanied by riders and qualifications, but they are a necessity to us as human beings.

Inseparable from thought, words make it possible for us to link our intuitive understanding more firmly with our overall outlook and to the entire ordering of our life. Thoughts about God are not something blasphemous.

Quite the opposite: Christian theologians, starting with St Paul, have always insisted on the importance of reason in the interpretation of faith. St Basil the Great wrote that we have been given reasoning souls by which we can comprehend God, fathom with our intellect the nature of what exists and reap the sweetest fruits of wisdom. St John of Damascus pointed to reason as one of the godlike traits of human beings. We just have to remember that theological concepts are always approximate and metaphorical in comparison with reality. There is nothing in this that diminishes the significance of theology. Natural science also comes to a point where modelling and adequate verbal descriptions become impossible and then symbols come to the rescue. In religious consciousness, on the other hand, facts of inner experience are combined with the interpretation of it. The more harmonious the union of these two elements, the more perfect is the system of the religious rites. Sarvepali Radhakrishnan wrote:

> Simply because [a mystic insight] is incommunicable, it does not become less valid than other forms of knowledge. We can describe this experience only by metaphors . . . intellect need not be negated, but has only to be supplemented. A philosophy based on intuition is not necessarily opposed to reason and understanding. Intuition can throw light on the dark places which intellect is not able to penetrate. The results of mystic intuition require to be subjected to logical analysis. And it is only by this process of mutual correction and supplementation that each can live a sober life. The results of intellect will be dull and empty, unfinished and fragmentary, without the help of intuition, while intuitional insights will be blind and dumb, dark and strange without intellectual confirmation. The ideal

of the intellect is realised in the intuitive experience, for in the supreme are all contraries reconciled.[12]

This is the *higher reason* which serves as the foundation for realist philosophy and theological thought.

Rational reasoning, operating with the data of experience and revelation, acts as a barrier protecting the idea of God from faulty thinking. But reason must clearly see the limits of its jurisdiction. The Catholic theologian, Jean Daniélou, writes:

> So we see at the same time how the knowledge of God is a work of reason and a challenge to reason. It is in this sense that 'nothing is more reasonable than the disavowal of reason.' Reason is the necessary means of knowledge in that it prevents us from placing God where He is not.[13]

We must moreover bear in mind the essential difference between philosophy and dogmatic symbolism. Philosophy, although based on intuition, formally follows the inductive path and is concerned not with realities but with ideas. It is different for dogmatic symbols. They are not arrived at with the help of the intellect although they are expressed in the language of concepts. Consequently those who attribute the Orthodox creed to Greek rationalism are making a great mistake. The truths expressed in it were given in a form alien to the abstract speculation of the philosophers. Hegel already noticed this. In general, fundamental Christian doctrines are marked by *inner contradictions*, para-doxes, antinomies, which cannot be smoothed out by the methods of formal logic. If the dogmas had been the fruit of philosphical speculation, they would most probably not contain these contradictions; rational conceptualization loves good order. The doctrines of the Three-in-One and of Godmanhood, however, are born out of mystic contemplation and in the imperfect language of concepts take on a dialectic, contradictory form. A dogmatic symbol reveals something *given* to inner intuitive contemplation, whereas speculative philosophy inter-prets it as a *fact* to be brought as far as possible into agreement with discursive thinking.[14]

And so we are not doomed to an isolated existence on islands of individual consciousness and experience. Between these islands are bridges: they are concepts and signs, symbols and dogmas.

God and humanity

One of theology's first problems is the question of how our limited, conditioned existence is related to the unconditioned absolute Being of God.

The spiritual experience of mankind testifies to the fact that God can be *close* to the soul in the deepest and most intimate way. So no gulf exists between him and us. In moments of inner enlightenment can we not sense his unseen presence in all nature, in the breath of the forest, the blossoming flower, the mysterious life of earth and sky?

> And You revealed yourself to me: You are the world,
> You are all, You are sky and water,
> You are the voice of the storm, You are ether,
> You are a poet's thought, You are a star . . .[15]

This is the tremendous truth of the *pantheism* which found final expression in the *Upanishads*, in Daoism and in some Greek and Western philosophical systems. Pantheism, however, is not able to contain all truth. It is widespread because it reveals God in the world of nature; in what is most readily accessible to visual contemplation. It translates its own finitude into the absolute and identifies God with the impersonal force that pervades the universe. However, impersonality is characteristic of the lower orders of existence; at the summit of the world hierarchy are personal, intelligent and self-conscious beings.

Even from our own experience we find how much higher is our 'I', our spiritual personality, to our unconscious and bodily nature. How much more difficult it is then to conceive of God as impersonal, who himself is the highest perfection. In the Bible we have a direct testimony of the revealed Creator as the supreme Person.

Of course in the depths of his being, the divine person is infinitely different from the personhood of a limited created being. The immeasurable, mysterious, incomprehensible essence of the absolute transcends us, surpassing both our intuitive and our discursive faculties. But God has turned towards the world, and the creator God, the God-Logos is revealed to the soul as will, reason and personhood. In this creative act God has annihilated the gulf between the absolute and the relative, between himself and the world. It is God who calls the creatures into being, who steers the cosmogonic and anthropogenetic process towards perfection, towards the supreme aim of the God-man,[16] which is to bring the world into communion with the fullness of divine life.

The problem of evil in the world

At this point, however, we are inescapably faced with a puzzle: one that the religious mind has always agonized over: how did *imperfection* come into creation? How can we reconcile the revelation of God's beneficence with the fact of the reign of evil on earth? The tragic question was posed long ago, not by Dostoevsky or by Camus, but by the book of Job and ancient religious teachings.

Our concern now is not with the issue of evil in human life. We must turn first to the world of nature. The harmony and adaptability in creation which people always find astonishing cannot hide the other side of created existence. All life processes are constantly accompanied by struggling and devouring, by suffering and dying. Even in the days when human beings knew little of the world, they saw this dark shadow cast by nature. Ancient demonology is nothing more than the personification of cosmic evil. But now that science has penetrated into the fabric of matter, the scale of these destructive tendencies has become even more apparent. Let others rightly claim that where consciousness is absent there is neither evil nor sin, but who dares deny universal suffering? Pain and death overtake all that lives, putting their terrible stamp on all biogenesis. Granted that pain may to some extent have a beneficial role in signalling danger, it nevertheless remains true that pain appears only because the danger for the living creature is perfectly real. Moreover the battlefield is not confined to the sphere of life. Thermodynamics has revealed a tendency in the movement of the cosmos *opposed* to the process of becoming. This tendency leads to the collapse of structures, to the degradation of energy and to an increase in entropy. 'As entropy increases,' says Norbert Wiener,

> the universe and all the closed systems it contains tend naturally to be used up and to lose their definition, and tend to pass from a less probable to a more probable state, from a state of organization and differentiation where there are distinctions and forms to a state of chaos and uniformity.[17]

Such is the fate of lifeless nature, while living nature appears to be like a gigantic beast devouring its children and itself trembling in agony. Death overwhelms life, chaos overwhelms organization. The world of creation is constantly being undermined by forces of destruction.

Religious thought has long recognized the presence of this cosmic evil. As a rule, it has considered it from three points of view.

The first approach had its birth in India. There the philosophers of Brahmanism gave a *monistic* answer to the question of the imperfection of the world. According to the *Upanishads* this imperfection rises from the depths of the Absolute itself: the spectre of ephemeral existence from time to time disturbs the divine Brahman. Pouring his strength into non-being, he embodies himself in corruptible forms, entangling himself in the nets of false existence. Only at the end of an immense period does the Absolute free itself and find the peace of unconditional perfection once more. Cosmogenesis is, consequently, something meaningless which essentially should not be.

The trouble with this teaching, which is difficult to accept, is the denial of value to being and above all, the fact that it makes the Godhead itself into the source of cosmic evil.

The second answer, at a first glance a more attractive one, is based on the doctrine of *dualism*. The most ancient myths of mankind draw a picture of a struggle between the primordial principles of order and chaos. This idea is most fully developed in the religion of the Iranian prophet Zarathustra from which it was borrowed by the Gnostics, Manicheans and the Albigensians. Dualism, however, for all its points of correspondence with what we see in the world, does not ultimately resolve the main issue. If two primordal opposing principles exist, neither of them can be the absolute which both faith and knowledge aspire to. It follows then that the ultimate reality must be sought beyond them, above them.

The Christian answer does not deny the partial truth of Indian pessimism or the relative truth of dualism. Christianity agrees that our present existence bears within itself marks of imperfection, and that cosmogenesis is inseparable from the struggle of diametrically opposed principles. But the Bible, in speaking of the world as the creation of God, takes the view of the universe as something *dynamic*, something in the process of perfection. The Old Testament knows of the forces of chaos, but does not treat them as divine; it looks on them rather as a created principle which opposes the designs of the Creator. According to the Bible, God *cannot* be the source of evil. Evil is the *violation* of God's designs by created beings and not simply a 'procrastination on the path of perfection' as Lessing said.

The monstrous images of chaos and Satan which we find in scripture are signs that a catastrophe has taken place in the spiritual world. Out of this catastrophe came demonic 'self will' and the rebellion against harmony which all nature reflects. 'For the creation', says Paul, 'was subjected to futility, not of its own will but by the will of him who subjected it in hope . . . We know that the whole creation has been groaning in travail together until now . . .' [Rom. 8.20,22]. These mysterious words point to the dependence of the present state of nature on a cosmic Fall. Is not the very irreversibility of time with its cruel implacability, an illness of creation? The book of Revelation predicts that in the future cosmos, time will be no more [Rev. 10.6].

Christian theologians do not give an unequivocal answer to the question: 'How did the poisoning of creation by evil come about?' Some of them, for example Vladimir Solovyev, explain it by reference to the ancient doctrine of the 'world soul', supposing it to have been seized by the element of cosmic evil. Certainly the Bible teaches that nature is not a dead principle, but has a certain spiritual dimension. This thinking is shared by very many theologians, philosophers and scholars. Very probably at a deep and immaterial level nature is somehow contiguous with the transphysical world and constitutes a kind of whole with it. Precisely because of this, nature has been infected with corruption at its very source. We might regard chaos and death as the results of a distortion of the spiritual parameters of the universe, a distortion which brought into cosmogenesis the blind destructive forces which impede its movement forward. From the moment of the cosmic Fall, in the words of the German mystic, Jakob Boehme,

> It is clearly seen . . . how the heavenly and hellish kingdoms in nature have always wrestled the one with the other, and stood in great travail, even as a woman in the birth.[18]

This idea may seem to deny divine omnipotence, but Christianity teaches that any act of God in relation to the world involves God's own self limitation, or as the Church Fathers say, the *kenosis* (self-emptying) of the absolute. It is this *kenosis* that leaves a space for the *freedom* of the created world without which all existence would be a distortion of the image of its Creator.[19] The elements in the universe which have self-consciousness – the spiritual worlds and human beings – are thus unthinkable without freedom; and this includes the freedom to seek 'one's own ways', to diverge from God's ways. The only thing which is beyond any explanation is the very urge itself to oppose God, an urge which by its nature is irrational. No words or concepts can shed light on this dark abyss. Berdyaev wrote:

> The mind without religion imagines itself correcting God's word and boasts that it could have done better, that God ought to have created the cosmos by force, ought to have created man incapable of evil, and he should immediately bring creation to a state of perfection in which there will be no suffering or death, and in which people would be drawn to the good. This

rational plan for creation is a fruit of human limitation and shows a lack of awareness of the meaning of existence, since this meaning is bound up with the irrational mystery of the freedom to sin. If evil were outwardly removed by force and compulsion, and if goodness were something necessary and inevitable, then the worth of each individual and the perfection of being would be devalued; such a plan does not accord with the intentions of that Being whose perfections are absolute. The Creator did not establish a cosmos that was forcibly and necessarily perfect and good since such a cosmos would not be fundamentally either perfect or good. The basis for perfection and goodness lies in love for God freely given, union with God freely joined, and this characteristic of all that is perfect and good, of all being makes the tragedy of the universe inevitable. According to the plan of creation, the cosmos has been set as a task, as an idea, which is to be creatively realized by the freedom of the created soul.[20]

The power of chaos cannot completely paralyse the forces contained in the universe. The Bible teaches about *wisdom* which is the reflection of the supreme reason in creation. This principle is revealed continually throughout all cosmogenesis in organization, in growth towards perfection, in order, and in progress. The work of creation is the work of the Logos overcoming chaos; it reaches the level of consciousness in human beings and is pointed towards the world to come. Thus struggle is the law of creation, the dialectic by which creatures come into being.

3

Faith and its Enemies

Every Soviet school child would have had instilled in him or her the idea that science and religion were incompatible, that religion was dying out, – and anyway hadn't Marx himself said that religion was the opium of the people? It was to readers brought up in this thought world that Fr Alexander began to address his great study of human religions, beginning with The Sources of Religion (1971) *from which this extract is taken. Writing this passage (the introduction) in the heat of the Khrushchev persecutions, Men identified those thinkers, artists and scientists, mostly Western, of this century who have been inspired by the truths of religion, in order to prove his point that religion is an inalienable attribute of humanity through all centuries.*

The extract is taken from Istoki religii, *Moscow 1991, pp. 13–24. The title to this translation has been supplied by the editor.*

No thinking person will deny that religion has, over the centuries, been a deciding factor in human life. From the stone age to the thermonuclear age, religion has, in its astonishing changes and metamorphoses, been indissolubly linked with the human spirit and with world culture. Egyptian temples and Babylonian hymns, the Bible and the Parthenon, Gothic stained glass and Russian icons, Dante's *Divine Comedy* and the works of Dostoevsky, the philosophy of Plato and Kierkegaard, the music of Bach and Britten, the social ideas of Savonarola and Thomas Müntzer, are all rooted in religion, for religion gives a higher meaning to earthly life and links it to what is eternal.

Religion has been the determining impulse in many historical movements. Asia's adoption of Buddhism, the preaching of the gospel in the ancient world, the expansion of Islam, the Reformation of the Western Church, all these were important landmarks in the life of mankind. Even the struggle against religion is an indirect acknowledgment of its significance.

Religious faith has influenced great social upheavals and the most secret depths of the human heart, and it is here that its chief strength lies.

Many people, however, while accepting the important role of religion in the past, say that for people of the twentieth century it is dead, or will soon be so. They say that the world is finally entering a period without faith.

Is this so? Is there not rather lying concealed behind the struggle against religion, which has been waged for the best part of this century, an unconscious fear of religion, and a doubt on the part of its enemies in the rightness of their cause?

Even in ancient times, people believed that there was not a single nation without any faith.[1] This still holds true today. As Arnold Toynbee remarked, even atheists should not be thought of as people entirely without faith.[2] Their views reveal a confused religious sentiment, even though that feeling is directed towards earthly objects, individuals and ideas. Anti-religious doctrines are often associated with inner impulses of a mystical nature. Ideological myths accepted in faith are in essence religion in a new guise.

One of the few atheists to risk taking their denial of God to its logical conclusion was Friedrich Nietzsche. 'God is dead!' he exclaimed, and worked feverishly to expel every reminder of God from people's lives. God is dead and consequently the universe is no more than a game of blind elements. Heaven is empty, the world is empty and everything is repeated in the endless flow of time. There is no meaning, there is no purpose, there is nothing that has value. How ludicrous therefore are human pretensions of grandeur. Mankind came out of nothing and returns there together with his pitiable civilization and planet. Nietzsche naturally rejected all the moral principles of Christianity, for the law of sovereign-nature is the survival of the fittest. He spoke with contempt also about the possibility of any kind of social transformations: for what is society if not a display of the same universal meaninglessness?

But few people have come to such radical conclusions. Most atheists have recoiled from the sombre scene of existence without values and have fallen back on what Nietzsche called 'the shadow of God'. In the dead wilderness of unbelief, they have strewn flowers taken from distant gardens among the stones and tried to soften the grimness of the landscape. (Nietzsche himself failed to hold out to the end and took refuge in the concept of superman.) Thus atheistic beliefs have grown up, which furtively insert meaning into meaninglessness, and are designed to reconcile people to what by their very nature they *cannot* accept. This is why many inconsistent atheists talk about the greatness of the good, about the inevitable radiant future that awaits mankind and for which we must be prepared to make the greatest sacrifices. They cherish selflessness, heroism and justice.

In our time this tension between an atheistic view of the world and the thirst for the ideal is vividly demonstrated in Albert Camus. While insisting on the 'absurdity' of existence, he nevertheless tried to find a prop, at least in the moral will of mankind. He struggled against tyranny for human rights, he debated, accused and preached. Such an attitude, though, hardly stems from his theory of the absurd. Camus himself confessed as much to his opponents:

> Et à la verité, moi qui croyais penser comme vous, je ne voyais guère d'argument à vous opposer, sinon un gout violent de la justice qui, pour finir, me paraissait aussi peu raisonné que la plus soudaine des passions.[3]

> [And in all honesty in my discussions with you, I had great difficulty in finding arguments other than a powerful longing for justice which, in the end, is just as irrational as the most unexpected passion.]

There is something tragic and moving about the atheists' attempt to take shelter from the abyss of an indifferent universe, from an empty cold sky. It is not simply fear and dread but an

unconscious attraction to those things which dogmatic materialism denies: to meaning, purpose, and to a rational origin of the
universe. This mysterious attraction, which is inherent in human
beings, cannot be eradicated by any doctrine. Even an atheist
such as the psychoanalyst Erich Fromm acknowledged its reality.
He wrote that 'The study of people forces us to acknowledge that
the need for a general system of orientation and for an object of
devotion is deeply rooted in human existence.'[4]

Where does this need originate? For everything in the world
surely has its real roots somewhere. No one, for instance, would
question that our bodily needs correspond to the objective
necessities for life. If through the ages, the human spirit has
longed for beauty, goodness, for something higher, something
worthy of worship, is it right to see this as mere self-deception? Is
it not more natural to recognize that just as the body is connected
to the objective world of nature, so also the spirit is drawn to the
invisible reality which is both kindred to it and beyond it? Is it not
significant that when human beings turn away from this reality,
superstitions and secular 'cults' spring up in its place? In other
words, if people turn away from God they inevitably turn to
idols.

Sigmund Freud, the founder of psychoanalysis, attempted to
derive the idea of God from repressed desires driven into the
unconscious sphere of the mind. But may we not turn the
question on its head? Are not atheistic substitutes for religion the
result of driving out the sense of God, which still makes itself felt?
We might argue that the very denial of the highest is nourished by
the unconscious element of faith.

Thus, in the period before the French revolution, the philosophy of the Encyclopaedists generated an enthusiasm very akin
to religious experience. After his conversion to the 'new faith',
Baron d'Holbach, patriarch of Enlightenment atheism, fell, it is
said, on his knees before Diderot in the throes of an atheistic
ecstasy.[5] His followers in the days of the revolution vowed 'to
have no other religion than the religion of nature, no other temple
than the temple of Reason'. Faith in humanity, the imminent
realization of 'liberty, equality and fraternity', faith in science, in
reason, in progress, have all from time to time inspired people to

reverence and even engendered strange cults. Think of the founder of positivism, Auguste Comte, and his worship of the 'Supreme Being' – mankind.

At the end of the last century, the German biologist Ernst Haeckel founded a 'monistic' religion of nature which was continued in the work of another biologist, Julian Huxley. Denying a personal God, Huxley thought that the vital force of the cosmos, the creative energy of evolution, could be made the object of reverence.[6]

The movement among the Russian intelligentsia to serve 'the people' patently bears religious characteristics.[7] In 'the people' they saw the salt of the earth, the anchor of salvation, the source of the highest wisdom. This cult gave rise to not a few heroes and 'martyrs'.[8] The history of the civil war in Russia in the twenties is a clear example of how faith in the future, in justice, in a kind of kingdom of Heaven on earth overcame all obstacles. The well trained and well armed enemy forces were opposed chiefly by conviction and enthusiasm in the face of which they had to retreat.

It is no accident that materialists, though in theory claiming the primacy of economics, in practice make appeal to 'consciousness', 'ideas' and 'faith'. Mao Tse-tung, for instance, admitted once that he deliberately fostered the cult of his personality to 'inspire' the masses. He made worship of a pseudo-god, and not the promise of material goods, the lynch pin of his struggle and his policy.

Many atheists, as we see, are not at all ashamed to label their views religious. Early this century, one of them wrote: 'We have all the more right to reject "Heaven" since we have all the more confidence in the strength and beauty of earthly religion.'[9] This 'religion' subsequently established its own infallible authorities, its dogmas, scriptures, rituals and saints.[10]

At the other end of the social spectrum, we find something similar. 'Today' wrote the National-Socialist ideologist, Alfred Rosenberg, 'a new faith is awakening – the myth of blood'. He and his fellows turned biological racism into a pseudo-mystical dogma, seducing a people whose Christian roots had at that time been undermined.

Many other examples could be given of how, when the idea of God is expelled from consciousness, it comes back to people though in a perverted, hardly recognizable form. This proves that people have an ineradicable need to link their lives to something higher, something holy.

Apologists of atheism attempt to represent their ideology as the result of intellectual progress, as the most 'modern' of ideologies. In reality, atheism existed long before the emergence of the major world religions and has always been a symptom of spiritual crisis, impoverishment and decay.

The 'mass atheism' of our tragic times is not an accidental occurrence. It is not at all the case that faith in God has run out among European peoples. The decline in faith has three principle causes. The first lies in the fact that Christianity was at the 'epicentre' of urbanization, a process which has inflicted heavy damage on the spiritual values and moral state of society. This hurricane has not affected the followers of Islam and other religions to the same extent. The full force of the blow fell upon the Christians. The second cause has to do with mistakes made by leaders of the churches, and the way some of them have perverted the true spirit of religion. The third cause lies in the shallow 'bourgeois mentality' that Berdyaev spoke about, in the ideas of secularism and of the Man-god.[11] These ideas originated in ancient times but were most clearly expressed at the time of the Renaissance. At that time, about 400 years ago, the Western world faced the temptation of pagan humanism and for the most part this temptation was not resisted. Man as the 'measure of all things' was raised to the rank of the divine, human reason was declared to be the supreme judge of the deepest questions of existence and human nature proclaimed to be essentially harmonious and sublime.

The ideologists of the Enlightenment and of rationalism created the theoretical framework for these ideas. A veritable cult of science grew up: social transformations came to be regarded as the only cure for all the world's ills and the idea of continual progress, which flourished in the nineteenth century, reinforced these attitudes.

Atheistic humanism, having repudiated Christian humanism,

continually announced the end of religious faith. However, faith not only stood its ground but continued to flourish. The period from the sixteenth to the nineteenth centuries gave the church a multitude of saints, ascetics, and theologians; missionary activity took Christianity beyond the borders of Europe; and new spiritual movements arose.

The answer to this was attempts to eradicate Christianity by force. Massive persecutions of the church erupted at the time of the Convention. Bishops and priests were executed, churches were turned into clubs, tombs of the saints were defiled (for example that of St Louis). Notre Dame cathedral was turned into a place for the worship of Reason.[12] A hearse was driven through the streets of Paris loaded with holy objects, which was intended to signify the 'burial of God'. But it soon became clear that the atheists had not 'buried' God at all but only a pile of church paraphernalia.

The 'storming of Heaven' did not end with the French revolution. Again and again, it resumed, now under the banner of evolutionism or of biblical criticism, now under the pretext of the struggle against reaction. Bismarck and the French ministers, the German social-democrats and Russian revolutionaries from their different sides unrelentingly attacked Christianity. At the turn of the century, however, a poll amongst members of the artistic world indicated that in the opinion of the majority, religion was far from collapsing. The American philosopher, William Hocking, wrote at the time: 'Hasten not to judge that the spirit of the age is becoming irreligious . . . Potentially, at least, men are becoming more religious. This development of religion is still a latent fact . . .'[13] As this fact became less and less hidden, atheism again resorted to violence.

During the first thirty years of the twentieth century, social upheavals in Russia, Mexico, Germany and Italy led to a veritable war against Christianity and other religions, a war which in the Peoples Republics of China and Albania subsequently became total. All possible weapons, from propaganda in the press and on the radio, tribunals and pillories to brutal mass executions, were unleashed to put an end to religion. Hand in hand with the militant anti-god movement went indifference, a cheap rationalism and the 'new' humanism – a poor imitation of the Renaissance. But the victory, so much hoped for by the persecutors, did not materialize.

Christianity long ago foresaw these battles which are foretold in the Bible; and from that same Bible the church draws confidence that she will never be overcome.

True, among Christians there have been those whose will has been paralysed by the pressure of secularism.[14] They were tormented by the question: does the church have a future? But they posed this question as if the church were *only* a human institution and they forgot Christ's words to Peter: 'I will build my church and the powers of death shall not prevail against it' [Matt. 16.18].

This promise is obviously not a call to passivity. What would have happened if instead of 'preaching the gospel to all nations', Jesus' disciples had shut their doors and stayed at home? Even then Jesus' message would have lived on in the world. Had the apostles fallen silent, then 'the stones would have cried out'. Jesus would have found himself other followers.

On the other hand, it is legitimate to ask has not the world lost the need for faith today? Is it not satisfied with what 'secular' culture can provide?

There is some evidence that this is so: the prolonged pressure of anti-religious forces have inevitably left their mark. Yet only a prejudiced person could deny that the hunger for faith is constantly reawakening even in the atmosphere of persecutions, secularism and denial of the spirit in the name of utilitarianism.

The contemporary situation makes it possible to see the very heart of religion, its true essence in sharper outline. If nowadays people no longer go to the hippodrome chanting prayers as they did in Byzantium, and do not drown heretics in the Volkhov river as they did in ancient Novgorod, then this is a gain, not a loss for faith. Faith, having lost its ties with the state, has been freed from the dead weight of its nominal adherents. When Christianity was made into an official ideology, the consequences were more often than not ugly consequences and church life was poisoned. It is far better for a 'pagan' of whatever kind to acknowledge himself to be what he is than to call himself a Christian to please surrounding society.[15]

Today's atheism is not a radical new stage of consciousness, rather, it reveals the reality of the spiritual dimensions in society. In the West, many church leaders deplore the fact that 'the churches are empty', but in so doing they forget how far worse it is if churches are full but hearts are empty. The outward fulfilment of ritual is by no means always a safe indication of a healthy faith, and conversely poor church attendance is in no way a proof of a decline in faith. Moreover, outer forms of church life were always changing in the past and will go on changing in the future. So there will inevitably be times when the need for changes affects the number of people regularly attending church.

But we must look deeper for the key to the problem: in the needs of the human spirit itself. Does not the revolt of the 'new left' – this contemporary nihilism – tell us that even when they have lost God, people passionately seek the absolute and are not satisfied with the reality to hand? Today the drama of Faust is being re-enacted: people are discovering in themselves the eternal longing for the things of the spirit and a dissatisfaction with what they have achieved. It is indicative that this longing is especially evident in the developed countries that have achieved material prosperity. The greater the power of 'mass culture', technology and urbanization becomes, the more keenly will individuals feel the weight of the new fetters laid upon them; whereas religion, as a contemporary writer has rightly remarked, 'remains the most personal of all forms of human activity'.[16] Lost in the labyrinths of civilization, it is in religion itself that the spirit again and again finds for itself a solid foundation and inner freedom. The individual person, the highest manifestation of what is human, will always find its refuge in the holy.

The progress of faith obviously cannot be measured by statistics alone. C. S. Lewis said that if the rebirth of Christianity has really begun it will develop slowly, quietly, in very small groups of people. And this imperceptible renewal is actually happening everywhere, even where it might be least expected.

It does not follow, however, that we should ignore those facts that do come to the surface. After everything that has befallen religion in the period of secularization, nearly 90% of the world's population consider themselves to be believers nowadays.[17] True, the Communist writer quoting this figure adds the rider that among the formal adherents of religion are quite a number of people who are indifferent; but then among those who subscribe to atheism there are many who are secretly believers or who are close to faith.

There are grounds for saying that in the twentieth century, contrary to the forecasts of sceptics, religion has begun to play a role in some ways greater than in past centuries. Evidence for this can be found in the most various cultural spheres. For example, whereas two or three hundred years back many artists who depicted Gospel themes looked on them in the main as formal subjects for a picture, nowadays we find a genuine mystical feeling in the work of prominent artists such as Marc Chagall, Nikolai Roerich, Georges Rouault and Salvador Dali. Religious and mystical problems engage writers today in a way that they did not a hundred years ago, with the exception though of Russia.[18] Prominent in the defence of spiritual values are Charles Péguy, Leon Bloy, Paul Claudel, François Mauriac, Julian Green and Antoine de Saint-Exupéry in France; G. K. Chesterton, C. S. Lewis, T. S. Eliot, Evelyn Waugh and Graham Greene in England; Thomas Mann, Hermann Hesse and Heinrich Böll in Germany; Mikhail Bulgakov, Boris Pasternak and Alexander Solzhenitsyn in Russia; J. D. Salinger, Ray Bradbury and John Updike in America; and Giovanni Papini in Italy. The drama of spiritual searchings and crises is forcefully portrayed in the writings of Franz Kafka and Rainer Maria Rilke. And many writers, even when criticizing the religious life of their contemporaries, aimed to purify faith and renew it. Such was also the intention of the denunciations by the prophets of old and the Church Fathers, who condemned any deviations from the true religion.

In the past, the overwhelming majority of scientists saw no contradiction between religion and natural science. We have only to think of Kepler, Newton, and Pasteur. Among scholars of our time, talk is about a synthesis of faith and knowledge. Charles Townes, Nobel Laureate, inventor of the laser, has commented on this. He said:

> The aim of science is to discover order in the universe and through this to understand the essence of things we see around us, to understand the life of man. The aim of religion, it seems to me, may be defined as comprehending (and consequently understanding) the purpose and the meaning of the universe and also the manner in which we are related to it. This higher ultimate force we call God.[19]

The words quoted are not a random or isolated opinion. This view is shared by those who are forming the modern picture of the world. Albert Einstein speaks of the meaning of faith for the scholar. Max Planck, Niels Bohr and Erwin Schrödinger speak about the connection between science and religion. Arthur Eddington, James Jeans and Pascual Jordan thought that knowledge of the world was the way to knowledge of God.

Leading twentieth-century scholars in many branches of science have adopted an anti-materialistic stance. In physics we think of Werner Heisenberg; in mathematics, of Georg Cantor; in biology, Theodor Schwann; in neuro-physiology, Sir John Eccles; in anthropology, Pierre Teilhard de Chardin; in palaeontology, the Abbé Breuil; in ethnography, P. W. Schmidt; in history, Arnold Toynbee; in psychology, Carl Jung.

The position in philosophy is indicative too. The greatest thinkers of our century, whether the intuitionist Henri Bergson, the Thomist Jacques Maritain, the 'organicist' Alfred North Whitehead, the existentialist Karl Jaspers, or 'the champion of freedoom' Nicolas Berdyaev, all proclaimed the supreme spiritual value of religion.

There is a flowering of new theology: Orthodoxy being represented by such figures as Sergi Bulgakov, Pavel Florensky, and Vladimir Lossky; Catholicism by Romano Guardini, Yves Congar, and Karl Rahner; Protestantism by Karl Barth, Paul Tillich, and Reinhold Niebuhr. There is new religious thinking in Judaism (Martin Buber) and in Hinduism (Aurobindo Ghose).[20]

Western interest in mystical teachings, in yoga and Zen, is on the increase. New movements are starting not only in Christianity, but in Islam, in Buddhism and even in paganism. Some of the social and political leaders of this century, for example Mahatma Gandhi and Martin Luther King, have been prompted to action by their religious principles.

It is not to decry these significant new developments to say that at times there is much that is immature and contradictory in them. The very diversity of the ideas and the quests (from the extreme left to extreme orthodoxy) shows how full to overflowing is the river of religion.

The upsurge is naturally also making itself felt in church life too. None of the last four centuries has known a pope as popular as John XXIII. The second Vatican Council which he summoned opened new perspectives in the dialogue between the church and the world, paved the way for new paths in theology, ecumenism, the apostolate, liturgy and understanding of the Bible.[21] The waves of discussion touched off by the Council, in their intensity reminiscent of the early church councils, demonstrated the strength and vitality of Christianity. Fearless free criticism of religious institutions coming from the faithful themselves and from theologians is a sign of a vigorous church life.

Protestantism, too, is exploring new avenues. The enormous success of the evangelist Billy Graham proves the strength of people's longing to hear the word of God. The Protestant initiative leading to the founding of the World Council of Churches is evidence of a thirst for the unity of all Christians which has never been known before in history. It is striking that ecumenism was born and lives at just the time when the world has seen an increase in racial intolerance and nationalism.

The vitality of the Orthodox Church is remarkable given the exceptional inner and outer ordeals it has suffered in the last decades in Russia. It is true that John Robinson, the English theologian, tries to minimize the importance of this fact in his well-known book by relating it to what he calls 'secondary religiousness', that is the intensification of faith in societies that are historically in decline.[22] However, to include Russia in this category shows a poor understanding of the dynamics of the contemporary world.

In the USA, this classic model of the 'consumer society', where the pursuit of comfort now threatens spiritual values, a widespread youth movement focussed on the Gospels has unexpectedly arisen, a movement which is called the 'Jesus revolution'. In Europe, the Taizé community attracts hundreds of thousands from different lands, members of different churches. In Africa and Asia, the number of new movements and preachers is increasing.

The fate of the Bible in the contemporary world bears strong witness to this. Not only are there astronomical circulation figures, annotated and illustrated editions, not only does the popularity of biblical themes in music, and television and screen testify to its undying attraction, but there are also hundreds of new researches and books resulting from an unprecedented flowering of biblical scholarship.

In the twentieth century, for the first time a serious dialogue has started between the churches, and between religions, between believers and non-believers. Even communists have been compelled to participate actively in this dialogue. Simultaneously in a number of countries, for example Latin America, the episcopate and the clergy are joining ranks with fighters for freedom and social reform.

If communists used to speak of religion as their implacable enemy, many of them are now obliged to change their attitude. A member of the central committee of the communist party of Chile, O. Millas, speaking about the social struggle of Christians, pointed out that they 'see the sense of their piety in the passionate love of their neighbour and unconditional faith in man. Catholics of this kind are not prevented from being revolutionaries by their faith, but on the contrary, it helps them in their struggle.' Taking this into account, Fidel Castro wrote that his revolution 'had never in any way been anti-religious'. Similar voices are also heard in Europe. Thus Georges Marchais openly affirms that 'Christians have a basis to join movements for democratic reform and to contribute to the building of a freer society'. This is far removed from the dismissal of religion as the 'opium of the people'.

It is not uncommon to hear that religion has only existed until now because it 'adapts itself' to the needs and conditions of the time. In recognizing this, atheism unwittingly testifies in favour of religion. It is well known that adaptability is a sure sign of an organism's vitality.

It is also said that religious conversion is 'bowing to fashion'. Maybe to some superficial minds, this is true. But 'fashion' by no means always plays a negative role. Has it not helped a large number of people to understand and appreciate icon painting and ancient church architecture? Is it not remarkable that the thing that they had stubbornly tried to suppress for so long has become a 'fashion'? Fashion is often nothing other than a simplified reflection of processes taking place in the depths of society.

The famous physicist Max Born spoke of a precipice towards which civilization is rushing, and emphasized that only religious ideas can return society to health. He wrote:

At the present time fear alone enforces a precarious peace. However this is an unstable state of affairs, which ought to be replaced by something better. We do not need to look far in order to find a more solid basis for the proper conduct of our affairs . . . [It is] the principle which in our own part of the world is taught by the doctrine of Christianity; the principle which Mahatma Gandhi had actually carried into practice.[23]

Thus we can safely assume that those who talk about the 'death of religion' are short-sighted, or have deliberately closed their eyes to reality, or finally, are victims of false propaganda.

Today as never before, the words spoken two thousand years ago by the apostle Paul sound out with greater relevance: they thought us dead 'and behold we live' [II Cor. 6.9]

4

A Credo for Today's Christian

This collection of Fr Alexander's sayings has been put together from his writings, interviews and lectures. The sayings are grouped thematically into sections on the Christian faith; the Bible and its interpretation; a large section on the church, tradition and Christian unity; the human person and society; and history and the coming of the kingdom. Some of the thrust of these sentences is directed towards a Russian readership who are confronted with tendencies towards a narrow nationalism and fundamentalism in the contemporary Russian Orthodox Church – note in particular the warning against literalism, the stress on the need for openness to change in church life, the call to understand other Christians, the importance of reason, and the call to service in the world. But the ideas summarized here express a confident and open Christianity, centred on Christ, not fearful of the world, a Christianity with its sights on the future, ideas which can be an encouragment to all Christians.

The collection was published under the title 'Basic features of a Christian world-view' in the volume, A. Men', Kul'tura i dukhovnoe vosrozhdenie, Moscow 1992, pp.26–30, where it is supplied with the subtitle, 'According to the teaching of the Bible and the tradition of the church'. In this translation the title and subheadings have been supplied by the editor.

Christianity is not 'an ideology', an abstract doctrine or a fixed system of rituals. The Good News entered the world as a dynamic force, encompassing all sides of life, open to everything created by God in nature and in human beings. It is not just a religion which has existed for the past twenty centuries, but a Way focussed on the future (John 14.6; Acts 16. 17; 18. 26).

I: The Faith of a Christian

A Christian

- centres his or her faith on Jesus Christ by whom all is measured and evaluated (Gal 2.20; Rev 1.8);
- understands the revelation of the inner life of God, of the mystery of the Trinity as evidence of the love of God and as a call to unity in love (John 3.16; 17.21; I John 4.8);
- believes that the coming to earth of the God-man was not a divine one-sided act but a call for people to respond to the love of God (Rev. 3.20).

II: The Bible and its Interpretation

A Christian

- does not look on faith to be an abstract conviction, but understands it to be total trust in God as revealed in Christ (Rom. 4.3);
- accepts the word of God which is recorded in scripture but guards against giving a literal interpretation to every line of the Bible especially of the Old Testament (Rom. 7.6);
- believes that one and the same God revealed himself in both Testaments; but that God revealed himself gradually as befitted the level of human consciousness (Heb. 1.1–2);
- does not ask for tangible signs (Mark 8. 11–12) but remembers that creation is a miracle (Ps. 19.1);
- refuses to point to human imperfection, or to 'the survival of animal nature' as the sole reason for the existence of evil in human beings, but believes in the reality of metaphysical evil (John 8.44);
- rejects the tendency to find in scripture or in the writings of the Church Fathers statements about natural science held to be valid for all time;

- views the academic study of the Bible and church history as an important means for clarifying the meaning of revelation and establishing the actual circumstances of sacred history.

III: The Church, Tradition, and Christian Unity

A Christian

- recognizes the presence and activity of Christ in the church, and in all life, even in the simplest and most mundane of its manifestations (see our Lord's parables, in particular Matt. 6.28–29);
- believes that the church lives and grows in the strength of Christ (Matt. 16.18; 28.20);
- believes that Christ reveals himself in the sacraments of the church, in her sanctification of the world, in her teaching and acts of service (I Cor. 11.26; Matt. 18.19–20) Rom. 6.11; Matt 28.18–20; Luke 10.16), but knows that not one of these aspects of the church's life is sufficient on its own, for Christ came as saviour, healer and teacher.
- recognizes the line dividing Tradition (the spirit of faith and learning) from 'traditions', many of which are associated with folklore and are impermanent accretions to religious life (Mark 7.8; Col. 2.8);
- respects the ritual forms of devotion without forgetting for a moment that they are secondary in comparison with love for God and other people (Matt. 23.23–24; Mark 12.28–31);
- believes in the significance of the hierarchical and canonical principle within the church, seeing them as structural features of an active organism which is called to be effective on earth (I Cor. 12.27–30);
- knows that liturgical rules and canon law have changed over the centuries and cannot (and should not) remain absolutely unaltered in the future (John 3.8; II Cor. 3.6, 17). This also applies to the theological interpretation of the truths of the faith. Such interpretation has had a long history, and has passed through phases when more of the truth was revealed and when interpretation deepened (for instance the Church

Fathers and councils introduced new concepts which are not to be found in the scriptures);

- is not afraid to look critically at the church's past following the example of the teachers in the Old Testament and of the Church Fathers;
- considers that all the inhuman excesses of the Christian past (and present) – the execution of heretics and such like – betrayed the spirit of the Gospel, and was an actual deviation from the church (Luke 9.51–55);
- knows that the opponents of Christ (illegitimate rulers, power-loving members of the hierarchy, fanatical supporters of the past), are to be found not only in the Gospel period but reappear under various guises at any time in history (Matt. 16.6);
- guards against authoritarianism and paternalism, which are rooted not in the spirit of faith but in characteristics inherent to the fallen nature of humanity (Matt. 20.25–27; 23.8–12);
- experiences the divisions among Christians as a sin which is common to all and a violation of Christ's will (John 10.16); believes that in the future this sin will be overcome not by a sense of superiority, pride, complacency, or hatred, but rather through a spirit of brotherly love without which the Christian calling cannot be fulfilled (Matt. 5.23–24);
- is open to all that is valuable in all Christian denominations and non-Christian beliefs (John 3.8; 4.23–24);
- considers that the separation of the church from the state is the most desirable situation for faith and sees the danger inherent in the very idea of a 'state religion';
- values the national character of each church as being particular, concrete emobodiments of the human spirit and of the mystery of the incarnation. However, this is not to deny the universal nature of the church;
- treats the works of art of the church over the centuries not as a mistake but as a way of realizing God's gifts.

IV: The Value of the Person, Human Relationships, and the Christian Vocation

A Christian

- knows that the dignity of the human person and the value of life and creativity are based on the belief that humanity was created by God (Ps. 8);
- professes that freedom is one of the most important laws of the Spirit, and in the light of this sees sin as a form of slavery (II Cor. 3.17; John 8.32; Rom. 6.17);
- believes that it is possible for a person to acquire the Spirit of God, but in order to distinguish this from a sick form of spiritual exhaltation ('bewitchment'), judges it by the fruit of the Spirit (Gal. 5.22–23);
- following the teaching of the apostle Paul looks on the human body, although imperfect owing to the fallen condition of nature, as the temple of the Holy Spirit (I Cor. 6.19); recognizes that it is essential to look after the body (I Tim. 5.23) so long as this does not turn into 'worship of the flesh';
- believes in the sanctity of human love if it is combined with responsibility, believes in the sanctity of the family and marriage (Gen. 2.18, 23–34; Matt. 19.5);
- according to the decisions of the church councils looks upon marriage and monasticism as equally honourable estates so long as monasticism is not undertaken for reasons of ambition and other sinful motives;[1]
- does not reject good even if it comes from non-religious people; but rejects force, dictatorship, and hatred even if they are perpetrated in the name of Christ (Matt. 7.21; 21.28–31; Mark 9.40);
- sees all that is beautiful, creative, and good as belonging to God, as the secret activity of Christ's grace;
- considers that when some area of life is infected by sin this should not serve as a reason for rejecting it. On the contrary, the struggle to establish the kingdom of God should take place at the centre of life;
- realizes that the Gospel understands 'asceticism' not so much

as an escape from the world but rather as a spirit of selflessness, a struggle against 'enslavement to the flesh', through recognition of the supremacy of eternal values (Matt. 16.24);

- sees that the Christian vocation can be realized in everything: in prayer, work, creativity, in active service and moral discipline;
- does not consider reason and science to be the enemies of faith. Knowledge enlightened by the spirit of faith deepens our understanding of the greatness of the creator (Ps. 104; I Kings 4.29, 33–34; Ps. 89);
- faces all the problems of the world, considering that any of them can be evaluated and made sense of in the light of faith;
- affirms with the apostle Paul that the witness of faith in the world is first and foremost the witness of service and active love (I Cor. 13);
- looks upon the life of society as one of the spheres where the principles of the Gospel can be applied;
- recognizes our duty as citizens (Rom. 13.1) in so far as they do not contradict the demands of faith (Acts 4.19);
- does not proclaim this or that system of government to be specifically Christian. The value of a system is measured by what it gives people: by its expediency and humaneness.

V: History and the kingdom of God

A Christian

- believes that history is moving forward through trials, catastrophes and struggle towards the future kingdom of God which transcends history;
- treats with reservation the idea of 'the flawed nature of history', that is the conviction that God's truth has been totally defeated on earth (this is contradicted by Rev. 20. 1–6);
- believes that, whenever the Last Judgment may come, people are called to work for the benefit of others, to create the city of God, the reign of the good;
- believes that the Last Judgment has already begun, that it began from the moment Christ began to preach (John 3.19; 12.31);

- sees the condition of the human soul after death as temporary and incomplete, waiting to be fulfilled at the general resurrection and transfiguration of all (Dan. 7.13–14; John 5.28; Rom. 8.11; Rev. 20.11–15);
- knows that the kingdom of God which is to come, can reign 'within us' even today (Luke 9.27; 17.21)

5

Christianity: The Universal Vision

*In this extensive study, Fr Alexander passes in review the ideas
of those thinkers who have in the past tried to define the
interrelationship of the world's great faiths and the course of
human religious development. First among these to engage Fr
Alexander's attention is Karl Jaspers who advanced the notion
of the 'axial period', that time during the first millennium* BC
*when simultaneously there came about in very different parts
of the world a change in spiritual perceptions: this was when
Chinese philosophy, the Hebrew prophets, the classics of
India, and Greek philosophy began. Because of the similarity
between these different movements, and the importance of the
issues they raised, the 'axial period' is held to be the starting
point for an understanding of the essential unity of all
humanity. Fr Alexander takes issue though with Jaspers for
excluding Christianity from this 'axial period'. He next
considers the historical process whereby the sense of human
unity has grown, and how Europeans became aware of the
great civilizations of the East. This leads on to a consideration
of two Russian philosophers of religion, Vladimir Solovyev
and Nicolas Berdyaev, and an Englishman, Christopher
Dawson, each of whom in their own way looked on Christianity
as the culmination of human spiritual development and the
final revelation of God for all humanity. In this universalist
vision, there is an honoured place for paganism and all the
great religions of the world, because truth does not come to
take the place of falsehood, but a fuller truth to enrich what
had gone before. This study illustrates some of the theoretical
underpinning for Fr Alexander's ecumenism and openness to
all forms of spirituality, in particular his debt to Solovyev and*

Berdyaev which is often acknowledged in his writings. It was work such as this which explains the appeal Fr Alexander had for members of the Russian intelligentsia.

This study, under the title 'On the problematics of the "axial period" (On the dialogue between culture and religion)', was published in A. Men', Trudny put' k dialogu, Moscow 1992, pp. 248–290. Subtitles are in the original.

In Russian society today favourable processes are at work, including a serious re-evaluation of many opinions formerly taken as axiomatic. In particular, the significance of our spiritual inheritance from the past in the contemporary world is hotly debated. Until quite recently, this inheritance was said to be something that had gone for ever; at best it was regarded as a survival, respected but lifeless. Even artistic treasures such as icons and church architecture were not understood (at the beginning of this century, for instance, [the art historian] Petr Gnedich characterized Russian iconography as a primitive, 'backward' form of art). It was easier still to disparage the religious, philosophical and ethical traditions which have come down to us from the remote past.

Ideas like this are not only a product of the twentieth century. They arose as early as the Enlightenment, and were elaborated in Auguste Comte's theory of the three phases of the development of thought and in other nineteenth-century doctrines in the philosophy of history. Up to a point, this attitude was caused by the impression made on people's minds by the progress of natural science which had begun in the seventeenth century. As a rule, the new scientific discoveries replaced much of what had been there before. Unconsciously (but sometimes consciously) an analogous principle, legitimate in the study of nature, began to be applied to the sphere of the spirit: that is, to philosophy, aesthetics, religion and ethics.

However, there is a qualitative difference. Even if chemistry meant the end of alchemy, and modern biology made ancient and mediaeval concepts obsolete, it would be rash to conclude that twentieth-century ethics has no need of the rules worked out in previous times.

The first step towards overcoming this arrogant attitude to the spiritual traditions of the past and of the non-European world was made in the field of aesthetics. Early in our own century, we find the beginning of a 'rehabilitation' of primitive, archaic and African and Asian art, which gradually ceased to be seen as 'barbaric' or 'unskilled', having nothing in common with 'advanced' modernity.

However, this tragic century of world wars, with its cruelty, destruction of the sense of law, its disastrous effects on the natural environment and its lack of spirituality, and the ensuing grievous social and ethical crises, has induced many people to ponder the reasons why this has come about. The realization then dawned that people, having hastily discarded the ideals of the past and declaring them to be fossils, had cut themselves off from cultural sources which were important for life.

Among various efforts to overcome this disastrous split, a prominent place belongs to the theory of the 'axial period' (*Achsenzeit*) put forward by the German thinker, scholar and publicist Karl Jaspers (1883–1969). This theory is distinguished first by the conviction that the ancient spiritual heritage of East and West is relevant today, and secondly by the effort to find a basis for the unity of mankind.

What was the 'axial period'?

Jaspers' theory is neither speculation nor an abstract scheme imposed on history. He himself emphasized that he had reached the idea of the 'axial age' empirically, from the study of established facts which were well known before the appearance of his book *The Origin and Goal of History (Vom Ursprung und Ziel der Geschichte,* 1949).[1] All that he did was to focus attention on the common starting-point from which the paradigms of thought in East and West had arisen.

What Jaspers had in mind were the events which happened simultaneously in the vast area between the banks of the Yellow River and the Graeco-Roman area in the middle of the first millennium BC. That was the time when the Buddha, Confucius, Zarathustra and the biblical prophets were preaching; that was when the *Upanishads*, the books of the Old Testament and the earlier parts of the *Avesta* and *Mahabharata* were written; then it was that the thinking of the ancient philosophers and tragedians, of the Jains, and of the representatives of the six classical systems of Indian philosophy, the *darshanas*, originated and flourished. All this comes under what Jaspers called the 'axial period'.

The human mind at that time broke through the limits set by geographical, cultural, ethnic and temporal frontiers. Indeed, even in our own time, Christianity and Islam, the teachings of the Far East and most secular doctrines have some hereditary connection with the cradle of the 'axial period'. We find in it monotheism and materialism, abstract mysticism and the search for a just social order, in aesthetic ideas and codes of morals. The question was whether that cradle should be considered to be only a monument of the past, or recognized as a vital reserve of spirituality, which is needed in the modern world. Jaspers attempted also to establish how far the heritage of the 'axial period' is universal, or whether its values are capable of nourishing no more than local currents of culture.

In his answers to these questions, Jaspers argued the case both for the relevance of the past for our own time, and for the universalizing tendency which lies at the heart of the 'axial period'.

One point must be made clear: when Jaspers gave priority in history to the spiritual sphere, he was not narrowing or impoverishing the question. Whatever the socio-economic correlates of the 'axial period' were, its spiritual wealth concerns that dimension of human existence which forms the very core of history. The true nature of humanity, that which raises it above the animal level, becomes apparent wherever we find achievements and discoveries of the spirit. Of course, people also 'humanize' processes which are common to them and to other living beings, but the content of their spiritual activity has no parallel in nature.

In a certain sense, the 'axial period' was a global revolution in consciousness. 'Mythological', undifferentiated thinking, as found at the beginning of history – the period which Jaspers regarded as the prelude to the 'axial period' – did not distinguish man from the universe. In the early literate civilizations of China,

India, the Near East and the Aegean, an outlook on things which may be described as 'magism' held sway.[2] Magism reaches back to pre-historic culture, when the universe was conceived to be a grandiose system of relationships in which the human race had quite a modest place. These relationships were seen as manifestations of the divine Nature, which had given birth to gods, people, animals, plants and the elements. All that people had to do was to submit obediently to the eternal cosmic order, of which they considered their own rituals to be part. However, since they knew its 'laws', people could make use of them with the aid of magic for their everyday purposes (hunting, war, agriculture, etc.).

The magic view of the world lasted thousands of years in a great variety of places on earth, creating stable and in many ways similar traditions, even in countries completely isolated from one another.[3] In itself this similarity has not yet been satisfactorily explained. Even harder to understand is the fact that the events of the 'axial period' occurred synchronically, since the period lasted only a relatively short time in history. It is true that in the first millennium BC numerous inter-cultural links were already at work, but, as Jaspers rightly noted, they were still too weak fully to explain this mysterious phenomenon.

We may take as an example what is called 'apophatic theology', that is, the doctrine of the ultimate reality as a principle which cannot be adequately expressed by any intellectual concepts.[4] It is easier to say what that principle is not than to give it an exhaustive definition. This was the teaching of Daoism in the tradition running from Lao Zi and Zhuang Zi, of Brahman in the *Upanishads* and the *Mahabharata*, Nirvana in Buddhism, of the Highest Good in Plato, of the One Who Is in the Israelite prophets – and in general the 'axial period' is characterized by the urge to overcome polytheism and find faith in one God. In all this, there is not the slightest reason to suppose that the Chinese thinkers knew anything of Greek ideas, or the prophet Isaiah anything of the Vedic texts. The same can be said of the astonishing interchangability of the moral maxims formulated in that period. Ethical values prove to be immeasurably higher than ritual systems, while the utilitarian psychology of magism gives way to a reverent search for truth and to mystical vision and prophetic faith.

Jaspers, being an existentialist philosopher, particularly emphasized that in the 'axial period', human beings became conscious of their separateness from the natural world and of the tragic quality of their existence, that is, that they found themselves in a 'frontier situation':

> [Man] experiences the terror of the world and his own powerlessness. He asks radical questions. Face to face with the void he strives for liberation and redemption. By consciously recognizing his limits he sets himself the highest goals. He experiences absoluteness in the depths of selfhood and in the lucidity of transcendence.[5]

It is a fact that soteriological doctrines, 'religions of salvation' arose precisely during the 'axial period'.

According to Jaspers, the 'axial period' began about 800 and ended about 200 BC. Christianity thus falls outside it, and becomes something secondary. 'From an historical viewpoint,' he writes, 'Jesus was the last in the series of Jewish prophets and stood in conscious continuity with them.'[6] Given that interpretation it is hard to understand, then, why Jaspers could not have extended the limits of the 'axial period' to the middle of the first century AD. However, this is a topic to which we shall return; all that we need to note at the moment is that in Jaspers' eyes, the 'axial' heritage is far from exhausted, and is capable of giving mankind new impulses for development.

> In this age were born the fundamental categories within which we still think today, and the beginnings of the world religions, by which humans still live, were created. The step into universality was taken in every sense . . .[7]

True, Jaspers did find something like a second 'axis' in the culture of the West after the Renaissance, which evoked a response in all mankind.

Europe's exceptional spiritual achievements from 1500 to 1800, that outshine science and technology – Michelangelo, Raphael, Leonardo, Shakespeare, Rembrandt, Goethe, Spinoza, Kant, Bach, Mozart – challenge comparison with the Axial Period of two and half millennia earlier.[8]

But Jaspers himself admits that this second 'axis' came fairly quickly into an *impasse*, which turned into a protracted crisis (we must remember that Jaspers wrote his book on the philosophy of history soon after the Second World War).

Jaspers saw the way out of this crisis in the openness of the European post-Renaissance mind, with its inherent pluralism and its receptiveness and sensitivity to other traditions. This is generally a fair judgment, if we do no more than recall the part played by Japanese art in the development of Western painting, and by Indian ideas in Schopenhauer's philosophy. We may also recall what the East meant to such writers and thinkers as Leo Tolstoy, Albert Schweitzer, Hermann Hesse and J. D. Salinger.

Jaspers' work has become a pointer for our times, which are marked not only by confrontations and explosions of chauvinism, but also by strivings for the unity of all mankind. The increasing interest of the West in the East is an eloquent witness to this. As has been rightly observed:

The ideologists of the Renaissance and the Enlightenment took as their standard classical man; the Romantics of the early nineteenth century turned to the world of the Middle Ages in their search for an ideal; although nineteenth century man, convinced of the triumph of reason, evolution and progress, discovered for himself the world of the Far East, he was nevertheless inspired by classical antiquity; but people of the twentieth century, and especially of its second half, are paying more and more attention to ancient eastern man.[9]

Following Max Müller, Radhakrishnan and Schweitzer, Jaspers held that Western culture and spirituality needed to be supplemented by something which could be found in Asia.

Unless the East had emerged from its seclusion, and the West had renounced its Eurocentrism which for so long it thought was the only possible model, this question and this way of thinking would not have arisen.

Overcoming cultural egocentrism

Although Christianity, which came from the East and was established in the West, bore within itself a mighty impetus to universalism, the mediaeval European and the inhabitant of ancient Russia identified the area of their own Christian culture with the actual historical world. Beyond the frontiers of this area, began the incomprehensible, dark and sinister 'world of the pagans'. A special exception was made for Islam, with which both the West and Russia entered into very close contact, and which was regarded as an anomaly, or a deviation from something familiar, almost as a Christian heresy. In a certain sense that is what Islam really was, for the Koran rests on the same biblical Old Testament basis as Christianity does (even if this biblical basis was given a rather free interpretation). Moreover the Moslems always revered Isa the son of Mariam, namely Christ, as a great prophet. Judaism was regarded as a similar deviation, adhering to the Old Testament, but supplementing it with its own later traditions.

However, at the time of the great geographical discoveries of the fifteenth, sixteenth and seventeenth centuries, Europe was brought face to face with the ancient highly developed 'pagan' civilizations, of which it had previously no knowledge at all, or only the vaguest idea. To judge by the memoirs of Afanasy Nikitin,[10] this meeting caused a real shock. Nikitin, a merchant from Tver', who was one of the first Europeans to go to India and Ethiopia at the end of the Middle Ages, recounts his inner struggles to remain a Christian while living among people of other faiths. Yet contact with these people gave him ideas which were certainly not intolerant. 'What is the true faith?', he writes: 'God knows. But the true faith is to know the one God and to call upon Him everywhere in purity of heart.'[11]

The encounter with new worlds put the Christian missionaries who had gone to African, Asian and American countries in a difficult dilemma: either to bring the gospel to the 'natives' as the 'religion of the whites', or to study and take account of the cultural and religious heritage of the indigenous peoples. For a long time, the first of these models prevailed. However, there were exceptions. We may mention among them the sixteenth-century missionaries Matteo Ricci and Roberto de Nobili. It was to such people, who called for respect for oriental 'pagan' traditions and for account to be taken of them, that Europe most frequently owed its first information about the cultures and beliefs of Africa, Asia and America. These were the ones who prepared the way for further re-orientation of the Christian understanding of 'paganism'.[12]

The eighteenth century saw the first translations of the sacred books of the East into European languages, including Russian.[13] However, the Eurocentric outlook still prevailed. For instance, [the German writer] Johann von Herder, [in his history of mankind, 1791] thought that although history began in the Orient, the oriental period was wholly pervaded by stagnation, despotism and superstition. This attitude did not change even after the archaeological discoveries in Egypt and Jean François Champollion's deciphering of Egyptian hieroglyphics (1822), which made Europe aware of the cultural treasures of the land of the Pyramids. G. W. F. Hegel, in his *Philosophy of History* (1830), relegated his cursory sketch of Egypt to the part dealing with Persia, on the grounds that it was only the Achaemenid dynasty who built an extensive empire (which included Egypt) in the Near East. For the same reasons, in the name of the statism which he proclaimed, Hegel gave a place in his philosophy of history to China and India; but in general his evaluation of Eastern cultures reflects a semi-contemptuous Eurocentric view of the East.

In particular, Hegel enshrined the four-stage scheme of history which continued to be accepted after him, according to which the first stage was the unchanging East; this was followed by the brilliant age of classical antiquity, after which came the Middle Ages, and then the modern era when the 'Christian-Germanic spirit' became dominant. Thus Hegel considered the Eastern element in world culture as the lowest. By contrast, Hegel's contemporary and adversary Arthur Schopenhauer came to recognize the profundity of Eastern wisdom, especially Buddhism. However, in coming to his conclusions, this pessimistic thinker was guided more by considerations of metaphysics than of the philosophy of history.

It was only Friedrich Schelling who, in lectures given in the later period of his life, made an attempt to find something lasting in the pre-Christian consciousness of the East by looking at it in the context of the religious and historical process as a whole. In these ancient Eastern and Western teachings Schelling found constituent elements of that universal truth which had been revealed to mankind in the Gospels during the decline of classical antiquity. According to Schelling, the distinctive feature of biblical religion as a whole, which distinguishes it from other faiths, is its historicism. Christ proclaimed the gospel at a particular and fateful moment of history, and everything that preceded his coming was, in its way, a preparation for the New Testament, 'Christianity before Christ'.

The information on the East available to Schelling was far from complete; but after the work of Friedrich Max Müller, and Paul Deussen,[14] many Europeans began to learn about the Eastern tradition, which they saw not as a stage of history wholly past or something exotic, but as a participant on equal terms in the spiritual creativity of the world. The development owed much to the English translation of *The Sacred Books of the East* which came out in 1875, edited by Max Müller, and to Deussen's exposition of the basic ideas of Indian philosophy (until then the history of thought had begun with the Greeks). Russian orientalists too, such as Iakinf Bichurin and Aleksei Vinogradov, made a considerable contribution to our knowledge of the East.[15]

In the second half of the nineteenth century, the study of culture began to acquire a secular, positivist, character. If Max Müller valued the traditions of the East for their spirituality (which did not prevent him from remaining a Christian), many of his contemporaries already regarded the East from a purely ethnographic standpoint. This was the key to the abandonment – whole or partial – of the old Eurocentrism. In any case, it is symptomatic that in two popular 'Universal Histories' published at the beginning of the twentieth century, Hegel's fourfold scheme was discarded, and large sections were devoted to pre-Columbian America and to Asia and Africa.[16]

Similar processes were under way in the East. Even before the rule of the Great Moguls, Hinduism had been engaged in a dialogue with Islam and Zoroastrianism. The Mogul emperor Akbar (1542–1605) tried to bring about a peculiar religious synthesis, recognizing the worth of various doctrinal traditions. Many representatives of the Indian renaissance in religion and philosophy, which began during the English rule, showed an openness to Western culture. One need only mention the names of Ram Mohan Roy, founder of the Brahmo Samaj movement, the ascetic Ramakrishna, the neo-Vedantic philosophers Vivekananda and Aurobindo Ghose.[17] Although their attitude to the West was quite critical, they knew, and to some extent adopted, the values of the Western world. The extent to which these values entered their philosophy of life would have to be the subject of special research, but the very fact that their views included a certain westernization and readiness for dialogue is significant. There is no doubt that Vivekananda derived a number of his philosophical ideas and his attitude to social action from Europe. The same process of dialogue with the West was carried on rather less intensively in China and Japan, where the main interest in European culture lay in the sphere of technological development.[18]

The reverse side of pluralism

The end of Eastern isolation and of Western Eurocentrism created the necessary conditions for a growth in tolerance and in a sense of common humanity, and for the fruitful mutual enrichment of East and West. But we must mention two extremely contentious and dubious consequences which this process was fraught with. One concerns culture in general and the other, religion.

Already in the nineteenth century, acknowledgment of the equality of civilizations had led to the idea that each was self-sufficient. One of the first to express this idea was Nikolai Danilevsky (1822–1885), a representative of late, 'secular' Slavophilism.[19] Rightly criticizing the fourfold (or, in another version, threefold) Eurocentric scheme of history, he questioned the West's right to claim an exceptional position, and to measure everything by its own scale. 'What has China or India to do with the fall of the Western Roman Empire?', asked Danilevsky. 'Even for neighbouring states beyond the Euphrates, the fall of the Parthian empire or the rise of the Sassanian kingdom were more important to them than the fall of the western Roman Empire.'[20] Every 'type' of culture was created as a distinct ethnolinguistic community, and therefore represents a complete whole, which cannot claim to be either eternal or universal.

But if Danilevsky, with his relativizing view of history, nevertheless recognized some continuity between cultural types, this recognition was wholly rejected by another historian who was thinking on the same lines, though he is hardly likely to have known of Danilevsky's work. This historian was Oswald Spengler (1880–1936), who wrote under the impact of the First World War and predicted the cultural extinction of the West.[21]

In his book *The Decline of the West* (1918–1922), Spengler – like Danilevsky – recognized the existence only of separate cultural organisms, but he thought their morphology was entirely autonomous and sealed off in itself. He went a good deal further than the antithesis expressed in the famous lines of Rudyard Kipling: 'East is East and West is West, and never the twain shall meet.' The West itself, in Spengler's thinking, is divided into separate impenetrable worlds. Thus he put early Christianity and the Church Fathers into 'Arab culture', in which there was no place for the Old Testament, and which was quite disconnected from the West European tradition. In a word, in Spengler, Eurocentrism was overcome at the price of completely losing any idea of the unity of mankind. In traditional Christian philosophy of history, represented by Augustine and Nestor the Chronicler,[22] the historical process is seen as a single purposive whole; in Spengler cultural bodies absolutely alien to each other are born, flower and die 'in solitude', subject to the inescapable fate of every living thing.

Spengler's book made a very great impression, since its publication coincided with the crucial years when the certainties of the nineteenth century were collapsing, and it really was possible to think that European civilization was coming to an end. But it is a curious fact that one of the most profound and significant answers to Spengler's pessimistic prognosis came from Moscow in the 1920s – the same Moscow which at that time H. G. Wells saw in an almost apocalyptic light.

Even before the second volume of *The Decline of the West* was published, a group of Russian thinkers responded in a book of articles specifically devoted to Spengler.[23] Recognizing the acumen and shrewdness of some of Spengler's observations, the authors showed convincingly that there were solid facts which sharply contradicted his thesis. These facts for instance include the numerous and durable links that bind not only the various stages of development of European culture together, but also the cultures of the West and the East. In particular, S. L. Frank, one of the compilers of the collection, observed that Spengler, by ignoring these facts, is further from the truth even than the supporters of the old fourfold model. Frank writes:

However one-sided, subjective and superficial are our conventional notions on the course of 'world history', they at least treat it as a connected whole and try – with varying degrees of success – to analyse the linkage or continuity between past and present. From this point of view, Spengler's division of the historical process which embraces and unites the so-called 'ancient', 'mediaeval' and 'modern' ages, into three completely different cultures, each locked into itself, and separated from the others . . . involves a palpable diminution and distortion of accumulated historical knowledge.[24]

It is not surprising that subsequent twentieth-century historians, though they took account of Spengler's idea of the morphological integrity of individual cultures, had to emphasize the mutual links, influences, and continuity between them. This was the keystone for the classic works of [the English historian] Arnold Toynbee, who substantially modified the Spenglerian model, and of [the Russo-American sociologist] Pitirim Sorokin, who pointed out the universal structure of world-views ('supersystems') which are common to the most disparate cultures.

Belonging as they did to the same generation as Jaspers, both these scholars collected a mass of empirical material, which reinforced the universalist tendency inherent in the idea of the 'axial period'.

The second, and more serious, difficulty in overcoming Eurocentrism made itself felt in the interpretation of religion.

Jaspers recognized that 'Christianity, in the shape of the Christian church, is perhaps the greatest and highest organizational form yet evolved by the human spirit', and that this church 'proved capable of compelling contradictory elements into union, of absorbing the highest ideals formulated up to that time and of protecting its acquisitions in a dependable tradition.'[25] However, as we have seen, he excluded Christianity from the 'axial period' on the grounds that the Christianity of the church is 'the result of later development', and that the teaching of the prophets, which preceded it, was more original. However, this is a weak argument, since all the religions which arose in the first millennium BC also relied on earlier ideas and, just like Christianity, once they had arisen, continued to develop and to be enriched. Vedantic doctrine, for instance, or Buddhism and Daoism did not spring up on bare soil, and did not remain static during the period synchronous with the European Middle Ages; and the teachings of Asvaghosha, Shankara or Tsongkhapa[26] evidently did not induce Jaspers to exclude Buddhism or Vedantic teaching from the limits of the 'axial period'.

Beyond that, Jaspers wanted to find in the inheritance of the 'axial period' some homogeneous soil for a spiritual synthesis of the present and the future. Once again, Christianity proved to be outside his scheme of things. Although he calls Christ 'the axis of history', his words show that he means the axis only of the Western world. That is why Jaspers tried to rise above religious differences, and proposed an 'eternal' or 'philosophical' faith, which would be able to bring people nearer to the Godhead irrespective of their specific religious traditions.

This was not a new idea. It had already been expressed in the *Bhagavadgita*, and by Plutarch. In the sixteenth century, Akbar worked out an eclectic kind of religion, in the seventeenth and eighteenth centuries the European Deists did the same, and were followed in the nineteenth by various representatives of theosophy and neo-Vedanta. Their 'omnivorousness' carried with it the danger of spiritual entropy, and in the last analysis turned faith into something amorphous, which could not match the creative power of the historical religions of the world. Superficially, this sort of 'pan-religion' might even seem desirable, in so far as it could stimulate the unity of peoples and cultures. But historical experience and a deeper understanding of the essence and practice of religions shows that this approach is destructive of spiritual values. What happens is a levelling down, a loss of form, and vital values are deprived of their unique essence. It is no accident that the Deists' efforts to create a 'pan-religion' led only to the disintegration of the foundations of religion and to the triumph of a mechanistic view of the world. It is worth remembering that even in India, the 'temple of all religions' is one of the least frequented of them all.

In this connection, Arnold Toynbee's case is interesting. In developing his religious and theocentric view of world history, he began by basing himself on Christianity, then tried to create an equilibrium between Christianity and Eastern religions. However, he was unable to sustain this intermediate position, and finished up prefering Indian pantheism.

All this proves once more that syncretism cannot give a satisfactory answer to the problem. For the Christian mind, it is in any case unacceptable. However, Christianity long ago ceased ignoring other spiritual traditions on the grounds that they were unworthy of attention, and now tries to find room for them in its own philosophical system.

The Christocentric interpretation

Christianity's first attempts to make sense of the religious and historical process came at a difficult moment for it, when there was a fierce struggle going on between the church and paganism in its many forms. We can understand how in the second century AD, the idea expressed by Tatian and Tertullian that pagans worship demons without knowing it, came about.[27] However, their own contemporaries, Justin Martyr and Clement of Alexandria, were already taking a different approach to the problem of pagan thought. They argued that before Christ, divine revelation was not restricted to the Old Testament, and that for pagans their own higher doctrines, which developed within their own milieu, played the role of the Old Testament. The pagan world, in this view, was not plunged in impenetrable darkness, for it had long since been made fruitful by the eternal Logos, which explains why many ideas are common to classical antiquity and to Christianity.

These arguments are biblically based, and in particular derive from Old Testament doctrines about the revelation to the Gentiles, and from St Paul's speech in Athens.[28] At the same time, patristic writers sharply resisted the attempts by Gnosticism and Manichaeism to create some sort of 'pan-religious fusion' out of a mixture of different religious traditions. While they recognized that there were elements of truth in pre-Christian consciousness, the Fathers of the Church never departed from Christocentrism in their theology and philosophy of history.

Later, in the Middle Ages, there were many church thinkers who did not reject pagan values. We only have to recall the place given in Christian thought to Plato and Aristotle.[29] However, this did not in the slightest alter the original Christocentric interpretation, which became both fuller and more concrete as the Christian world learned more about other religions and systems of thought.

It is impossible to go into the details of this process in the scope of an article. We shall therefore confine our examination to three representatives of the Christian philosophy of history, who were older contemporaries of Jaspers: Vladimir Solovyev, Nicolas Berdyaev, and Christophr Dawson.

The idea of the 'axial period' in the form proposed by Jaspers is not to be found in the writings of Vladimir Solovyev.[30] He does, however, examine and compare those doctrines which arose precisely in that period of history. He treats them not as forgotten 'fossils', but as natural moments in the dialectic of the spirit, which contain a partial or 'one-sided' comprehension of the Absolute.

Solovyev came to these conclusions while still a young man, after a swift transition from the nihilism of the 1860s to a Christian world-view. Already in his first published work, strongly influenced by Schelling, he treated religious and historical development as something integral.[31] This essay was devoted to the earliest times, but in his master's dissertation, *The Crisis of Western Philosophy* (1874), he analyses the crisis fully aware of the latest findings of European thinkers of his time. He showed how the development of rationalism had led their thinking into the *impasse* of positivism, and how they had found a way out of the crisis by overcoming their exclusive reliance on reason. In the systems of thought for which Schopenhauer had laid the foundation, Solovyev saw an indication that 'modern philosophy' was ready to accept 'the very truths which, in the forms of faith and spiritual contemplation, had been established by the great theological teachings of the East (partly the ancient East, and in particular the Christian East).' In Solovyev's words, 'this modern philosophy, with its Western type of logical perfection, aims to unite all the contemplative spiritual perceptions of the East.'[32]

For Solovyev this conclusion meant that the spiritual riches which had belonged to the East in the distant past had not lost their importance for the modern era at all. In other words, Solovyev had already in some ways anticipated Jaspers' view of the course of history. More than that, when Solovyev was working in the British Museum and in Cairo his writings are marked by the search for a 'universal religion' which is again reminiscent of Jaspers' theory.

But even then, the Gospels occupied a central place in the thoughts of the young philosopher, and the 'pan-religious' themes soon disappeared altogether from his work. Even earlier, in 1873, he had worked out a plan for a book on the philosophy of the history of religion. The first draft for this book had been made when Solovyev was an extra-mural student at the Moscow Theological Academy. 'The aim of this work,' he wrote, 'is to explain ancient religions, an explanation which is necessary because without it there can be no understanding of world history in general, or of Christianity in particular.'[33]

Solovyev's project was never realized, but it was reflected in a number of his works on the philosophy of history and on theology (*Lectures on Godmanhood, The Spiritual Basis of Life, The History of Theocracy, Russia and the Universal Church*, etc.). The ideas in these works are among the first examples in Russian thought to take the patristic assessment of paganism as their starting point.

According to Solovyev, spiritual knowledge and revelation have a definable dynamic:

> Just as external nature has only gradually been revealed to the mind of man and to mankind, which means that we have to speak of the development of experience and of natural sciences, so too the divine principle has gradually been revealed to human consciousness, and we must speak of the development of religious experience and religious thought.[34]

However, this process should not be identified with Comte's positivist theory, in which there is a complete rupture between the old and the new. In Solovyev's view there is no such thing as a 'completely false' religion, since

> The advance of religions is not a process whereby pure truth replaces pure falsehood, for in that case truth would appear suddenly and all at once, with no transition and no progress – and then the question would arise: why did this sudden appearance of truth occur at a particular place and time and not at any other? And if we were to answer that truth could only appear after falsehood had been exhausted, that would imply that the coming of falsehood was necessary for the coming of truth.[35]

At the first stage of consciousness, mankind was wholly immersed in the natural world in all the multitude of its phenomena, and this gave rise to polytheism. The second stage gave preference to the spirit, since it drew not on external phenomena but on spiritual experience. This 'internal liberation from nature in the self-awareness of pure personality was first clearly expressed in Indian philosophy', whose last word was apophaticism, 'which understands the unconditional principle as nothingness', that is, as free from all delimitations.[36]

The synthesis of naturalist and spiritualist thinking was achieved, according to Solovyev, in the idealism of the ancient world, which teaches that the invisible cosmos of ideas is the basis of the visible world. However, the pantheistic idealism of the Graeco-Roman world still lacked any understanding of the real in terms of life and personality. That is what we find in the Bible. Biblical doctrine, given first in the Old Testament, not only links humanity with 'the Living God', but sees an expression of the divine will in the ethical imperative. The idea of the covenant (alliance) between God and man, means, as Solovyev puts it, 'the free interaction between Creator and his creation'.[37]

However, Old Testament history itself passes through a number of stages. It begins with God's covenant with one people, and then gradually comes to a universal covenant. The decisive role here belongs to the prophets. 'In prophetic consciousness,' Solovyev says, 'the subjective, purely personal element of the Old Testament Yahweh (that is, of Being, of He who is) is united with the objective idea of a universal divine essence.'[38]

Not one of the links in the religio-historical process is wholly excluded in Solovyev's theory, but each finds its place in the final synthesis of the pre-Christian world, when the Old Testament meets Eastern and classical thought (in Alexandrian philosophy). The completion of the human perception of the Absolute as Person comes about in the central event of history, the coming of the God-man.

The entire life of the world and of mankind is determined by the interaction of the divine principle and the natural principle, and the whole course of this life consists in the gradual coming together and interpenetration of these two principles. At first they are distant from, and external to, each other, but then come closer and closer together, penetrating each other more and more deeply, until in Christ, nature becomes like the human soul, ready for total self-denial, and God [is revealed] as the spirit of love and mercy, giving to this soul all the fullness of divine life.[39]

For Solovyev, Christianity was not some abstract idea, but a life-giving impulse, transforming earthly existence. He was convinced that even those historical forces which seem to arise independently of Christianity in fact co-operate indirectly with the cause of Godmanhood on earth. It was only at the very end of his life that he reached the conclusion that these forces contain some ominous, destructive principle, and that their denial of Christ leads inevitably to an apocalyptic catastrophe. From this perspective, Solovyev's Christocentrism becomes even clearer. It is no accident that in his *Three Conversations* (1900), the best representatives of the three Christian confessions recognize the Antichrist by his attempt to obscure the God-man with things that are secondary (church ritual, church art, church scholarship).

Solovyev's writings inspired a whole school of distinguished Russian thinkers of the twentieth century. They all to a greater or lesser degree cherished the idea that Russian culture was called, and was able, to unite the divided principles of East and West (an idea frequently expressed by Solovyev and his predecessor Petr Chaadaev).[40] That is why the question of the spiritual heritage of the past and its links with the present was of exceptional importance for thinkers such as Sergi Bulgakov, Pavel Florensky, Evgeny Trubetskoi, Semen Frank, Dmitri Merezhkovsky and Vyacheslav Ivanov.[41] But it was in the philosophy of Nikolai Berdyaev[42] that this topic is most prominent.

Vladimir Solovyev, who was in some ways still a typical nineteenth-century thinker, came not long before his death to an eschatological vision. Berdyaev, wholly caught up in the storms and crises of the twentieth century, lived and thought almost from the beginning of his literary career along eschatological lines. He was acutely aware of the precipitate course of history, and his gaze was fixed on what was being revealed beyond its limits. He was not in a position to write, as Solovyev did, in a calm academic manner. The rapid succession of thoughts, insights and acute aphorisms turn his books into something like prophetic outpourings, full of tension and emotion. He was a passionate polemicist, but he knew how to respect his opponents, and though a Christian, he never allowed himself a wholesale denial of non-Christian values.

Like Solovyev, Berdyaev had not yet identified the 'axial period' as the most important starting-point for all subsequent spiritual history. However, again like Solovyev, he viewed the pre-Christian world in all its diversity, seeing in it distinct stages of human consciousness. In Berdyaev's words:

> The whole of the varied religious life of mankind has been nothing less than a continuous ascent towards the unique revelation made in Christianity. For when specialists in the science of religion attempt to prove that Christianity is not original, that pagan religions already had the idea of a suffering God (such as Osiris, Adonis, Dionysus, and so forth), that Totemism had its eucharist in the form of communion through the body and blood of the animal, that most of the elements of Christianity can be found in Orphism and the ancient religions of Persia and Egypt, they are failing completely to understand the significance of what they observe. The Christian revelation is universal, and everything analogous to it in other religions is simply a part of that revelation.[43]

The core concepts in Berdyaev's philosophy of history are personalism and historicism. Each of these is revealed in biblical teaching. However, since Berdyaev recognized that 'in paganism there was light, there was a thirst for the divine and for immortality', he considered that 'there is a sense in which it can be said that paganism was also the old testament of mankind'.[44]

However, this 'old testament' differs significantly from the biblical Old Testament. First, it was 'immersed in the cosmos', in its impersonal, non-specific element. Even in Indian mysticism, which Berdyaev considered to be 'in its own way on a very high level', the person is dissolved in the absolute. By trying to escape from the grip of matter, personhood loses itself. Nevertheless, according to Berdyaev, the principle of personhood is one of the greatest marks of spirituality. On this basis, he decisively rejected later occult modifications of Indian doctrines, and expressed the gist of his rejection in a lapidary phrase: 'It is as difficult to find God in the theosophy of Annie Besant as it is to find man in the anthroposophy of Rudolf Steiner.[45]

Berdyaev did not consider pagan 'cosmism' to be an error. The higher reality is hidden both in spirit and in nature ('the whole natural world is symbolic of other worlds'). That is why in ancient times the religions of nature and the religions of the spirit were dialectically linked. They are merely aspects or stages of a single religio-historical process – stages which form a regular succession on the way to the revelation of the highest principle of all, which is personhood.

Secondly, the Graeco-Indian mind is almost totally resistant to the notion of a progressive movement of history. It is in essence extra-historical. Berdyaev explains this by saying that the non-biblical world had no strong idea of freedom. Indian mysticism sought and found freedom at the cost of personality. Greek thought was in thrall to the idea of necessity. 'Submission to fate', Berdyaev writes, 'is the most characteristic feature of the Hellenic spirit. It had no conscious knowledge of freedom, that freedom of the subject to create history without which neither its fulfilment nor comprehension is possible.'[46]

The Old Testament, according to Berdyaev, is different. 'The Hellenic world had been content to contemplate a harmonious cosmos; but this was foreign to the Jews who were destined to reveal the historical drama of human destiny. It constitutes their specific contribution to the history of the human spirit.[47]

In fact, the Old Testament is the beginning of the philosophy of history as such, rather than just a description of events following one another (as in the classical historians). For the prophets, history is a process or path leading up to a great eschatological messianic event. Among ancient religions, Berdyaev finds only one analogy – namely the religion of Iran, with its faith in the ultimate victory of divine light over the darkness of evil.

In spite of all this, the Old Testament – like other forms of religion – remains only a partial revelation, a preparatory step towards the fullness of Christianity. This fullness, however, cannot simply be reduced to a synthesis of ideas, as many historians have done. As the ancient world neared its end, such a synthesis was reached more than once. Berdyaev writes:

> In the Old Testament, in India, in Socrates and the Stoics we can find almost all the elements of Christian morality . . . The one absolutely new and original thing in Christianity is Christ himself; he had not been in the world before, and there will never be another Christ. Christ is the one unrepeatable point of contact between the divine and the human . . . Through Christ, God became both akin to and close to man.[48]

The events described in the Gospels, in which Old Testament eschatological messianism found fulfilment, open the new age in history. The impulse of God made man, bursting into the world and overcoming its inertia, is from time to time fettered by 'objectivization', and becomes clouded over. 'Until the world and history come to an end, dualism will reign; monism, unity and wholeness can only be established after the end, that is, outside objectivization and outside the predetermined world of phenomena.[49] In other words, the eschatological intention retains its full strength and significance in Christianity.

In evaluating the development of Christian consciousness, Berdyaev focusses sharply on the question of demythologization – and this is long before it was raised in Western, Protestant theology. His approach is far more profound than that of Rudolf Bultmann, who was the first person in the West to discuss the problem. For Bultmann, the essence of demythologization was merely to 'translate' the symbolic, mythological language of New Testament doctrine into a language comprehensible to modern man.[50] Berdyaev, on the other hand, regards the 'social formation' of many Christian concepts as a concession to inert objectivization which is deadening and foreign to the spirit of freedom found in the Gospels. There in the history of Christianity an inescapable struggle between 'objectivized' religion which lives 'by the principles of this world', and the religion of the spirit. The religion of the spirit exalts man, and makes him a creative partner in the movement towards the Kingdom of God. All values created by mankind before the coming of Christ and after it are part of this movement. This is Berdyaev's answer to the question of spiritual continuity.

We cannot, however, simply equate Berdyaev's 'religion of the spirit' with Jaspers' 'philosophical faith' or the 'pan-religion' of theosophy. Berdyaev agrees with those 'who see light in all religion', but considers that the theosophists give this truth 'a false syncretistic sense'. As he puts it, 'the only world religion is the religion of Christianity, real and entire'.[51]

Almost at the same time as Berdyaev, the English historian Christopher Dawson was analysing the dialectical development of pre-Christian thinking, though his most important book, *Progress and Religion* (1929), came out after most of Berdyaev's works.[52] According to Dawson, sociologists and historians have often underestimated the role of religion in the formation of social consciousness and of culture in general. However great the significance of the material bases of civilization, it is indicative that 'when culture loses its spiritual basis, it becomes unstable.'[53] The spiritual factor is the active and creative source of culture.

> It emancipates man from the purely biological laws which govern the development of animal species, and enables him to accumulate a growing capital of knowledge and social experience, which gives him a progressive control over his material environment.[54]

Twenty years before Jaspers, Dawson clearly formulated the idea of the 'axial period', and showed that it was connected with 'the first appearance of new spiritual forces, which . . . still influence the minds of men today'.[55] Dawson, however, tries to trace the connection between this era and the long period before it, which Jaspers called 'the beginning of history'. That was when the principles of material culture were established, when literacy began, when the most important technical inventions were made, and it is from this era that the most impressive monuments of architecture, sculpture, painting, and crafts have been preserved.

Dawson asks: what was the spiritual force which drove these ancient cultures? From his point of view, they owe much to a primaeval world-view, which amounted to a great deal more than is allowed by such definitions as 'primitive' or 'savage'. Progress in the study of peoples who have maintained features of a way of life from the remote past has put an end to a condescending attitude towards them, which arose from a lack of understanding and from cultural isolation. In considering the beliefs of the Australian aborigines and the American Indians, and the traditional cultures of Africa, Dawson concludes that they originate in a particular way of looking at the world, but certainly not in 'primitivism'. This is borne out by their ideas of a higher principle, and by the mysticism which has developed in the framework of shamanism. 'Primitive' peoples have their own philosophy, though it is as a rule without abstract forms of expression. 'The dynamic element in primordial culture,' Dawson emphasizes, 'is to be found rather in the sphere of direct religious experience than in that of a conscious rational enquiry.'[56] He also argues that the ancient intuition of divine universal reality is almost identical with the intuition of the most recent mystics.

When a seer is joined by an interpreter, the latter turns into a priest. The priest orders and interprets what the seer sees, but the structuring activity of the priest is directed not so much towards metaphysics as towards the formation of a system of ritual; and that system in turn exercises an enormous influence on the social basis of culture.

The teachings of the 'axial period',[57] in Dawson's view, had not yet broken with the ritual period which had preceded it, but had only given it a different meaning, putting ethical and speculative elements in the first place. The ritual-cosmic world order took on features of a moral world order, in which a faint intuition of unity is expressed in the apophatic idea of the Absolute.

Most of the teachings of the 'axial period' preserve the most ancient view of life, which is inspired by the cycles of nature. In

Brahmanism, too, as well as in the teachings of Greek philosophy, the world is seen as an unchangable rotation of events, ruled by the principle of the eternal return. However long the cycle lasts, there is nothing new in it: it remains within the limits of a circle foreordained for ever.

The only exception to this is to be found in the Old Testament prophets. Their insight discovered something greater than the divine law determining the cycle of the world. According to Dawson,

> While the philosophers of India and Greece were meditating on the illusoriness or the eternity of the cosmic process, the prophets of Israel were affirming the moral purpose in history, and were interpreting the passing events of their age as the revelation of the divine will. For them, there could be no question of the return of all things in an eternal cycle of cosmic change, since the essence of their doctrine of the divine purpose in the world was its uniqueness.[58]

True, the Old Testament too had its static and cyclical elements, reflected in certain tendencies towards apocalyptic and legalistic positions. However, the core was the prophets' line, and it was this which provided the basis and point of reference for Christianity, 'the new religious movement which was destined to transform the ancient world'.[59] The historical coming of Christ united the eternal and the temporary, and made the unconditional and the finite into mutually interpenetrating principles. Christianity, even more than the Old Testament, discloses the uniqueness and value of history, and its purposeful movement forwards. This became, according to Dawson, not the result of some natural evolution of beliefs, but a breakthrough to something absolutely new, 'which forced European civilization out of its old orbit into a path which it would never have followed by its own momentum'.[60]

However, as Dawson shows, the mediaeval subjection of the church to the state, and the Christian theologians' recognition of the value of nature, history and reason, gradually led to the transition of European culture to the path of secularism. This could not be done, of course, without some sort of faith as its basis. At first, it was Deism and rationalism which claimed this role, later to be replaced by the 'religion of progress', a secular variant of biblical eschatology. When the crisis of the West and the World War led to disillusionment with this new religion, the whole structure of European culture proved to be shaken to its foundations.

Like Jaspers, Dawson holds that the most important stimulus to the renaissance of a culture must be a return to lost spiritual values, but for him these are first and foremost the values of Christianity. Return to these values 'would restore to our civilization the moral force that it requires in order to dominate external circumstances and to avoid the dangers that are inherent in the present situation'.[61] Science, on which the 'religion of progress' rested, has failed to become a moral force. This does not mean that it should be rejected. It is a legitimate and organic element of culture, which may do good, provided that there is a 'progressive spiritualization of human nature, which is the function of the Christian religion'.[62]

In this way, Dawson reaches a position distinct from the views of Jaspers and Toynbee. Although he recognizes both the greatness and the profundity of the legacy of the East, he can see a dynamic spiritual principle only in Christianity. Moreover he calls on us to free Christian consciousness itself from those elements which had been introduced into it and had weakened its capacity for cultural creativity and social activity.

Beyond syncretism and confrontation

There is one common and exceptionally important feature which makes Jaspers' theory akin to the ideas of the three Christian thinkers whose views we have just cursorily touched on. Although they speak of the remote past, they all concentrate on the problem of mankind in our own time. Indeed, the inadequacy of technological progress for the development of mankind becomes clearer and clearer nowadays. In particular, even before the Second World War, Dawson spoke of the disastrous consequences of the technological revolution, which is not terrible in itself, but mainly because it has proved to be the instrument of a spiritually immature and morally weakened humanity.

Hence, it is quite understandable that many people should turn to the ethical ideals and spiritual values of the world religions. However distinct Jaspers' views are from the Christian philosophers of history they, like him, were convinced that these ideals and values must again become a living signpost for people. A person who stands on the brink of an abyss has no right to consider these ideals and values exhausted. The breaking of the link between civilization and spirituality has not gone unpunished. But overcoming it is a complex task. One of the most serious obstacles on the path towards achieving it is the confrontation between the world religions themselves and the various currents within them.

Jaspers, Toynbee, Radhakrishnan and many others see the solution in the creation of some universal variant of faith, which would be able to unite everyone. Similar claims are made today by the so-called 'non-traditional cults' which are spreading quickly in various parts of the world. Some of them follow the path of syncretism, while others offer themselves as an alternative to all the classic religions.

The opposite of such tendencies is religious exclusiveness and intolerance, which can take very diverse forms. Thus, in the opinion of the Protestant Karl Barth (especially in his early period), the truth is not to be found anywhere outside the Bible, while for the American convert to the Russian Orthodox Church Abroad Serafim Rose, anything outside Orthodoxy is no more than the machinations of the devil. It hardly needs saying that such a position in practice has frequently led to religious wars, violence and reprisals against those who held a different view.

Neither of these extremes is acceptable in the light of the Gospels. The former is inconsistent with the Christian understanding of truth, the latter with the Christian doctrine of love.

In our view, everything should be based on mutual understanding, tolerance and dialogue, i.e. on what has become known as 'superecumenism'. It would seem that the views of those Christian thinkers whom we have discussed above, can be of great assistance here. Based on the patristic tradition, they saw the history of the spirit as a single if contradictory process, in which separate stages are linked together. With this approach, Christianity could, for instance, remain open to any values which it could accept, while retaining still its identity and uniqueness. According to Berdyaev:

> Christianity is not a religion of the same order as others; it is, as Schleiermacher said, the religion of religions. What does it matter if within Christianity, supposedly so different from all other faiths, there is nothing original at all apart from the coming of Christ and His Personality; for is it not precisely in this particular that the hope of all religions is fulfilled?[63]

It is important to note that Christianity has long since ceased to be 'the religion of the whites', and is spreading intensively in contact with African and Asian cultures. Thus, in India, there are now Christian monks who include in their life certain features of Hindu asceticism. There are a great many tendencies in Christian art and rituals which have absorbed oriental and pre-Columbian American traditions. Originating in Palestine, Christianity absorbed Hellenism and Latinism, and then shaped the culture of Byzantium, Russia and Europe, though preserving national characteristics. Today it has crossed even these frontiers, creating 'new churches' in Africa, Asia and among the Northern peoples.

Today's world crisis shows that there is no future for hostility, or defensive isolationism, or eclecticism, but that dialogue can be fruitful for all participants. The followers of the religions of the world have something to say to mankind. Christianity brings the gospels, its service, its love. Of course, it is not so easy to learn tolerance and openness while remaining true to one's own fundamental principles. Christians, though, have never thought that spiritual life was an easy matter, but rather an ascetic and heroic deed. The whole earth now needs this deed. On the eve of the two thousandth anniversary of the foundation of the Christian church, the world has reached a critical frontier. That is why dialogue has become not a luxury for intellectuals but a necessity of life.

Part II

The Russian Experience

6

Religion, the 'Cult of Personality' and the Secular State

The question how did it happen that Russia, alone of all the countries with a Communist regime, endured it so long and in such an extreme atheistic form is an issue which today gives rise to much soul-searching and many debates. Blame is variously ascribed to the lack of democratic structures in Russia and the failure of Tsarism, to the Bolsheviks themselves, to Stalin, to Lenin – and to the Jews. But Fr Alexander approaches the problem from a quite different angle, looking at the moral failures of the nominal Christians of the past.

'Do you seriously think that it was the atheists who were guilty of destroying our churches? The real guilty ones were the false Christians, all those merchants and aristocrats, blood-suckers, who tormented their serfs, went in for drunkenness and debauchery, and then on their deathbeds tried to redeem their sins and gave money for building churches. And our clergy were guilty too, the ones who went drinking with the civil authorities and sucked up to them and gave their blessing to all kinds of illegalities. The atheists came along as an instrument of God's wrath. Read the prophets in the Bible and you'll see what I mean.'[1]

'Nothing happens by chance in history . . . What we sow, we reap. And if today we are weeping over the ruins of our churches, we should weep no less for our past sins and our mistakes as Christians, and those of our forebears . . . Christ said, "Now is the judgment of this world" [John 12. 31] . . . and this judgment is continuing now.'[2]

But there were also historical and sociological factors as well which date from the church reforms of Peter the Great in the early eighteenth century and lasted right up to the fall of the monarchy in 1917. Fr Alexander lists them in an interview he gave with the journal Youth:

1. *The abandonment by the educated classes of traditional church culture in favour of the ideas of the Enlightenment. This rift began to be healed only at the beginning of the twentieth century with the Russian religious renaissance.*

2. *The low status of the clergy, their poverty, forced social segregation, and low level of education.*

3. *The subservience of the church to the state from the time of Peter the Great, so that the church was administered by a government department and priests were expected to betray the secrets of the confessional.*

4. *The veto on any new thinking in the church, on Bible translations. All this meant that when the revolution came the church was mentally quite unprepared. Within a few years of the establishment of the Bolshevik regime, the religious intelligentsia had either been exiled or perished in the camps, and the mass of uneducated people were defenceless against the pressures of atheism.*[3]

In the following article Fr Alexander looks at the phenomenon of Stalinism as a kind of spiritual sickness, a longing for God which was perverted into the deification of a dictator. In a historical survey he discusses the religion of 'emperor-worship' from the earliest times to this century, and concludes with some recommendations for a secular state which would prevent a recurrence.

This study was first published in Kul'tura i dukhovnoe vozrozhdenie, *Moscow 1992, pp. 378–413.*

The whole earth followed the beast with wonder. Men worshipped the dragon, for he had given his authority to the beast, and they worshipped the beast, saying, 'Who is like the beast, and who can fight against it?' And the beast was given a mouth uttering haughty and blasphemous words, and it was allowed to exercise authority for forty-two months (Rev. 13. 3–5).

This idea first came to me back in my school years, when one of my classmates was killed in an accident during PT. Those who were around him in his last minutes said that while he was dying he spoke with Stalin, who 'came to take him to himself'. It struck us, his comrades, as bizarre. We had not noticed that he was particularly 'ideological' in any sense of the word. And then for the first time an idea came to me that explained it – so that's it, it's religion! In the soul of a dying youth the holy image of Stalin had acquired an elevated, sacred quality – Stalin the father figure whom we had become used to thanking for our happy childhood. Over the years my idea has become a certainty, reinforced by many observations. In the end, it has helped me to understand the gigantic historical tragedy that formed the backdrop against which the youth of my generation grew up.

An urgent issue

As Russian society today begins a difficult cure, comes to its senses and is restored to health, the question 'how could it have happened?' is ever more frequently and ever more insistently being asked. What caused that long 'polar night' of our history which is associated with the names of Joseph Stalin and his accomplices? What induced them to wage war against their own people with such incredible cruelty? And how could a person who was behaving like a conqueror on occupied territory come to be treated like a kind of earthly god?

This riddle cannot be left to historical science for it to make a dispassionate and unhurried study of these 'deeds of by-gone days' as if we were studying the campaigns of Genghis or Batu Khan.[4] Quite the reverse. The subject is something extremely important for all of us right now. It concerns a grievous social disease which gave rise to an endless stream of crimes witnessed and perpetrated by millions who are still alive today.

It is difficult to cure a disease if you do not understand its causes, and if no treatments have been found there is still the danger of a relapse, even if the first crisis has passed. That is why people fear a return to lawlessness. The disclosure of new, monstrous facts about the Terror brings not only the satisfaction that truth has seen the light of day, but also – understandably – fears about the future, not least for the future of our children. So it is quite natural that economists, sociologists, writers and psychologists should all be urgently looking for an explanation for Stalinism. They study it from all sides and are proposing innumerable hypotheses about its nature and origin.

References to Joseph Stalin's evil personality are the most superficial and unconvincing of the explanations. There have always been plenty of power-hungry and unprincipled people, sadists and intriguers, in all countries. But how can it be explained that one-sixth of the earth came to be in the hands of such a person, and why was he surrounded by the aura of divinity? Stalin's character alone cannot explain this.

Then what if Stalin really was a universal genius (as his apologists believe), who by right won the adulation of all and by right was set on a superhuman pedestal and even above the law? But this too is not convincing. Stalin was never noted for the charisma of a Mahatma Gandhi. He could not match Lenin's intellect. He was not a great writer like Julius Caesar, and he never showed personal bravery as a military commander like Alexander the Great, Suvorov[5] or Napoleon. He was not even a brilliant orator with the ability to infect crowds with his enthusiasm. Although Stalin claimed to have the last word in all fields of science and culture, his pretensions were pure fiction. A dropout seminarian, he reduced philosophy to the notorious 'fourth chapter',[6] transformed history and economics into a pack of lies, choked genetics and sociology, linguistics and cybernetics and for decades obstructed the development of art and literature.

That all the successes of the people, including victory in World War II, were attributed to Stalin, might be called the '*Little Zaches* effect'.[7] In the Hoffman story the befogging of people's

minds, which led to their ascribing good to the credit of the evil
dwarf, was the result of witchcraft. But then who bewitched and
darkened the consciousness of millions of adults in those days
when the country was wracked by hunger, when the cream of the
peasantry died, when writers, scholars, musicians, artists,
veterans of the revolution and military officers were morally and
physically destroyed?

Those unscrupulous experiments at huge cost of human life, all
those great canal projects, 'transformations of nature', the
genocide carried out against whole nations and classes, the
barbed wire of the camps, the degenerative effect on the morals of
society which became infused with the spirit of mistrust, fear and
denunciation, and alongside all that – a blind faith in the genius,
wisdom and kindness of the 'father of the people': there is
something truly inconceivable about it all which the brain simply
refuses to grasp.

Certain historians and publicists, especially in the West,
maintain that the Stalinist regime was a purely Russian phenomenon, caused by the weakness of democratic conditions in the
former tsarist empire. But if this is the only factor, then how are
we to explain analogous phenomena in other countries: the
deification of Mao Tse-tung, the dictatorship of Pol Pot,[8] and
the 'minor cults' in eastern Europe? How, finally, can we explain
dictatorships however they are dressed up in Germany, Italy and
many Latin American countries? We find a depressing similarity
in the basic symptoms of the illness regardless of the different
ideologies and the particular slogans in people of different
cultures, traditions and races. When the cult of a leader has taken
the place of democracy, it has led, as a rule, to the ecstatic worship
of the dictator. Many of us were prompted to think about this
after seeing Romm's film *Obyknovennyy Fashizm* (Ordinary
Fascism).[9]

The people who come closer to understanding these phenomena are evidently those who look for the causes of what happened
not only in socio-political factors, but also in socio-psychological
ones, in the very nature of human beings.

The tendency to avoid freedom, to place the responsibility for
risk, initiative, actions and words on someone else's shoulders is

just as characteristic of people as their love of freedom. This tendency is very accurately described in articles by the psychologist, Leonid Radzikhovsky. 'People fear the world,' he wrote. 'They fear reason, they fear the unknown. They are reluctant to think for themselves, to use their senses. They need faith, mystery and authority. They need everyone to merge together, to lose their individuality, to become part of the crowd – only thus can they live without fear, in this they see some kind of higher meaning, a pledge of immortality.'[10]

Most autocrats consciously or unconsciously exploit these complex feelings. We have to admit that something similar occurs in the history of religion. But we will return to that later. For now, let us note that in the psychological complex under discussion, two heterogeneous elements are strangely intertwined: the first is the so-called 'herd instinct', the hunger for submission to firm government. The second is the fundamental and quite proper striving of the human spirit to seek a higher truth and the meaning of existence.

However closely these elements intertwine in the course of human history, their roots are quite distinct. The thirst for submission is atavistic and instinctive, inherited from our animal origins where groups are as a rule led by herd leaders. Whereas the search for the meaning of existence, for the ideal, is an integral part of culture and a characteristic of humans as spiritual beings.

The well-known psychiatrist and philosopher Erich Fromm considered that an essential condition for a harmonious consciousness is orientation on some higher values. However, it is very important where this orientation is pointed. If the object of orientation is merely something limited, temporary and perishable, it risks resulting in one or other form of idolatry. There is a risk of this type in the idea of man as the 'measure of all things', which has come down to us from antiquity.

By way of explanation, let me give you a concrete example. In one of his poems, Evgeny Evtushenko[11] (one of our veteran democrats) burns with righteous anger about Hitler, Beria and Pinochet. Yet he declares his 'faith in man', though of course, alas, Hitler, Beria and Pinochet and other criminals and their henchmen are also members of the human race. So for the poet, the 'measure of all things' is not simply man, but something else that lifts people above the level of the Hitlers, the Berias and the Pinochets.

One of the secrets of the success of Stalinism lies in the fact that, having created a religious vacuum, it united people's atavistic and spiritual drives into a common course. It fused in people's consciousness the supreme ideal, the 'measure of all things' with the mythologized figure of The Leader and thereby endowed him with attributes of divinity and limitless power. The anatomy of this process is nowadays becoming clearer and clearer and its fatal consequences more and more apparent.

I have to say that I am not one of those who totally condemn the present-day defenders of Stalin. Their fate, their spiritual condition, seem to me to be deeply tragic. It is perfectly understandable why they close their eyes to the uncontrovertible facts produced in party decrees and other authentic documents and testimonies. The point is not so much that to accept these facts means wiping out the value of much of their own past. The dethroning of the dictator and his henchmen strikes at the heart of the sacred beliefs of the Stalinists, cuts the ground from under their feet and demands of them a radical rethink of everything on which their worldview was based. In a word, what's at stake is *faith*, which is one of the most important cogs in the machinery of dictatorship.

The term 'cult of personality' was first used as a kind of shamefaced euphemism for Stalinism; and at the beginning even conveyed the impression that a purely academic problem about the role of personality in history was under discussion. But the word 'cult' was well chosen. It faithfully expresses the religious, or if you prefer, the pseudo-religious nature of the phenomenon.

Only in the future when the picture of the disaster becomes fuller will it be possible to give an exhaustive explanation for what happened. I just want to touch on one aspect of the question: what place does the cult of Stalin take in the history of religion precisely as a *cult*. Then I want to pose the question: what antidotes are there available to us today to prevent a relapse?

From the age of the sorcerer to the Roman emperor

We have to begin by looking far back into the mists of antiquity. As far as I know, the first thing written in Russian on this subject was L. S. Shaumyan's article 'The cult of personality' in the three-volume *Philosophical Encyclopaedia* (Moscow 1964). Although the author concentrates mainly on the political side of the matter, his work is undeniably useful as an explanation of the genesis of the 'cult' and its connections with the sacral theocratic monarchies of antiquity.

Certainly, the practice of deifying those who wielded absolute power was widely known in many states of the classical East. Emperors there were often perceived, not simply as people whose regimes were sanctioned by religion, but as direct descendants of the gods, and the embodiment of superhuman powers.

For hundreds and thousands of years, this view continued undisputed, as something self-evident, in other words, it belonged to the category of ideas which the ethnologist Lucien Levy-Bruhl has called 'collective representations'.

Faith in the divinity of rulers was a constituent part of the world-view in ancient Eastern societies and was an important element in their cultural and social life. It was precisely that faith which inspired the Egyptians to construct the 'eternal homes' or pyramids for the pharaohs. Note that the pyramids were not just graves or memorials, but were considered to be the abodes of the spirit of the pharaoh, who continued to participate in the affairs of the country even after his death.

An instructive analogy for our time is the fact that the 'god-kings' did not overly rely on people of creativity and initiative. An extensive network of bureaucrats were the obedient instrument of their will. Enormous finds of pottery and papyrus records unearthed by archaeologists testify to the activities of ancient officialdom (and how many more such documents have disappeared without a trace!).

In certain cases it is possible even to date the beginning of ruler-worship: for instance, in the Mesopotamian cuneiform script, 'the sign of god' i.e. a star, began to be joined to the name of the monarch in the third millennium BC under Naram-Suene.

For the most part, however, evidence of the origins of royal cults are lost in the mists of time before written history began.

There are grounds for believing that the ruler-worship cult was preceded by primitive forms of power relying upon magic and on magism as a belief-system. Magism was based on the belief that there is an eternal cosmic order to which human beings have to submit, but over which they can exert influence by performing certain actions, namely magic rituals.

Although in practice magism often seeped into religious consciousness, it was essentially antagonistic to religion. In religion there is a genuine reverence of the Transcendental, but in magism instead the idea that, through magic, cosmic forces can be compelled to serve the selfish interests of human beings.

So we can understand why in the Bible magic is contrasted with true faith which is expressed in love and trust for the Creator. We see this in the story of Adam who aspired to equality with God. Adam's claim to autonomous power ('knowledge') over nature, over 'good and evil' – which in biblical terms means over the whole world – is depicted as destructive and dangerous pride.

The history of primitive society fills in the outline given in the biblical story with quite specific detail. Those who were credited with powers of magic – exorcists, shamans, sorcerers – wielded immense power and influence in society. In the words of Sigmund Freud, the magus and the wizard 'at the dawn of humanity were those very supermen which Nietzsche anticipated would only appear in the future.'[12]

However we interpret this phenomenon (whether it was the effect of social factors, paranormal phenomena or hypnosis), what is important to us now is that it served as a precursor to the cult of monarchs and dictators. In *The Golden Bough*, James Frazer even tried to research how the idea of sacral power, which developed at much later stages of civilization, arose from the magician's supernatural authority.

Nonetheless, however paradoxical it may seem at first glance, the power of the 'god-king' could never be absolute in the full sense of the word.

The ancient Eastern world did not fully identify the will of the monarch and the supreme divine will with its ethical teachings and religious traditions. In spite of their sacral prerogatives, rulers in one way or another were compelled to reckon with these teachings and traditions and to act in such a way as to uphold them as the 'agents' or 'defenders' of them. This is why the kings of Egypt, Babylon and Iran constantly had to demonstrate their piety and declare their loyalty 'to truth and justice'. In other words, the concept of the monarch, even though surrounded with the halo of sanctity, was not seen in principle as *the ultimate source of truth*.

The same attitude put certain limitations on autocracy and restricted its actions. These restrictions can be seen most clearly in two cultural areas, that of the Old Testament and that of ancient Greece. In the Old Testament, the law of God was in no uncertain terms proclaimed to be the standard of conduct for any person, whether simple peasant, leader or anointed king. Moreover, monarchical power itself was regarded in the Bible as merely a tolerated evil, a kind of concession given to imperfect people. 'For they have not rejected you' said the Lord to the prophet Samuel, when the people asked that a king should be found to rule over them 'but they have rejected me from being king over them' [I Sam. 8.7]. And the book of Deuteronomy bids the monarch constantly to read the scroll of God's law 'that his heart may not be lifted up above his brethren, and that he may not turn aside from the commandment, either to the right hand or to the left' [Deut. 17.20].

Any departure from the law of God by the anointed leaders was publicly denounced by the prophets. The very status of a prophet itself as a free herald of divine will permitted these preachers to castigate the rulers openly and severely, though of course from time to time the prophets paid for their bravery with their liberty or even with their life.

We find another type of control over the powerful in the West: in democratic Athens. It was here that the idea of *law* first appeared. As Fustel de Coulange has shown in his well-known work on antiquity,[13] this idea had a religious origin and in that sense it was close to the principles of Old Testament society. But in time, it acquired a rational and almost secular character.

Of course, at that time, Athens and Jerusalem were but tiny islands among a sea of states ruled by the principle of sacral monarchy. Thus, it is not surprising that even the expansion of Greek culture whose centre was Athens could not democratize the world. On the contrary, the Greeks themselves subordinated themselves to Alexander the Great and thus returned to the ancient idea of a divine emperor.

In the course of this retrograde movement, the monarchs of the Hellenistic period enjoyed using many ploys of political mystification. But they apparently justified this to themselves by saying that they were meeting the desires of the people to have 'living gods' as their leaders.

The great religious and philosophical movements which preceded Hellenism such as those associated with Buddha, Lao-Zi, Zarathustra, the Israelite prophets, and other thinkers of antiquity undermined many long-held beliefs. But those who could not accept these new ideas first passed through a stage of scepticism and then nostalgia for the old forms of life and thought. As a result, the king cult caught its second wind in the Hellenistic period.

An example is to be found in Alexander the Great who, having usurped the privilege of the pharaohs announced himself to be the son of the Egyptian god Ammon. And after the death of the conqueror, kings and dictators appeared one after the other, actively claiming to be divine. Without going into detail, let us simply note the titles which they took for themselves: Ptolemy I was Soter – 'Saviour'; another was Epiphanius – 'the Revealed God' or even simply 'Theos' meaning 'God'. In Syria, Antiochus IV claimed to be the incarnation of Zeus, whereas the well-known rival of Rome, Mithridates of Pontus was called 'Mithra-Dionysus'. When Demetrius Poliorcetes took the Parthenon temple as his residence, Athenians welcomed him with an enthusiastic hymn:

Other gods are far away or have no ears.
Perhaps they do not exist at all,
Or do not look down at us.
But you are before us, not wood or stone

But in the flesh, alive
So now we approach you with prayer.[14]

This process was completed by the second sacralization of power in the Mediterranean area with the cult of the Roman emperors introduced by Octavius Augustus in 29 BC.

But this time, political calculations bordering on cynicism were glaringly obvious. For Augustus, the cult of his personality was just an instrument in a political game, a means of strengthening his autocracy and the ideological integration of the numerous peoples of the empire. Before he triumphed over his competitors, Octavius had witnessed how Julius Caesar had been raised to the ranks of the gods after he was killed by the republican conspirators. But Augustus did not want posthumous worship. Gradually, beginning with the eastern provinces, temples were erected in honour of the 'emperor-genius'. Augustus was depicted in the pose and clothing of Jupiter. Incense was burned before his statues. Even Roman intellectuals, weary of civil wars, accepted the cult of the man-god and joined in the chorus of his praises. Virgil greeted his reign as the eternal age of Saturn, and Horace in his epistles addressed Augustus thus:

You in your lifetime, however, we fully acknowledge and
    honour,
Setting up altars where vows may be made by invoking your
    godhead,
Sure that your equal will never arise nor has ever yet risen.[15]

After the death of Augustus, in the period from Tiberius to Diocletian, the cult of the emperor continued to escalate, leading to new temples and ceremonies. Nevertheless, the claims of the regime to absolutism were not entirely successful. On the one hand, many educated people, especially those of philosophical bent, played along with the cult of the emperor with ill-concealed irony, and on the other, paganism itself prevented worship of a man-god from becoming the only religion. Even those who made sacrifices on Caesar's altar worshipped other gods along with him.

Finally, it was during the rule of Augustus and Tiberius, the 'authors' of the Roman monarchical cult, that a new spiritual force arrived in the world which was radically opposed to worship of the head of state. This force was Christianity.

Christ and Caesar

One of the main reasons for almost three hundred years of Christian persecution in the Roman empire was precisely their refusal to recognize the emperor as a living god. In other instances, Rome was inclined to religious tolerance, but in the case of the Christians, compromise was impossible. They demanded from Christians just a formal act: all they had to do was to throw a handful of incense on a brazier in front of the altar to Caesar. But thousands of men, women and young people preferred exile, prison, torture and death because for them even such an apparently innocent gesture was a betrayal of Christ . . .

Christians were not anarchists at all or rebels fighting for an alternative state order. The new faith was a spiritual movement. It was not trying to create a political utopia. It accepted the existing order and its laws as a positive reality. For all its imperfections, the Roman empire had inherited and developed the Greek idea of law and legality. Hence St Paul's words about obedience to the governing authorities. According to his teaching, the principle of government itself – the alternative to social and political chaos – comes 'from God'.

But the church also affirmed another principle expressed in the words of St Peter. A pupil of Paul's, St Luke, records it like this in Acts: 'We must obey God rather than men' [Acts 5.29]. Peter's speech was specifically concerned with religious matters, and consequently these words refer to the need for freedom of conscience.

Moreover, Christianity did not give up its right morally to judge the acts of the emperor. In particular, the book of Revelation portrays a tyrannical empire at war with God in the shape of a monster, an image which is borrowed from the Old Testament book of Daniel, the first 'manifesto of religious freedom' in history.

When Christianity spoke out against the deification of the emperor, it also threw down the gauntlet to that tendency in religious psychology which is made up of mixed feelings of submission and fear, of delight in and craving for a strong hand, of adoration of the power of a capricious Master who arbitrarily punishes and shows mercy, before a heavenly Despot whose image was easily confused with earthly rulers.

The image of the divine as revealed in Jesus of Nazareth is free from any such characteristics. In Jesus least of all do we find any projection of those secret desires on which the cult of an earthly power is nourished.

Indeed, the prophets of the Old Testament in their protest against the seduction of 'divine despotism' prophesied that the Messiah would come to earth without the traditional attributes of earthly rulers. And in fact the Gospels do not contain anything that might suppress the *freedom* of human choice and decision-making. Christ was born and lived among poor, un-important and despised people. His disciples were not an elite but simple common people. He did not perform a single miracle in order to demonstrate his power. He did not have an obedient army like Muhammad nor did he use coercion to win souls. Neither the religious nor the secular authorities supported him. He went about the earth not in triumph as a conqueror but as an outcast, someone persecuted and met by a wall of incomprehen-sion. He came to know the bitterness of betrayal, slander and condemnation. He died, not like Buddha in advanced years among faithful friends, but in the prime of life, nailed to the cross like a common criminal before a jeering mob and deserted by all. Even after the mysterious events of Easter, he did not appear to his enemies in order to break their will or force them to believe in him.

Although there were times when Christ could be severe – even frightening – he always respected human freedom. He sought children, not slaves. There are no 'knock-down' arguments in the Gospels designed to paralyse the will, whether in the form of irrefutable miraculous phenomena or incontestable logic. St Paul expressed this clearly when he said: 'For Jews demand signs and Greeks seek wisdom, but we preach Christ crucified, a stumbling block to Jews and folly to Gentiles, but to those who are called, both Jews and Greeks, Christ the power of God and the wisdom of God. For the foolishness of God is wiser than man, and the weakness of God is stronger than men' [I Cor. 1. 22–25].

No wonder Dante says that the greatest miracle of Christianity is that it conquered the world without miracles. Like the ministry of Jesus, the preaching of his disciples was a call for spiritual freedom which appealed to people's free conscience. 'For you were called to freedom, brethren', declares Paul [Gal. 5. 13]. The apostles went forth to conquer the earth, without any external power to rely on, and so setting the ideal model for all future Christian generations. And this ideal, established by the Gospels and the apostles, will never be obscured by any of the betrayals of it which have occurred many times in the course of history.

'A Christian empire'

At the beginning of the fourth century AD, the Roman empire changed its tactics in its battle with Christianity. It recognized Christianity, and even made it the state religion, but in so doing it imperceptibly subordinated Christianity to itself. In many ways, this marked the beginning of a tragic period for the church, the period conventionally known as 'Constantinian', when the political authorities pursued their own aims in the name of Christ and of his church.

In the light of the Gospels, the very ideas of 'state religion' or 'Christian state' are very doubtful and arguable. Any state, even the most perfect, is nevertheless an instrument of coercion which is difficult to reconcile with the spirit of Christian freedom.

In paganism, the social order was usually conceived of as part of the cosmic order. State and religion were simply different aspects of one universal order. Christianity, on the contrary, divided its own spiritual domain – 'God's domain' – from that of 'Caesar'. In this polarization lie the premises for the separation of church from state, although this formula was not yet current. But when the emperors chained the church to their chariot, that oppression of the spirit began which led to religious-political dictatorship, and to 'Christian' persecutions of dissenters . . .

But how could the religion of love behave like this?

Any empire will strive for a single ideological structure of society, one that is convenient to the authorities. At the end of the classical period and during the Middle Ages, the state religion became the means of enforcing conformity. Emperors, kings, princes and other rulers often resorted to forced Christianization and a repressive assertion of confessional unity. So, if the emperor was an Arian, he persecuted the Orthodox. If he was Orthodox, he persecuted the Arians. This false, though perhaps historically inevitable, union of church and Caesar dealt the church an enormous moral blow. Adopting the style of secular politics, the church leadership came to copy its tactics and methods and transformed the church – especially in the mediaeval West – into the likeness of the state.

However, as happened already in the Old Testament when the prophets exposed the power of the establishment, so in the history of the church there have always been those who kept faith with the Gospels and opposed the incursion of Caesar into spiritual life. We only have to remember the protests of St Ambrose of Milan and St John Chrysostom; the resolve of Pope Martin and St Maximus the Confessor, the defenders of icons and the Russian *nestyazhateli* (non-possessors), the activities of Savanorola and Jan Huss, St Maxim the Greek and St Filipp of Moscow.[16] These centres of opposition within the church were a constant reminder to the autocrats that there is a divine 'measure of all things' which stands above earthly power.

In exactly the same way, though in the Middle Ages the image of Christ was at times replaced with the image of the Thunder god, again and again the half-forgotten Gospels were 'discovered' with their message of spiritual freedom and love: for instance, in the West the teachings of St Francis of Assisi, and in the East the icons of Andrei Rublev.

The concept of a sacral Christian state was ultimately doomed to failure, if only because the good news of Jesus is alien to coercion and to the idea of earthly autocrats. Addressing the apostles as members of the church of the New Testament, Christ says 'You know that the rulers of the Gentiles lord it over them, and their great men exercise authority over them. *It shall not be so among you*; but whoever would be great among you must be your servant' [Matt. 20. 25–26]. In relying on religious sanctions, the monarchs of 'Christendom' were attempting to circumvent that teaching by using principles of state religion, of the 'symphonia' and the theory of the 'two swords' – the secular and the ecclesiastical. But all this turned out to be unsustainable, and the period of the decline of feudalism ended with the bankruptcy of theocratic power and the birth of the idea of the secular state.

The secularization of power

This secularization process was nourished by two main sources. First, the confessional pluralism which gathered force in the West as a result of the Reformation called into question the very idea of a state creed. The religious wars which burst out in Europe in the sixteenth and seventeenth centuries showed that government had to take account of the different churches and could maintain peace and stability only by following the principle of religious tolerance.

Secondly, the Renaissance initiated new thinking about the theory and practice of the state independent of religious sanctions, by resurrecting the republican and democratic ideas of antiquity.

Niccolo Machiavelli [1469–1527] is usually considered the father of political secularism in modern times. Speaking out against the status of Christianity as a state ideology, he in fact rendered it an important service and freed it from extraneous, worldly elements. But in his reflections on the foundations of society, Machiavelli went much further. Being a pragmatist, he considered self-interest to be the main moving force in history. He gave pride of place to the worst aspects of human nature. As a result, Machiavelli not only cut religion out of politics, but all morals as well.

So, for the first time ever, there came about a theory of absolute power without any restraints whatsoever. This power turned into something self-sufficient which meant that any means it employed were justified. True, Machiavelli himself thought that the sovereign should act for the good of the people. But he envisaged this good – as Thomas Hobbes did later – as a harsh order, an iron bridle, which the sovereign must always hold in his hands.

The theories of Machiavelli gave justification to one of the strongest human passions – the will to power. Thousands of examples are known of people who for different motives voluntarily forego wealth, family, home and many other things, but only a few isolated incidents are known to history of people voluntarily foregoing power. 'Machiavellianism', therefore, became the most tempting model for any autocracy striving to free itself from religious constraints.

Running ahead, we can say that this aim was only achieved in the totalitarian regimes of the twentieth century. But for the time being that lay far ahead. In the eighteenth and nineteenth centuries, 'Machiavellianism' did not become dominant and had to be content with isolated and temporary victories. The religious and moral ideas, absorbed together with Christianity, remained too strong for the authorities to leave them out of account. Even the leaders of the French revolution who started out with atheism soon found it necessary to take up religion again even if it was a form of Deism – the cult of the supreme Being introduced by Robespierre.

Democratic tendencies too were developing concurrently, first appearing already in the Middle Ages (Novgorod in Russia and the city communes in the West). They should logically have set society on course towards the separation of church from state, of God from Caesar. That this was inevitable was confirmed in the West by the ever growing ideological and religious pluralism.

In contrast to dictatorship, democracy is known only in human society; it is unknown in the animal kingdom. Democracy is founded on two things: consciousness of the high value of the individual, which is nourished on the soil of religious personalism, and secondly the effort to give society a rational structure.

The growth of democracy in the last century went hand in hand with the development of scientific rational thought, which, according to the theory of English historian Christopher Dawson, is the second fundamental element of European culture along with the first, which is Christianity. The faith of Europe is rooted in the gospel and in antiquity, especially her science, including political science.

The Church Fathers of the first centuries AD had already shown how there could be creative interaction between these two mutually complementary elements, Christianity and science. But in practice in modern times, a spirit of division has grown up between them, a schism which threatens the destruction of the whole edifice of European culture. In particular, this division has affected the area concerned with the task of creating an optimal social structure.

The fact that the leaders of the churches have to a greater or less extent opposed the secularization of the state, of science and of politics has been one of the more tragic chapters in the history of Christianity. Hundreds of years of inertia and the habit of seeing religion as a form of state ideology and of shoring up Caesar have led to the most lamentable results. Those very church figures who, like Lamennais[17] held out their hands to democracy and secularism, found themselves under suspicion and in isolation.

In the eighteenth and nineteenth centuries, the divide between faith and science deepened with the anticlericalism of democrats and educationalists which gradually turned to aggression against religion as such. In religion, they saw the ally of reaction, monarchism and of conservative tendencies, and indeed in some ways this view conformed with reality. To attack religion, they used the achievements of various sciences, evolutionism, biblical criticism and social and economic theories. But the elimination of the religious and ethical foundations of society was to have its effect. It was precisely this which fuelled that pathological crisis of culture that marks the boundary between the nineteenth and twentieth centuries.

The Christian expectation of the kingdom of God and the transformation of the world and of humanity came to be replaced by faith in Progress – a secular version of biblical eschatology. According to this faith, the developments of science and technology as well as enlightenment and social institutions by themselves would make people happier and more humane. However, the prognoses of the self-confident nineteenth century were not destined to come true. On the contrary, history was on a headlong course towards the epoch of two world wars.

The Russian variant

Any objective student of Russian history has to agree that at the time of the revolutions of 1905 and 1917, the majority of the population of the Russian empire were believers. They belonged mainly to two world religions, Christianity and Islam. Other religions in Russia had a comparatively small number of adherents. Not even the most gifted leaders can bring about a revolution without the support of the masses. But if the destruction of the old order was carried out by believers, how are we then to understand all the ensuing course of events? For an answer we must once again return to the distant past.

Rus' – Russia – the nucleus of the future tsarist empire, adopted its ecclesiastical and political systems from Byzantium together with Orthodox Christianity. In particular, early Russia adopted the idea of *symphonia*, the harmonious interaction between the power of the Christian state and the church with its hierarchy. This system undoubtedly played a major part in establishing the Russian state. The church reconciled the princes, fought against centrifugal tendencies and, by its authority sanctified the right to the throne of the grand princes. Under the Tatar yoke, the church became the main influence preserving national culture and inspired the unifiers of the Russian lands. But the first grand prince who was officially crowned tsar, Ivan the Terrible, rejected the moral authority of the church which, in the person of metropolitan Filipp, spoke out against his bloody tyranny.

The patriotic role of the church in the Time of Troubles is well known. However, no sooner had the monarchy been renewed after that catastrophe, when it again began a systematic attack on the church while keeping up the appearance of a 'Christian' government. The second Romanov tsar [Aleksis] deposed patriarch Nikon, and his son Peter the Great abolished the patriarchate and created the synodal system which subordinated the church to the autocracy to an even greater extent than in

Byzantium. Catherine the Great formally announced herself to be 'Head of the Church'. A pupil of the French Encyclopaedists, in doing this she was following the advice of Diderot 'to keep the priests in poverty and ignorance'. No wonder that ordinary priests, as Pushkin observed, almost all went over to the side of Pugachev.[18]

All historians of the Russian Orthodox Church consider that the 'synodal period' was a difficult and stagnant time for the church. Autocracy, protected by its own sacral privileges, constantly and brutally interfered in church affairs and even in religious education and theological debate. This brought into church life a spirit of officialdom and bureaucracy and discredited the authority of the clergy in the eyes of the people. Sufficient to say that the authorities required the clergy to abuse the secrecy of the confessional for political purposes. There were also instructions to give out certificates to those receiving communion as a guarantee of trustworthiness. It would be hard to think up a more certain means of discrediting the church.

Of course, these policies could not entirely paralyse the inner life of the church. Even in this synodal period, the church had its great saints, ascetics, clergy and theologians. But almost all of them had to carry on a difficult struggle for spiritual existence. Think of the kind of situation described in Leskov's novel *Cathedral Folk* [Soboryane].[19]

Towards the end of the nineteenth century, the ecclesiastical-political picture in Russia was characterized by the following traits:

The guardianship and control by the state had deprived the Orthodox Church of its independence. It was placed under the watchful eye of the Procurator-general. Religious dissenters such as the Old Believers and sectarians were brutally repressed. Changing your denomination, in the sense of leaving the 'majority faith' was considered (until 1905) a criminal offence.

The union with the autocracy which had been historically imposed on the church undermined any trust in her which those who wished for a transformation of society might have put in her, and the same is true also of the many cultural figures, including among them believers, for whom freedom of thought was of incontestable value.

The moral energy of Christianity was siphoned off into non-religious, oppositional liberation movements. It is remarkable how many revolutionary democrats came from a clerical background and were educated at church schools.

The crisis of autocracy, made more acute by the Russo-Japanese war [1905] and World War I, gave many believers hope for radical changes for the better. This is why the leadership of the Russian Orthodox Church did not perceive the collapse of the monarchy in February 1917 to be a catastrophe. After all, it was precisely this event which finally allowed them to convene an All-Russian Church Council to resolve many of the long overdue complex problems.

The Bolshevik government declared the separation of church from state, i.e. the same principle which was already applied in the United States, France and other countries. And for a vast republic of millions of Orthodox, Old Believers, Catholics, Armenians and Georgians, Lutherans, representatives of different Christian sects, Jews, Muslims, Buddhists and adherents of archaic traditional cults, this approach was the most right and natural one. The very idea of 'state religion' had effectively outlived its usefulness. 'Not one state official', wrote Lenin, 'should even have the right to ask someone about their faith: it is a matter of conscience into which no one should dare interfere. There must be no "state sponsored" faith or church.'[20] This idea was also expressed in the Soviet government's 'Appeal to the Muslim Workers of Russia and the East' adopted soon after the revolution. 'Henceforth', it says, 'your faith and customs and your national and cultural institutions are declared free and inviolable.' Religion, free from the supervision and pressure of government and government free from religious sanctions and built instead upon a rational and democratic foundation, this, it would seem, was the ideal and aim for future development.

The revolutionary decrees about freedom, together with the idea of people's power and the fact of religious pluralism in the country – these were the preconditions needed for this. Especially important in this regard was the freedom of conscience declared by the Bolshevik revolution. The decree of January 1918 guaranteed that 'each citizen may belong to any religion or none'. In July that year, a paragraph included in the Constitution of the RSFSR stated that 'freedom of religious and anti-religious propaganda is recognized for all citizens'. Explaining this point, Lenin said in a speech at a meeting in Moscow that 'religion is a personal matter. Let each believe or not believe in what they want . . . the Soviet republic does not recognize any religious differences. The republic is outside any religion, it has separated religion from the Soviet state'.

That was an unambiguous indication that the new government was oriented on a *secular* model, which should theoretically have excluded any confrontation between the church and the state.

However, history, as is well known, does not run in a straight line. In spite of these hopes, confrontation began and very soon.

Today, from the perspective of decades later, it becomes more and more obvious that this conflict cannot be blamed entirely on one side or the other. Any revolution inevitably unleashes spontaneous violence which is exceptionally difficult to control. Among those institutions connected with the old regime was the church, which explains the negative attitude towards it. At the same time, the hastily-published decree on the separation of church from state evoked protests from religious circles who perceived it as an act of discrimination. This impression seemed to be confirmed by numerous anti-clerical and anti-religious excesses.

I think it is high time to lay to rest the legend which still crops up in books that patriarch Tikhon pronounced an anathema on the new regime. In fact, he only excommunicated those believers who participated in acts of lawlessness, cruelty and vengeance. And the general Church Council had stated on 1 September 1917 that 'the Orthodox Church does not take part in the battle between political parties'. The patriarch reprimanded the *émigré* schismatics who elected for political reasons to take the path of autonomy.[21] However, it must be admitted that a significant number of the hierarchy and church people were not ready for radical changes and reacted to him with open or silent animosity.

All this facilitated the unleashing of a real war against religion in the first years after the October revolution, a war which had no legal cause but was prompted by the general tendencies and atmosphere of the times. It became particularly violent in connection with the question of the 'confiscation of church valuables'.[22]

The church has through all ages considered the material assets under her control to be the common property of the people and was accustomed to give them away readily at moments of national need. This might have happened again during the famine at the beginning of the 1920s. But in practice, forced 'confiscation' took the place of this tradition, and the results were protests from believers, bloody skirmishes, trials and death sentences. Patriarch Tikhon was arrested. After his release, he took a series of steps in an attempt to normalize relations with the authorities, but this did not produce any tangible results.

How illusory any hopes for reconciliation were can be judged from the experience of the so-called Renovationist schism,[23] whose leaders spoke up energetically in support of the Soviet authorities. It became apparent that even a change of direction like theirs altered things very little, just as the declaration by the head of the patriarchal church, Metropolitan Sergi, in 1927, did not save the situation. Repression fell upon all: 'Tikhonites' and 'Renovators', the 'non-commemorators', and sectarians, Catholics and even shamanists. By the end of the 1920s sectarian communes had been annihilated, including those established by Tolstoyans. Religious schools were closed, religious publishing had been gradually eliminated, publishing of the Bible ceased, churches and monasteries were closed and 'monuments of architecture' were turned into warehouses or blown up. Books and icons were burned. The extent of anti-religious propaganda grew even wider and often sinking to outright desecration and blasphemy. Atheist extremists started 'Komsomol Christmases' and 'Easters' during which young people organized comic processions, dressed in the vestments of clergy from different cults.

No wonder that the heroes of Alexander Blok's poem, *The Twelve* (1918), the twelve apostles of the 'new gospel', cry 'Let's fire bullets at Holy Russia'. The war against the church turned imperceptibly into an anti-national one, since the popular traditions of the land flowed in the same stream as that in which from time immemorial had flowed the traditions of Christianity, Islam and other religions. The 'storming of the heavens' provoked the kind of cultural suicide whose bitter fruits we are still reaping today.

So then where was faith in all this? How could people who were brought up in a thousand-year-old religious tradition allow this to happen? Some were killed or sent to the camps, others emigrated and those who were spared after the hurricane went into a sort of spiritual underground, isolationism. From the legal point of view, believers recognized that they were pariahs, outcasts, second-rate citizens and they were considered enemies of society. Many experienced a sort of conversion to another faith. The people's dreams about paradise on earth, so vividly described by Andrei Platonov,[24] the elemental eschatology of the masses, found fodder in utopianism, which inspired the builders of the new order. Many agreed that the slogan displayed in Solovki concentration camp was justified: 'With an iron hand we are driving humanity to happiness!'

Similar sentiments were expressed in the literature of the time, for example in Sergei Esenin's poem *Inoniya*.[25] In it he imitates the denunciations of a prophet and curses the old world, 'damns Radonezh' and 'the baying of the bells' in the name of a mysterious city which he glimpses ahead:

> With my tongue I lick
> the faces of martyrs and saints on the icons.
> I promise you the city of Inoniya
> Where the god of the living resides! . . .

In sacrilegious ecstasy, spitting out the host, he proclaims:

> A new saviour on a donkey
> is coming to the world

Our faith is in power
Our truth is in us!

And the 'new saviour' did not take long to appear. Only he did not come riding on a donkey. Comrade Stalin, although a man from the mountains, did not like to be seen riding in public.

'All of us lived under god'

In revolutions there is almost always a risk associated with the legal vacuum. When the legal system of the old type has been destroyed, people are not immediately ready to settle down under a new legal order or to take it seriously. The urge to destroy is sometimes still raging when the time has come to start building. History shows that power-seeking leaders easily take advantage of this. Cromwell, Robespierre and Napoleon all rose to power in this way. The October revolution did not escape this danger either.

Another alarming symptom came about with the Bolshevik revolution: the abandonment of the principle of the secular state. Such a state by its very nature is obliged impartially to protect its citizens, and among their freedoms, the freedom of conscience is one of the most important. In the heat of battle and the intoxication of victory, this obligation was in fact forgotten. At the time when he was decimating the peasantry in 1929, Stalin issued legislation about cults which is blatantly discriminatory. In the words of Konstantin Kharchev,[26] past chairman of the USSR Council for Religious Affairs, this Stalinist legislation flouted the decree on the separation of church and state and established 'the complete dependence of the church on the regime'.

By this time, all opposition elements among church congregations had disappeared. Almost all of them had openly declared their loyalty to the state as citizens. But still Stalin continued to tighten the pressure.

To some degree, this was part of his general campaign against culture, spirituality and against the people; but there was another secret motive that was important to the dictator personally. Unswervingly and single-mindedly, following the precepts of

Machiavelli, he built the edifice of absolute dictatorship. With cold calculation, he cleared from his path everything and everyone who might represent the merest shadow of a threat to his absolute power. No longer could science, art or literature exist independently of his personality and will. And least of all, religion. But to preserve it even as a 'tamed' version was risky. There must be only one god, the one in the Kremlin, and belief in him was to become the dominant state ideology. The dictator was to be the only oracle and embodiment of truth. He was not even limited by Marxism to which he formally adhered, since he himself was his own doctrine incarnate.

And so, the 'final battles' began. The Stalinist constitution left out the point that religious propaganda was permitted. A symbol of the victory of the Stalin cult was the blowing up of the church of Christ the Saviour.[27] Before World War II, the religious structures of the country were in tatters. Stalinist religious politics during the war were clearly a tactical manoeuvre, taken in the face of terrible danger and as a concession to the war allies.

From the moment the leader decided that the religious vacuum gave him sufficient space, there began the short history of the new religion, which brought unaccountable suffering, a religion that harked back to pagan Man-god worship. 'The Father of the Peoples' ascends to his lonely Mount Olympus whence all other divinities, ideals and principles had been expelled in advance. The emperor Augustus himself could not have dreamed of such absolutism . . .

Portraits of the General Secretary, resembling icons, were drawn according to strictly laid down canonical rules. They were distributed everywhere, just like icons. An insult to them was punished as if it were an attempt on the person of the dictator himself. His triumphant statues were just like those of the pharaohs. Many people remember a picture of those years called 'Morning of our Motherland', where there was no motherland but only he himself, looking like a visitor from outer space. The museum of gifts he had received became a shrine full of totemic, sacrificial objects. His biography was printed in large type like the Bible. Sayings of the 'Luminary of all Sciences' were quoted as if they were the ultimate word, like holy scripture.

Eastern storytellers and folk poets competed to compose hymns embellished with eastern fantasies in honour of 'The Father'. By his power the sun rose. His power held winged eagles in the sky and it was not just Asian rhapsodies that were adapted for these kind of panegyrics. Our generation still has embedded on its mind the words of superstitious prayers written all over the country. If you were wounded in battle, do not despair, 'press your wound, dry your tears and repeat the sacred name aloud' and then 'with the blue air, with the running of the river, that Person will send you strength'. He ruled everywhere.

> He is with us in battle and at work,
> He has been the Thunder in the sky
> He carries airmen in their flight
> And he has guided the hands of pianists.
>
> We know the country nurtured us
> We trust in our destiny
> Whoever is with Stalin has happiness and power
> Wherever there is Stalin – there is glory in battle.
>   (Dzh. Althauzen, 'Song about the Leader').

The Master could not be hoodwinked. He could do things, using someone else's hands. He knew how to pretend to be tired of these raptures and treat them lightly, patronizingly, as if they were childish naiveté. This is the way Stalin behaved with dupes like Feuchtwanger[28] and other guests of the Soviet Union. But he knew exactly what he was doing. He was sure that his cult had successfully taken over the space left by the destruction of all his religious competitors. And to some extent on the surface of life this was true. But there was a terrible price for achieving this goal. As the gulf between myth and reality increased, the violence became more and more cruel.

According to M. I. Kalinin, Lenin said in 1920: 'I suppose that, except for the theatre, there is no institution, no organ with which we can replace religion.' This was historical foresight of a sort on his part. A grandiose, ominous spectacle unfolded in the country. Its directors, actors, artists and stagehands hoped that they would be rewarded for their efforts, or at least spared. But such was not the logic of the inexorable Moloch. Even the closest accomplices of the leader disappeared without trace, or their lives constantly hung by a thread . . .

Of course you can object: does not faith in God also appeal to a higher authority? Have we not seen violence done in the name of other religions? We have to agree that this is true, but with two conditions.

First, in the course of the ages, no perversion of religious-ethical principles has ever entirely eliminated them. These principles have always remained as a source of renewal and of repentance. Stalinism, however, for a few years simply hi-jacked all the worst traits of religions through history in their periods of crisis: the inquisition, intolerant dogmatism and witch-hunts.

Second, there is a substantial difference between faith in a higher Being who creates, embraces and pervades the universe, and a conscious lie, a myth prepared in a laboratory by political counterfeiters. Even an atheist who approaches the question objectively must agree that the idea of the supreme Good and Reason, which demands ethical behaviour from man, contains deep spiritual meaning. It is no coincidence that in the history of humanity, most people have accepted this idea. And what spiritual value is there in a faith imposed on people, a faith according to which the head of state is omnipotent, omniscient and omnipresent – especially when that person is in reality an executioner, falsifier and a destroyer of people's lives and souls?

There may be differing opinions about the historical religions and differing assessments; but there can be no two opinions about the cult of Stalin if we do not want to go back to that chaos and bloodshed. There may even still be people today who will remind us how soldiers went in to the attack with the name of Stalin: obviously they did not mean the *real* Joseph Dzhugashvili at all, but a political phantom, a surrogate of the eternal idea of God.

People sometimes say that Stalin created for atheism a kind of 'Constantinian age', that is, an epoch of state support. But to say that is to speak a half-truth and to miss out what is really important. In the 'cult of personality', state power came to total self-deification, and established itself as the only absolute value.

The terrible experience of dictatorship in the twentieth century may also serve as a lesson to us believers as well. It enables us to see from the side what spiritual tyranny looks like, and paternalism, and games played on infantile feelings and mass neurosis. This experience should lead us to refuse the very idea of state religion, which has had so many analogies with Stalinism – whether Geneva under Calvin or Teheran under Ayatollah Khomeini.

Towards a secular state

To bring this cursory survey to a close, let us return to a question raised at the beginning: is there an antidote capable of preventing the return of the cult? I think the antidote has to do with the honest and consistent application of the principle of the secular state, the state which serves the interests of its citizens regardless of their religious affiliation.

Nikita Khrushchev whose greatest service was to be the 'dragon killer', did not fully understand the importance of this principle. He preserved from the past the habit of managing all areas of national life as if the country was his own private property, brutally imposing his own personal tastes in literature, art and economics etc. According to his caprice, brutal violations were sanctioned even of the already cruel religious legislation dating from Stalin's time. The illegal closures and at times the destruction of thousands of churches and other places of worship as well as the oppression of religion and believers were grotesque echoes of the 'Master's' times. And the situation was essentially very little different after Khrushchev, although the brake was applied to the violence to some extent. Stagnation is, after all, stagnation.

The 'fifth Russian Revolution', as *perestroika* has come to be called, marked a bold – and to many people, unexpected – change of course. The new course put into practice the demands of real life. The meeting of Mikhail Gorbachev with the patriarch and members of the synod of the Russian Orthodox Church and the national celebrations marking the millennium of the Christianization of Russia, ushered in a change, unprecedented in all Soviet history, to a new and positive attitude to religion. It was emphasized that all of us, believers and atheists, have one fatherland and one history. Effective steps were undertaken to overcome the isolation of believers.

Of course, all the same Christians remain Christians, Muslims remain Muslims and atheists are still atheist. But in contrast to the prolonged and painful division of society according to the religious principle, we now have the idea of the secular state, which equally defends the rights of Buddhists and Hindus, agnostics and Baptists. In a society where many peoples live and there are tens of millions of believers, there can of course be no other way.

All our people will benefit from the secularization of the state. The government, by guarding the holy of holies within man – his convictions and his freedom of conscience – is helping to unite its citizens in a unity based on religious tolerance.

This change of course will also make possible a return to our lost cultural values. After all, the great art of Russia, the Baltics, Caucasus, Central Asia and our rich legacy of thought were born precisely within the traditions of religion. If we accept the values of this religious legacy the way will be opened to a more careful and responsible attitude to our national traditions. As far as problems of inter-faith relations are concerned, besides the state, no small responsibility is vested in the leaders of religious congregations who now have more means of influencing the thoughts and feelings of believers.

Besides which the new opportunities given to religious institutions will result in a raising of the general spiritual level among the followers of the different religions. After all, until recently, they were deprived of even the most elementary sources of information, deprived of everything to improve religious-moral education – even of their basic books like the Bible.

Finally, today it is becoming more and more obvious that the decisive factor in all spheres of life is neither tinkering with administration nor the deification of power, but the moral growth of people. May the ethical principles grown on religious soil one way or another enter the flesh and blood of our society; but without a return to the sources of them, this is not enough. A return to religion would play a significant role in the country's moral rebirth: in family and inter-ethnic relations, in the work ethic, in production, in ecology and in charity.

It would be a mistake, however, to think that all work in this direction can be done only by those in authority, whether political or religious. Their efforts will be futile if they are not consciously helped by many, many people. The development 'from below' of a series of informal organizations such as 'Memorial',[29] 'Cultural Renaissance' and others, is a positive sign in this connection. Never mind if it will be difficult to avoid mistakes, disappointments and excesses. But life is life and we must go forward without fearing the risks.

I want to believe in the victory of reason, freedom and humanity, even if that victory will never be complete in this world. I am sure that 'in spite of everything' these hopes are shared by many of our compatriots, regardless of their religious beliefs.

7

Russia in Crisis

The dramatic changes that have taken place in Russian society since perestroika *have induced in many people a sense of alarm and despondency: too many familiar markers have vanished and the much vaunted freedoms of democracy have left many people in a dark mood of 'chernukha', a kind of black pessimism. The interviewer in the dialogue that follows represents something of this attitude and gives voice to the issues which many ordinary Russian people are concerned with. Fr Alexander argues from a long historical perspective to present the Christian hope, and to take issue with the materialist assumptions of the interviewer and the audience listening to him. In Russian the notion of culture [kul'tura] is wider than the English equivalent: it is closely bound up with the questions of national identity as well as spiritual and moral values, and not just to do with the arts and learning. This interview, under the title 'What is happening to Russian culture?', was published in A. Men, Trudny put' k dialogu, Moscow 1992, pp. 78–93. It has been slightly abridged in translation. Title supplied by the editor.*

Interviewer: Fr Alexander, what do you think is happening to Russian culture? Everyone agrees it's in crisis. But what of the future? Total collapse?

AM: It's not only nowadays that people have been saying that culture, and even the human race, is coming to an end. In Rome, before the birth of Christ, they were expecting the immediate end of the world. And many times since there has been much talk about the same expectations. It's understandable for them to crop up again in this century of world wars and nuclear armaments, the age of moral and cultural crises.

For people of my generation and the previous one, predictions like these are startling only because for too long we had drummed into us the idea that history is inevitably getting better and better. Many people accepted that idea, though no one has ever proved it to be true. Incidentally, that idea too has a long history. In the eighteenth century the French thinker Condorcet[1] expounded it, and after him the idea of limitless progress was a typical feature of many philosophical, social and political systems.

Yet actual history hardly bears this out. In reality, too much in life does not get better but comes round full circle. And the grandiose scientific and technological progress of this century has come about at such a cost that involuntarily one asks, is this progress? Of course, transport is getting better, as well as means of communication and ways of getting energy, but far too often this is at human cost. Declarations are made about freedom, justice, humanity, but the degradation of human beings is worse than ever before. On the one hand, progress in medicine; on the other, the growth of new diseases, including terrible ones like AIDS.

A crisis of culture comes about when people lose their spiritual markers, when the moral ground slips away from under their feet, when they break with the eternal values and hanker only for the latest trend. There are symptoms of this crisis today in all the developed countries. And the symptoms are especially acute in Russia.

Interviewer: We live in an age of shortages – both material and spiritual ones. It seems to me that there's hope of salvation in the fact that we've begun slowly but surely to admit that these shortages do exist [. . .] Some people argue that without a spiritual rebirth there'll be no soap, though others, even very clever people, are saying that the talking must stop and first we must feed the people. Perhaps there is some sense in this? Perhaps there's nothing terrible in leaving culture for later?

AM: It wasn't so long ago that it was held to be axiomatic that social and economic measures are all that is needed to change the world. That illusion cost us dear.

People need medicine and housing and food. But that's no more than animals need. When people start ignoring what it is that raises us above the natural world, society will inevitably be in crisis. That's what happened in the waning years of the ancient world, and towards the end of the last century, and that's what's happening now.

The Bible rejects the idea, which was typical of classical times, that humanity is inevitably degenerating, and it also rejects the theory that the development of humanity on this earth is limitless. The Bible starts from the idea of the parallel growth of two opposing forces: good and evil, and the constant struggle between them. And a human being cannot be a passive observer of this struggle, but is called to take part in it. People choose for themselves which side to stand on.

Think of the picture [of life under the Roman emperors] Suetonius describes in his *Lives of the Twelve Caesars*.[2] Around that time, many Christians had made up their minds that the universal catastrophe was imminent, they abandoned their work and waited for the inevitable end. Thereupon the apostle Paul sharply criticized them. The mystery of the fulfilment of history, he taught, is hidden from human eyes. People must live and work, carry out their duty on this earth without speculating about 'the times and the season' (I Thess. 5.1).

The Bible recognizes that civilizations are not everlasting: it predicted the fall of the Assyrian empire, and the Babylonian one, and other empires as well. The predictions came true. But the collapse of culture isn't something preordained in the Bible. The book of Jonah tells the story of how the prophet Jonah was sent to the city of Nineveh, capital of the kings who had taken Israel captive, with the dire news that in three days the city would be destroyed. Jonah himself looked forward happily to this retribution which would confirm his prophecies. But the inhabitants of the city all repented in time and so averted the disaster.

Interviewer: So repentance then is the way to salvation is it? But is it realistic nowadays to expect people today to be saved by repentance alone? It wasn't that simple in the past either. Didn't Moses have to spend forty years leading the Jews out of Egypt to their homeland, leading them through the wilderness, waiting for the death of those who remembered being slaves, waiting for a new generation to grow up able to start living as free people?

AM: Yes, but the Gospels offer us a way out. The apostles showed people that spiritual change is possible by calling them to be compassionate. This call has come again and again in human history and often at the most critical times. In the Middle Ages it was revived thanks to St Francis of Assisi who taught that we should love people, and the whole natural world. In the history of the Russian Orthodox Church a comparable role was played by St Sergius of Radonezh [. . .][3]

I believe that just as in previous ages, people emerged to lead the world out of its spiritual dead end, so in our times too the right people will be found. And as regards repentance, the good news of Christ was preceded by a call to repentance; this is what John the Baptist called people to. And the very first word of Jesus' teaching was, 'Repent'. And remember that in Hebrew this word means 'turn round', 'turn away from the wrong road'. While in the Greek text of the Gospels, it is rendered by the even more resonant word, *metanoite*, in other words *rethink* your life. This is the beginning of healing. Repentance is not a sterile 'grubbing around in one's soul', not some masochistic self-humiliation, but a re-evaluation leading to action, the action John the Baptist called 'the fruits of repentance'.

That's why there is so much hope in the numerous attempts now being made to rethink our recent history, to 'change our minds'. The abscess must be lanced, otherwise there will be no cure.

Interviewer: But many people find the cure is more frightening than the disease. They think that concentrating on the past 'distracts' them from attending to the problems of today [. . .] We must think of the future.

AM: That's wrong. It's always a risky business to make the future into a tranquillizer, an 'opium' (saying that things are bad now, but they'll get better later). Haven't we had enough painful lessons from the recent past? By itself, nothing automatically gets better. And social changes on their own help no more than the manoeuvrings of Krylov's 'Quartet'.[4] Contemporary civilization may have no future at all unless it looks truth in the eye, unless it finds a firm foundation for moral principles. For true spirituality, as for art, the 'past' doesn't matter. There is a 'past' for science and technology, but not for the actual foundations of our life. To tackle current problems without regard for how the world solved them over the course of centuries means foregoing our human inheritance. In Russia at last we have come to value the beauty of the ancient church art. But it's no less important to value the spiritual inheritance of the past. And we must take from that inheritance all that is most beautiful, most vital, most effective. Especially as spirituality never died out. Its creative stream was merely driven 'underground' in the [Soviet] years that were 'without time and without legality'. But it never dried up.

Our worst disaster is the erosion of moral values. I've mentioned Pitirim Sorokin before: the Russian scholar who is well known to the world but forgotten by us (last year was the hundredth anniversary of his birth).[5] He said something like this: If you compare the levels of energy production and consumption with the present level of ethics, then we have to admit that we are in the Stone Age as regards our production of Christian love.

Moral regeneration has always been based on spiritual and religious foundations. I don't at all mean that people without religion are excluded. Simply that they today are nurtured by this primordial wellspring of morality, though in an indirect way.

Interviewer: But atheistically inclined people might ask you why you keep referring to a mythical God in the search for truth? Why not start with people and the ideals of humanism?

AM: The Renaissance tried to create a secular morality derived solely from man. In doing this, the humanists quite rightly reproached the Middle Ages for devaluing human worth. However, by taking humanity as the starting point and making it the ultimate measure and criterion of truth, humanism itself has led in the final count to dehumanization. Indeed, the idea that we are merely 'thinking animals', in whom good and evil are equally inherent, that we are our own measure, opens the door wide to the forces of destruction. The age of the Renaissance itself was the first to prove this – it produced modern Christian humanistic civilization, but also a model of moral dissolution. And as a result of this arrogance, people became ever more frequently to be perceived as the 'mass', just insignificant specks of dust, the chance result of the blind forces of nature [. . .] fit only to be despised. Even the Utopians, whom one might have thought desired the good of all, based their thinking on the concept of the 'mass' which could and should be manipulated. In their theories, freedom and the value of the individual – however much they intended otherwise – were reduced to nil.

That's what it came to. And we've all in some way or another experienced the consequences for ourselves.

Many people nowadays think that salvation lies in a return to a mediaeval mind-set with its fanaticism, its denial of the value of earthly life. That can't be right. The criticism of the dark sides of the Middle Ages by the humanists was, I repeat, in many respects correct. But I do want to remind you that there were quite a few humanists, for instance Mirandola, Savanarola, and Erasmus,[6] who called people not to a secularism deriving from the classical period, but to a rebirth of the spirit of the Gospels, the spirit of freedom, of love, of tolerance, and respect for the person, made in the image and likeness of the Creator. So far, we haven't paid enough attention to this aspect of the Renaissance, of which Dante was in part a precursor. But it was just this aspect that held enormous potentialities for the future.

In civilization people have free choice. But this freedom does not shield them from the devastating consequences of a wrong choice. That is why it is important for people today to make the right choice. I think the English historian Arnold Toynbee had a profound idea when he said that the decline of any culture is the result of a wrong 'answer', a wrong choice.

But how are we to make the right choice? How are we to distinguish a true prophet from a false one? Especially as nowadays, as in all unsettled times, there are any number of soothsayers, healers of body and soul, around. They are extremely popular, because people are agonizing over the past, have no joy in the present, and are frightened of the future. People are ready to believe anyone who gives an answer to the 'accursed' questions and who promises immediate changes for the better. Incidentally, that's how dictatorships arise.

Interviewer: But doesn't the church itself consist of people with their weaknesses and failings. At the time of the Inquisition, and today too, it lays itself open to accusations of formalism, intolerance, and persecution of the non-orthodox. What 'guarantee' is there that the church can show the right way forward?

AM: The empirical history of religion presents a very mixed picture. And its critics, if they are honest and conscientious, have done a service to believers by helping them to understand their historical sins more clearly.

Augustine, a great teacher of the church, spoke of the two 'cities', of the two types of spirituality. The watershed between them often passes through religious communities themselves. Christ meant it when he said, 'Not everyone who says to me, Lord! Lord! will enter the kingdom of heaven, but the one who does the will of my heavenly Father' [Matt. 7.21].

The Russian religious thinkers, Vladimir Solovyev, Mikhail Tareev,[7] and Nicolas Berdyaev, following Augustine, made the point that there are two forms of religious attitude: there is an 'open' attitude which is free and humane, and a 'closed' one which is life-denying and debases the individual. The antithesis between the gospel and Phariseeism is an eternal example of this conflict.

I say all this because I cannot share the view that any kind of religion serves the ethical renewal. St John spoke against this view when he gave the warning, 'Do not believe every spirit' [I John 4.1]. He also gave criteria for the discernment of spirits when he said, 'If anyone says, "I love God" and hates his brother, he is a liar' [I John 4.20]. In this St John was being true to the gospel of Christ and to the prophets of the Old Testament who said that you cannot serve the truth and God without being true to the moral commandments which God has given us.

Who will bring about a return to the spiritual values which we have lost? In your question there was hidden an unconscious desire to put the effort and the responsibility on to someone else, perhaps even, for example, on to the church. But the church is part of society. And today everyone knows that it too suffered grievous losses. Of course, we Christians want to do our modest bit for moral regeneration. But over the years, we too have accumulated our own internal problems, and besides we cannot function creatively unless we too repent, unless there is a change in the general climate in Russia. We need the combined efforts of people of different views sharing the same ground which unites believers and non-believers. That common ground is the revival of law and order, compassion, the protection and development of the cultural heritage.

As regards prophets, there is no general criterion applicable to any belief system. For the Bible teaches us that the true prophet is one who proclaims the word of God revealed to him and who does not make any compromises with paganism or with human vanity whether it is personal, political, class or national vanity.

When the prophet Isaiah accused the instigators of the war, and challenged popular opinion and the authorities, he was acting as a divine emissary. When Metropolitan Filipp single-handedly challenged Ivan the Terrible, he showed himself to be a true prophet. In our times, Martin Luther King was another such prophet. Each of them was the mouthpiece of high spiritual and moral ideals.

The process of natural development has been directed towards the creation of a being who would be capable of becoming a bearer of spirit. That being is man. But humanity is still far from true spirit-bearing. Whatever helps this process is helping the universal purpose for the world. Whatever hinders it is opposing the divine purpose which, in the language of the Bible, is called the kingdom of God. We Christians have no doubt that the kingdom will come, that our imperfect history will move into another dimension and that the way to eternal life will be opened for us. Everything that has served the kingdom will come to supreme fulfilment there. Everything that has gone against it will vanish. Each one of us is a participant in this process of divinization. We might call it evolution. But this word sounds impoverished to me since it implies a blind course of events; while I believe in the meaning, the spiritual purpose, of existence. And that lays an enormous responsibility upon all of us.

Interviewer: But then how do we today connect our obvious responsibility for the future with Christ's words that we should live for the present day, without thinking of the morrow (like 'the birds of the air'), without speculating about the 'times and the seasons'?

AM: When Christ said 'Do not be anxious', he was not calling us to be frivolous or careless. He was warning us only against that painful and fruitless mood of constant worrying which often afflicts people, and which doesn't help anything, which makes them feel afraid, nervous and impotent. We are too bound up with what is temporal, what is transient. This is a sickness of the West and of the East. We need to develop inner freedom in ourselves. This was the freedom that Christ had in mind when he said, 'Do not be anxious'. Christianity gives its blessing to work and service, regarding them as a means for spiritual growth. Remember that the saying, 'he who does not work shall not eat' comes from the New Testament, from Paul. Paul also taught us our responsibility towards nature.

Interviewer: [. . .] We've got to become aware of our lack of spirituality, we must throw a bridge over the abyss that separates us from the past, we must knit up the threads. For many long years, all we had in philosophy were over-simplifications, so-called 'criticisms' and biased interpretations. We had no access to the primary sources. That, it seems to me, was our misfortune.

AM: The path of culture is an integral, organic, process. Interruptions can only do it harm. The fact that whole generations in our country were cut off from traditions, including ethical, religious and philosophical ones, dealt society a grievous blow. Of course not everyone was capable of getting to grips with the intellectual wealth of Russian religious philosophy, yet its ideas would somehow have seeped into people's consciousness, and might have been 'in the air'. But since 'the oxygen was cut off', our culture became unbelievably impoverished. I'm glad that this gap is now being filled, even if belatedly.

Interviewer: For our generation, the generation who grew up in the seventies, one of the most important sources of knowledge about the Gospel events, about Christ, was Bulgakov's novel *The Master and Margarita*.[8] Now that we can read the Gospel itself we can judge how far our ideas were correct. But the paradox of the situation was that the novel became a barrier between us and the primary source. Bulgakov the artist described the Gospel scenes so convincingly that many of us who read the Gospel according to St Matthew after the 'gospel according to Bulgakov' saw before them not Jesus Christ, but Yeshua [. . .]

AM: That's a topic for another time. But to be brief. Of course *The Master and Margarita* is a masterpiece. But Bulgakov's Yeshua has almost nothing in common with the real Jesus of Nazareth. He is a dreamer, a naive wandering philosopher, who addresses each and every person he meets as 'good man'. The Christ of the Gospels was not like that. He radiated strength. He could be stern and even harsh. He sharply castigated the authorities: Herod, the scribes and the Pharisees. He was not a searcher after truth, but he was himself the Truth. He didn't 'wander about', but, as Chesterton said of him, he waged a campaign against the forces of evil. That's not to mention that the actual Gospel events are distorted in the novel. The author made use of the then fashionable hypothesis according to which the evangelists conveyed the facts incorrectly (Henri Barbusse, for instance, whose book on Christ was translated into Russian in 1928, took this line). The only genuine Gospel motif to be found in Bulgakov's book is the motif of 'hand-washing', the motif of betrayal. Both Pilate, and the Master, and many others, each in their own way betray themselves and other people. This theme was especially cogent during the period of denunciations and unbridled lawlessness [the 1930s]. [. . .]

Interviewer: Your thoughts lead us once more to the idea that art is incompatible with 'evil-doing' and cannot serve evil. We've somehow forgotten about the close link between ethics and aesthetics [. . .] What do you think about the idea of saving the world through art? Today our avant-garde claims the role of saviour. But it's driven by quite a strong destructive impulse.

AM: I'm not very expert in the nuances of the so-called avant-garde. Of course in many respects, I think it reflects the ugly, pathological state of morals. It has an element of youthful *épatage*, bravado, wanting to throw down a challenge to the whole establishment. That has often happened. In the distant past, a protest against all that was rotten, stale, boring was sometimes expressed in the most eccentric way. They shaved their heads, grew long hair, went around in rags. One moment they shouted 'Back to nature', and then 'Away from nature'. This was all so much froth, unavoidable in natural development, where good and evil, intelligence and stupidity are amazingly mixed up together. But sooner or later the hubbub subsided, unless, that is, it was kept alive by persecution and oppression.

Nonetheless, the idea that every avant-garde, every search for new forms of art is something destructive is highly debatable. Haven't people often perceived what is new and unusual as destructive? In its time, icon-painting was the avant-garde if we compare it with classical art, so was Gothic art and eastern Orthodox architecture and Christian philosophy which the conservatives thought was a compromise with paganism.

People often complain about modern music, and with some justification. But we mustn't throw the baby out with the bath water. Think of jazz which was born in a particular religious culture (among the North American negroes) and though it doesn't appeal to everyone you can't dismiss it out of hand.

Interviewer: No one today denies the need for us to link our culture with world culture. But as one American has wittily observed, we have mixed up the plumbing and instead of the water pipes, we are connected to the sewers of world culture. And there is a real danger that mass culture will swamp true culture.

AM: Forgive me if I, as a historian, take another example from the past. In the second century BC Greek influences began to spread in Rome. This appalled the Romans of the older generation. And to some extent they were right. Their fellow countrymen were being influenced by Hellenistic Greece at a time of decline. They got from Greece not so much Plato or Sophocles as 'the dregs of culture', debauchery, scepticism, agnosticism, the cult of pleasure and entertainment. Something similar is happening in our links with world culture. Many important artists, thinkers, profound writers, serious scholars are still unknown even today in Russia. They haven't been translated, their work isn't known. They were known by hearsay, by very biased 'accusatory' criticism. It is much easier for what is superficial, trivial, banal to get through. Here's a typical example. Videos are rapidly becoming available now in our large cities. But those who are in charge of our culture haven't lifted a finger to ensure that people can see the classic masterpieces of Western cinema. And the video dealers are quick to supply a torrent of pulp films directed at the lowest possible tastes.

The way to combat this is not by prohibitions but by making the best works available to people. You can't graft on taste by making prohibitions. This is true of all aspects and manifestations of culture. What is bad must be combated by affirming what is valuable, enriching, beautiful. I am sure that in free competition it will win.

Nowadays, many young people want to think independently and are capable of doing so. Provided the right to open discussion of problems which previously were taboo isn't taken away, we won't do too badly. There's still hope.

8

Two Understandings of Christianity

*What follows is the text of a lecture which Fr Alexander gave
on 25 January 1989 in Moscow. His first topic takes its starting
point in the contrast between two monks depicted by Dostoevsky in* The Brothers Karamazov: *Zosima, the famous spiritual
guide, a lover of nature and experienced man of the world who
believes the Christian path is to be lived in the world and
therefore sends his young protégé Alyosha Karamazov away
from the monastery and back into the world to deal with the
troubles of his family; and the ascetic Ferapont, living a life
turned in on himself, full of hatred and portrayed by Dostoevsky as semi-crazed. These two monks represent two different
models of Christianity: the one open to the world, like the
famous monastery of Optina Pustyn, and the other withdraw-
ing from it. Fr Alexander draws a telling portrait of the present
weaknesses and distorted ideology of many adherents of the
Russian Orthodox Church today and shows how this tendency
is rooted in Russian history.*

*The second theme of the lecture is to weigh up and assess the
relative importance of the inner life and of outward works in
the Christian life in general, arguing for a balance of each. The
talk concludes by drawing out the point that has been running
like a leitmotif through the lecture: a plea for pluralism and
understanding in the religious life.*

*The text was published as 'Dva ponimaniya khristianstva' in
A. Men', Radostnaya vest', Moscow: Vita-tsentr, 1992,
pp. 309–318. The conversational style has been retained in the
translation.*

Dear Friends! Perhaps the subject of this talk of mine may seem

strange to some of you, but I want to remind you of a scene from
Dostoevsky's novel, *The Brothers Karamazov*, and you will
realize that my subject has not been idly or casually chosen; it is a
topic that has a deep relevance to the history of spiritual culture,
to the history of literature and to the history of Christianity in
Russia and in other Christian countries.

You remember, I'm sure, two characters in *The Brothers
Karamazov* who are polar opposites: the *starets* Zosima and his
antagonist Ferapont. Remember how the *starets* Zosima is
described by Dostoevsky as a radiant personality with broad and
enlightened views about the world, human destiny and about
people's attitude to eternal life and to God. Some literary scholars
think that Zosima is modelled upon the famous *starets* Amvrosy
of Optino,[1] who was canonized at the time of the thousandth
anniversary of Christianity in Russia [1988]. Other specialist
historians reject this idea because there are important differences
between the real, historical Amvrosy and the character which
Dostoevsky imagined. Even so, there definitely is a connection
between the prototype and the literary character.

The monastery of Optina Pustyn was not a typical one, and
indeed it was unique in the history of our Church. That was why
so many cultural figures made a point of going there: Khomyakov, Kireevsky, Dostoevsky, Solovyev, Leo Tolstoy, Leontyev,
Sergi Bulgakov and many others.[2] They didn't stream off to any
other monasteries, but specifically this one which was so unusual
and unexpected.

In one of the issues of the literary almanac *Prometei*, there is an
article entitled 'Optina Pustyn – why did so many famous people
go there?', written by the well-known poet Nadezhda Pavlovich,[3]
who started publishing her work in Blok's lifetime. She worked at
Optina Pustyn and managed to meet the last *starets* there. She
shared her impressions with me of her meetings with this amazing
character. In her article, Pavlovich names many more of them
whom I have not mentioned.

The *startsy* and other inhabitants of the monastery were
concerned with the same problems which preoccupied the
cultured section of society at that time. That's why both Tolstoy
and Dostoevsky were able to discuss with the *startsy* not only

their own personal problems but also general human and cultural issues. Yes indeed, the place was exceptional. That was why Dostoevsky created his Zosima with Optina Pustyn in mind for he found there a kind of open variant, an open understanding of Orthodoxy and an open understanding of Christianity.

But in this same monastery, which is described in Dostoevsky's novel, there is another character – *starets* Ferapont, a famous ascetic, a powerful old man who walked around bare-foot, dressed in a rough belted overcoat, like a beggar. He hated *starets* Zosima and even on the day he died, had no shame about denouncing him over his grave. If you haven't read it already, read this great epic novel, and you will see how within one Orthodoxy, one Church, one culture and even one monastery, two seemingly completely antagonistic elements clash – and clash quite sharply. The situation which Dostoevsky describes gives us as it were the first intimation that within Christian culture not everything is identical and not everything can be reduced to some sort of unity.

I do not intend now to discuss those divisions within the Christian world which have happened over the last twenty centuries – the split which occurred as early as the first councils of the church, divisions between Arians and Orthodox, between Orthodox and Monophysites and finally the great and tragic schism of the Christian world between West and East: that is between Catholicism and Orthodoxy. This division took place in spite of the fact that each side adopted the same names: the Eastern church called itself Catholic and the Western called itself Orthodox, but still the schism took place.

Of course, two understandings of Christianity clashed there too. If we turn to history, then we shall see yet another great clash within Western European culture: the rise of Protestantism. This again was a new interpretation of Christianity: Catholicism and Protestantism are two different understandings of it. And finally, within Protestantism itself, the orthodox and radical movements clashed with each other. I do not intend to discuss this because it is a large special subject. For the present I shall be dealing only with problems related to that culture in which we Russians have grown up and were educated and which is closest and most comprehensible to us.

Orthodox culture derives from two sources. The first source is the fundamental and most important one, namely the Gospels. That source is the teaching and proclamation about God-manhood, in other words, about the mystery of the eternal and the mystery of the human. It is the teaching that humanity is exceptionally important and valuable for the Creator. It is the teaching that humanity is raised above all creation because the Eternal itself made contact with it, because human beings are created in the image and likeness of the Creator and in them lives a kind of programme for the future: to develop from beings akin to the animals to beings akin to heaven.

But there was another tradition too, born long before Christianity, and that is the tradition of ascetic practice. It is an exceptionally important tradition. It contains some of the richest experience of self-observation and the richest experience of inner practice, that is, of spiritual work designed to make the human personality grow. But this ascetic tradition, which came mainly from India and Greece and which was adopted by the church several centuries after the appearance of Christ, came to regard the surrounding world as something alien and external to it, something which had to be recoiled from and shunned.

Were there good grounds for this tendency? Of course there were. Every one of us can readily understand how energetically a person seeking depth, stillness, contemplation and eternal wisdom must push away the cares and noise, the superficiality and futility of life which surrounds them, if they are to find themselves. And then by picking out a few words from the Gospels (true, taken out of context) such as 'He who hates his life in this world will keep it for eternal life' [John 12.25], this tendency began to predominate, firstly in monastic circles and in certain strands of the church, but then, gathering ever greater strength thanks to its inner spiritual energy, this tendency began imperceptibly to be the dominant one, and almost overshadowed the other source, the principle of the God-man. If in the Gospel it says, 'He who hates the world', it also says in the same Gospel of St John that God so loved the world that he gave his own Son to save it. This is the contradiction, and this is the dialectic in which we have to distinguish the two understandings of the world.

In practice, of course, it was not so straightforward. And so the other-worldly type of Christianity which shunned the life surrounding it, shunned history and creativity and culture, developed along its own lines. It could not, of course, be totally consistent, and it did create things of cultural value. We know that within the walls of monasteries of the ascetic tradition there were great artists, chroniclers, masters of historical narrative, and architects. But this culture developed there in spite of the basic tendency which set Christianity outside the world and above it.

And then in our own national culture, these two lines have clashed, and the clash grew into antagonism. For educated society at the beginning of the nineteenth century, this other-worldly Christianity was identified with Orthodoxy itself. And what is more, Orthodox circles themselves easily slipped into the same identificaton. That is why almost all initiative was left to the secular world. Social justice, the structure of society, agonizing problems such as serfdom – all were left to the sphere of the state and were disregarded by the church. These matters seemed to be of no concern to Christians. Hence the indifference, the apathy to things of this transient world, and hence the bitter inner split.

Though the process had begun in the eighteenth century, the division deepened throughout the nineteenth century. Even Christian writers like Dostoevsky did not fully understand the true tradition of the church. And what of the church people who were far removed from society? There grew up two languages, in the literal sense – a church language and a secular language. The church language absorbed a mass of Slavonicisms (you will find, for example, a large number in the works of Leskov). This was why Russian versions of the Bible in the nineteenth century were immediately outdated for they didn't correspond either to the language of Pushkin and Gogol, or to that of Tolstoy and Dostoevsky. Secular language developed along its own lines.

At that time, in the reign of Nicholas I [1825–55], a person who became well-known as a writer was Archimandrite Fedor Bukharev. He was a monk who lived at the Trinity St Sergius monastery and a learned theologian and biblical scholar. He published a book entitled *Orthodoxy and its Relationship with the Contemporary World* in which he first broached the question of the need to bring the two understandings of Christianity together. He pointed out that the problems which concern everyone – culture, creativity, social justice and many more were not matters of indifference to Christianity; rather the contrary, that in the resolution of these problems, the spiritual ideals of the Gospel could be important and might be an inner resource for their solution.

But Bukharev was attacked, abused in the press and reduced to such a state that he left monastic orders and the service of the church, became a journalist and soon died in poverty and oblivion. But his memory lasted long. At the beginning of the twentieth century, Pavel Florensky made a collection of his letters. But to date, his works have not been published in full.

Then Tolstoy came along and posed the problem in a completely different way. For him, the traditional understanding of Christianity as a sum of traditions which had grown up from the Gospels was only a useless burden, the dead weight of centuries. He proposed casting all of it aside and returning to the original nucleus. One might say that he was following a Protestant line. But that's not really so, for Tolstoy as a thinker never was a Christian. His ideas were different and much more Eastern, closer to the Eastern philosophies of India and China. That's why his conflict with theology and with the church was not an indication of the conflict between the two understandings of Christianity but merely a side issue.

Then Vladimir Solovyev came along, a great figure of world philosophy. He was a person who, in an era dominated by materialism and positivism, had the ability to raise questions about spiritual values in such a way that the most cultured people of the time were compelled to acknowledge the seriousness of the problems. He was a man who was at the same time a poet, critic, philosopher, theologian, historian, and historian of philosophy, and publicist. People like that with universal gifts are born only once in a century. In his *Lectures on God-manhood*,[4] he put the question like this: is the Good News of Christ really only a method of salvation for the individual soul? Is it only a personal route for someone on the way to perfection to achieve eternal bliss after their death? Indeed, if that were so then this is no different from several other religious systems. We find essentially the same thing in Islam and in Eastern religions. Solovyev saw things from a completely different point of view: Christianity is the line which joins higher things with lower, the divine with the human. If this is what Godmanhood means, then there is nothing in history which is a matter of indifference to spirituality. Therefore, the Christian ideal can absorb into itself everything, including social problems, the moral problems of society, and even problems of art. Solovyev created a great synthesis whereby the two understandings of Christianity could be united.

His follower in the twentieth century was our well-known compatriot Nicolas Berdyaev, a bold, enlightened thinker with a most brilliant mind. The whole world knows him and international conferences gather to discuss his works. Unfortunately, his works were not published in Russia and to many Russians his name for a long time has hardly meant anything at all.

Berdyaev wrote several articles which had the same title as our lecture today – 'Two Understandings of Christianity'. He clarified and reformulated the subject. He defined two points of view: personal salvation and creativity. These two points of view are as it were hostile to each other. To one group of Christians, the most important thing is simply inner self-perfection leading to salvation. Everything else is rejected. Creativity is left to the secular world, outside the domain of the church: it is left, as it were, outside the spiritual realm, without the light inherent to the impulse of the Gospels. This position led to a strange outcome: humanity was demeaned. The great word 'humility', which Christ spoke about, was turned into a synonym for compromise, appeasement and a wretched collusion with evil.

Collusion with evil means, in the final analysis, working for evil. Hence the unwillingness to make any kind of protest and the unwillingness to take any bold initiative. Submission means acknowledging evil. And although Christ said of himself that he was 'gentle and lowly of heart' [Matt. 11.29], he never taught us to compromise with evil. This was the source of human demeanment which offended Berdyaev so exceptionally. He said that faith and spirituality should elevate people, and help them to stand tall because people are made in the image of God and are the most valuable of beings. The gospel preaches about humanity, about the greatness of humanity on which the light of heaven shines. So Berdyaev treated humility in a completely different way: as openness to everything, as the readiness to accept other points of view, as the readiness to listen to and hear the voice of other people and the voice of God. This understanding of humility is the opposite of pride, for pride hears only itself. Pride, locked up in itself, feeds on itself, as the saying goes, lives in its own world, in its own prison. So Berdyaev sought to find a way of uniting these two opposing trends which were tearing the church apart.

This propensity for the two understandings of Christianity to clash continues even today. You can easily find it in literature. In Leskov's story *The Mountain*, you will immediately see two types of Christian: one is the artist Zenon and the other is the crowd which hangs around the patriarch's palace. There are also many legends and stories which Leskov makes into serious parables. Even Belinsky, in his letter to Gogol which you certainly remember from school, described his understanding of Christianity – true, in a very incompetent, irritable and inaccurate manner. He said that Christ proclaimed freedom, equality and brotherhood and so on – in short Belinsky treated Christianity as an egalitarian liberation movement of social opposition.[5]

Why is it important for us to be aware of this now? – important for all of us, believers and non-believers? Because today our culture is getting back those lost and half-forgotten values from the past and, together with them, the age-old values of the Russian Orthodox Church and of Christianity as a whole. And people who lack a clear understanding of the richness and deep antinomies of the phenomenon that is Christianity, think that Christians are all the same and that the church is something which has one clearly defined official view and a systematic ideology fully worked out in theory and practice. And they will be discouraged when they see that within this historical stream are many diverse and even contradictory currents. And we must bear this in mind. It must be borne in mind by those who wish to start on the Christian way and by those who are interested in Christianity simply as a cultural phenomenon and who want to understand it and make their own minds up about it.

In periods of social freezes and social storms, as in war, people get quickly divided into two groups: those for us and those against us, believers and non-believers and so on. This is an over-simplified picture. And for those people who are just joining the church the picture still seems valid. But it may happen that a pagan, someone far away from the church, may become spiritually closer to a Christian than their fellow believers. It's a paradox but it's true. This can happen because there isn't one single interpretation of Christianity which wholly corrsponds to it.

There was a time when the antagonistic and seemingly irreconcilable principles of other-worldly culture-denying Christianity and the Christianity which strives to share in creativity were in fact united in the church. But that was long ago. When Christianity first appeared in the ancient world, it faced the question: how to treat all this heritage? How to treat the philosophy, art, literature and in general all the great edifice of ancient culture? Should we say it's all rubbish? That it's all out of date? That it should all be thrown away? Many people said precisely that. Many were willing to go down that road.

The main answer given by the classic Christian thinkers, who are known as the patristic writers or the Fathers of the Church was, however, a positive one. Christianity could and should be open to all these questions. That's why the Church Fathers were most often the outstanding writers, thinkers, poets and social activists of their time. They did not consider that such things were alien to or unworthy of Christianity.

So in the case of John Chrysostom you will find not only discussions about injustice in his writings but also in his life too efforts to fight social oppression and the unjust distribution of material goods.

You will find in the writings of Augustine the famous words that a state without law is in principle no different from a band of robbers. That was written in the fourth century. You will find among the writings of Basil the Great a special work on the meaning of pagan literature for Christian youth. You will find in the works of Gregory the Theologian (also the fourth century) marvellously humorous letters and poems which he wrote to his friend.

But often something else creeps in to this general orientation. In the great legacy of the Church Fathers there is a special section, a special part and that is the legacy of the Desert Fathers, of the supporters of monasticism. It was collected in the huge anthology the *Philokalia*.[6] This is a magnificent and, in its own way, eternally valuable book which has much to offer people. But then this tradition of the *Philokalia* began to be accepted as the only one. Yet it was intended for people who were called *inoki* [Russian for 'monk']. *Inok* means 'a person living a different way of life'. This means a person who deliberately lives apart from the world, not at all because he despises the world but because he personally has chosen for himself that special way. This was when the mistaken idea grew up that the legacy of the Church Fathers was to be regarded as the rejection of culture, whereas in fact this was not the case at all.

The return of contemporary Christian thought (by contemporary I mean over the last one hundred years) to the traditions of the Church Fathers, is the return of Christianity to an open model, which participates in the whole movement of human society. Berdyaev called this 'the churching of the world'. But understand me correctly: that word doesn't at all mean that some historical church incidentals are imposed on the secular culture of the world. It means that there is no such thing as the secular.

I myself, I don't know what the word 'secular' means. It is a conventional historical term because there is a spiritual element in everything – or not, as the case may be. Even though the title under a picture may say 'The Virgin Mary', if the picture is painted in an uninspired way, if it has something superficial, banal and flat about it, then it won't have anything to do with spirituality. And it's very important to understand that there isn't some literature which is spiritual and some which is unspiritual or 'secular', but rather there is literature with spirituality and literature without spirituality, there is good literature and bad literature. And truly good literature will always have a bearing on the eternal problems.

We can say the same of all types of art and also of the most varied kinds of creativity. Christianity has nothing to fear in all this. It's open to it all. The narrow, other-worldly model is a legacy from the past. It's something mediaeval (in the worst sense of the word) which, alas, is still extant. It often attracts new recruits who think they become true Christians if they put on black head scarves and walk around with a special mincing gait. None of that's necessary. That's parody, that's a caricature.

There's a complex relationship between the inner and the outer. There is a tendency for some people to say: my spiritual life is going on here inside and I don't need anything from outside. But this is a serious mistake because somehow or other, a person expresses all their experiences. No one can be a bodiless spirit who looks indifferent and only experiences things somewhere deep inside them. No. Everything is expressed, is embodied, in gesture, facial expressions. Experience is a matter of body and soul together.

But at the same time what is outward, for instance, rituals are slippery customers, they are like dangerous underwater rocks: they have a tendency to become sufficient unto themselves. It is very good when a person makes the sign of the cross when they stand before the icon of God. But it's possible that person may gradually forget the important thing and just continue to cross themselves. Indeed, in popular speech, the words for 'to pray' and 'to cross oneself' have become interchangable. When a grandmother says to her grandson: 'Say your prayers, say your prayers', she is not thinking about what is going on in his heart. She is thinking about him waving his hand and making the sign of the cross. In this way, the external can gradually squeeze out the internal.

Is this a danger for Christianity? Not at all. This danger is not specific to Christianity. Pharisaical mechanisms are at work in all spiritual movements, because the externals are always easier. That is why the Pharisees of gospel times observed thousands of rituals but inside, their spiritual lives were often dead. And this pharisaical external piety can exist in all places and all times. In the dialectic tensions between these two elements: the external and the internal, what is open to the world and at the same time concentrated, lies the deepest truth of the scriptures. And when we look deeply into it, we find there eventually the ultimate and final formula.

A spiritual community of people who are moving towards the supreme aim will undoubtedly still look like an exclusive group, but at the same time, this community is open to all and to the whole world.

The foundation of the church goes back to ancient Old Testament times. When God called Abraham, he said to him: separate yourself, leave your country, leave your father's house, become a wanderer. This meant cutting himself off; but at the same time, God said to him: but through you will all the tribes and peoples of the earth be blessed. This contradiction, this paradox in the Bible, is still alive today. Yes, the person who wishes to develop in a deeply spiritual way must build some sort of defence around their soul. Otherwise, the noise of the world will deafen it. But at the same time anyone who does not wish to turn his soul into a small reservation, into a stuffy lamp-lit little world in which the spirit cannot live, must ensure that their defence is not absolute. It's like breathing in and breathing out. It's like talking to many people and talking to one. It's like solitude and company. It's like day and night. It's like what joins things together.

So the conclusion at least for me is clear: neither of the two understandings of Christianity is wrong, but each as it were takes one side and wrongly develops it. Fullness of life lies in the synthesis of the two.

Florensky, the well-known theologian and philosopher, said that complete truth when it comes to our world is fragmented into contradictory parts and we see only this fragmented world, but somewhere in a higher dimension all these paradoxical, disunited and antinomic fragments are united in one. That's the mystery of life. That's the mystery of the two understandings of Christianity.

I hope, after this short digresson, that you may feel that the variety and even the contradictions within the Christian church, and even more, the contradictions between the different Christian denominations – Protestants, Catholics and Orthodox – are not a sign of decay and breakdown but rather manifestations of parts of the whole, the united whole which we have to reach at greater depth. Then what seems to us to be impossible to unite will be united. Then the source, the profound source of spiritual life will nourish not only individual souls or small groups of individual souls in their interior lives but will also go beyond the limits of the merely personal and become for us a social force, a force in society, a force that will help us live in this world, and bring to the world our value as human beings and the light which each of us has been given to the degree that we are in communion with it.

It follows, therefore, that this is not just a question for literary scholarship although you will find in it many literary aspects. Nor is it purely historical, although, of course, it has a direct relationship to history. It is a subject for today.

And it seems to me that such pluralism, such interaction of different points of view, is an important pre-condition for the vitality of Christianity. And perhaps it was providential that Christianity was split into different tendencies, because without this it would probably have been something uniform and forced. It is as if, knowing people's tendency to intolerance, God divided them so that each person in their place, in their own garden could bring forth their own fruit.

And the time will come when all the different fruits will come together into one stream, in which will be preserved all the best in the spiritual culture of humanity and of each person who is made in the image and likeness of God.

9

The Russian Orthodox Church Today

This was the last interview Fr Alexander gave. It took place on 5 September 1990, four days before his death. There are grim clues in his answers to the Spanish journalist, Pilar Bonet, as to the likely reasons why he was murdered and by whom. The text is reprinted in A. Men', Kul'tura i dukhovnoe vozrozhdenie, Moscow 1992, pp. 445–450, with additional excerpts from the newspaper, Panorama, *December 1990.*

PB: What changes have there been in the Russian Orthodox Church since Gorbachev came to power?

AM: Gorbachev has revolutionized the relationships between church and state. The Bolshevik system was conceived as a system of absolute authoritarian control. But total authoritarianism is only possible when no other form of authority exists. From the outset, therefore, the Bolsheviks sought to destroy those institutions which represented another, spiritual, authority. That's why the Bolshevik regime was aggressively anti-religious from the very start and this attitude did not alter in principle for the whole seventy years.

But Gorbachev changed this policy by a deliberate act. That's a historical fact. Not merely the details changed, but the history of the church in our country changed.

PB: What tendencies are now apparent in the Russian Orthodox Church?

AM: The conservative tendency is fairly powerful: it is strongly anti-Western, hostile to all reforms and idealizes the past, taking the harshest models from the past, even I'd say mediaeval ones. This tendency is very popular in certain circles. In Western terms, we could call it 'right-wing', it's a profoundly right-wing trend.

You might ask why this should be so in the church. One of the reasons is the artificial selection which went on over several generations through the merciless suppression of all forces in the church that were alive and ready to experiment. If a bishop displayed any spirit of freedom or independence of thought, or propensity to experiment, he was immediately despatched to the provinces or forcibly retired.

PB: In other words, what happened in the church was a reflection of what was happening in society in general.

AM: Yes, and that's why the most conservative and right-wing elements have been preserved, have survived, and multiplied. They found favour with the functionaries and with the KGB. It is no secret that the authorities liked the church which looked like an ancient relic from the past, a museum.

In the 1960s, there were some independently-minded and forward-thinking individuals among the clergy.[1] They were pushed aside. The bishops were conservative. Today, there are more open-minded people among the bishops, but among the rank and file clergy, there are more conservatives. But even so, the tendency towards protectionism, i.e. conservatism, is prevalent everywhere. Besides, the liberals are a bit afraid of it.

PB: Would you say then that in a sense the liberals are living underground?

AM: Yes. The general trend nowadays is a reaction against the destruction of national values. Since the Communists can't get things done, then let's have a monarchy, an idealized monarchy; since the Party's failed, then let's restore the church just as it was before the revolution. Though we forget that it is precisely because the pre-revolutionary church was the way it was, that the catastrophe happened. But nobody is interested in this any more. It's all nostalgia for the past.

PB: To what extent would you say that this is dangerous?

AM: It causes a great deal of disappointment to people who are weary of the ideological yoke. They looked for open positions among Christians, but instead they've found a new version of the closed society.

PB: Are you not disturbed by the fact that today the Russian

Orthodox Church is proving itself to be wholly incapable of renewal? In this respect, the church could really only be compared with the Communist Party, don't you think?

AM: Of course, the only difference is that God helps the church but not the Party.

PB: What is your opinion of the so-called Karlovci Church?[2]

AM: That church is even more conservative than the Russian Orthodox Church and it is a monarchist church, which is what people find attractive. That is all I have to say. In general, religious awakening is a natural thing. Our society is, on the whole, potentially quite religious. When it was deprived of its faith, it transferred its religiosity to the political sphere. Now, disappointment with the old gods has set in and there is a return to tradition.

It is understandable that Communism did not like anything national because it wanted a levelled down society. It wanted citizens, not nations. The communists acted just like the rulers of ancient Assyria. When they conquered a country, they deported the peoples they had defeated and settled people from other subjugated areas in their place.[3]

Why was this done? So that people lost their national identity. So that there was no centre of resistance and all people became mere subjects of the king. Nationalism is a completely understandable reaction, it's to be expected, it's self-defence to keep some form of cultural identity. Nationalism is not a completely normal state of affairs, it's reactionary, but still the reaction is legitimate.

PB: Do you think this is a temporary phenomenon or . . . ?

AM: Yes. The fact is that people will tire of it. People cannot spend all their time engaged in a form of cultural narcissism, they'll get fed up. At the end of the day, even the most committed patriots will tire of it.

PB: So is Russia currently living through a phase of narcissism?

AM: No, I'd say it's just beginning. But it's harmful and dangerous because it makes society idealize itself. This is very characteristic also of our clerical circles. They think they're wonderful. When we believers celebrated the millennium of Christianity [1988], there was not a single word of repentance, not a single word about the tragedy of the Russian Church, only triumphalism and self-congratulation.

I understand that every culture, every nation, must to a certain degree love its own identity, but now this has got to the point where we love ourselves and no one and nothing else. Even the Catholics in our country have become nationalists. Take the Greek Catholics in Ukraine. You might think they belong to the one universal international church, but they are behaving like a group of nationalists. The Lithuanian Catholics are also nationalists.

The process of returning to national traditions has started after long years when these were suppressed. We should respect this process. I do respect it and I understand the fact that art in its actual forms has to be national. But, at the same time, it is imperative to avoid the dangers of a shift to the right. You see, the open model is acceptable to those who are sure of their own ground. Those who stand on shaky ground prefer a closed model because it is easier for them.

Around fifteen years ago, a young man at my church started making occasional visits to the Baptist Church. I told him, you are Orthodox, of course you can go there because the church is everywhere, Christ is everywhere, the gospel is everywhere. Do both: go to the Baptist Church and don't forget your own spiritual roots. And when I explained the open model to him, he said, Oh dear, how uncomfortable! He ended up by becoming a Baptist.

That person could only be either a Baptist who did not recognize Orthodoxy, or an Orthodox who cursed the Baptists. He wanted to have a little hole to hide himself away in. Apparently Peter the Great also suffered from a psychological disorder – the fear of open spaces. He built himself tiny little rooms and so on. There is an illness like that – the fear of open spaces. In the history of religion, there is also this fear of open spaces.

PB: Now more and more Orthodox are turning to the Karlovci Church. Is this some sort of shift to the right?

AM: Yes, it is.

PB: What about people looking for something more to the left? Where can they go?

AM: Nowhere. They can stay within the Moscow patriarchate. Some people are trying to go off to the Catholics. Two or three people from my parish have done that.

PB: Have you ever considered this course of action yourself?

AM: No, because I believe that the church is one, so it wouldn't make any sense to me.

PB: How would you describe Pope John Paul II?

AM: Some of my parishioners knew him when he was still a bishop. Everyone liked him. The fact that he is a little strict is perhaps not a bad thing as a counterbalance to the general disintegration. He is criticized for his attitude towards family life, for example, for his views on abortion, but abortion is murder after all, all the more so now when contraception is available.

PB: So, you think contraception is normal?

AM: This is not my own opinion. I have consulted with our bishops and they are of the opinion that a person has a right to practise birth control. Otherwise, they may bring more children into the world than they can support, in which case they will become animals rather than human beings.

PB: Is the conservative tendency in the church reflected in military and political circles?

AM: Yes, our nazis support this tendency and there are many of them. Take 'Pamyat';[4] it is full of nazis and fascists and their numbers are mushrooming. Why is there anti-ecumenism? Because ecumenism demands that you respect another person's model of Christianity. Instead of this, we have hatred. The word 'catholic' has almost become a term of abuse now, like in the times of Taras Bulba.[5]

PB: Have you witnessed any particular disturbing symptoms recently?

AM: Well, if you don't call the growth of Russian fascism disturbing, what else is? Of course I have! And very many church people are very actively supporting it.

There has been a joining up of Russian fascism with Russian clericalism and nostalgia among church people. It's of course shameful to us believers because society was expecting to find in us some kind of support and instead support goes to the fascists. Of course not everyone shares these attitudes – it's only a tiny percentage. I can't say what that percentage is because I haven't studied the figures. But wherever you go, whoever you meet, this one's a monarchist, this one's an antisemite, that one's anti-ecumenist and so on. And people keep putting labels on, even those people who never used to be like this. Do you understand? It's typical, a feature of our times, the era of reaction. When Gorbachev opened the floodgates, reaction as well as democracy poured in. But reaction is always more aggressive.

PB: What is your opinion of Patriarch Alexi?

AM: Well, he's an intelligent man. For example, when he was still metropolitan he was the first publicly to condemn Soviet neo-fascism and antisemitism. He was the first and, as far as I know, the only one to do so.

PB: Recently, I visited [the town of] Tyumen' and there I met a priest. I had a conversation with him and he seemed a perfectly ordinary, pleasant person until suddenly he said, 'well, of course, I do not trust Moscow, it is full of Zionists. There, the church is full of Jews . . . '

AM: This fear of Zionism is typical. In 1975, fifteen years ago, I gave an interview which was published in Paris.[6] They asked me then whether there was any antisemitism in the church. I said that I hadn't come across any, not on a mass scale. Fifteen years later and the picture has completely changed. I wouldn't say the same thing now. Antisemitism has become, unfortunately, one of the distinguishing features of the church.

PB: Are you of Jewish descent?

AM: Yes.

PB: I feel uncomfortable asking you this.

AM: Why should you feel that way?

PB: The point is that you in your position are an ideal target for antisemitism.

AM: Of course, that goes without saying. I feel it. I have been a priest for a long time, thirty or so years, but this has only started to happen now. I feel it in the way people behave towards me, in the way they talk to me, in everything.

PB: What do you personally think of the problem of antisemitism?

AM: I think this is a question of social psychology. There has to be a category of people who are held responsible for the sins of society. They are the personification of society's own sins.

Instead of admitting that we destroyed our own sacred things, people say that it was Kaganovich[7] who gave the order to destroy the church of Christ the Saviour. If the people hadn't wanted to desecrate it, it wouldn't have mattered who had given the order. They would have killed Kaganovich and saved the church. But the people went and blew up thousands of churches. That means people are to blame. But it's a very difficult thing to admit and so you have to find someone to blame. It's easy to swear at the Jews. A coward will always pick on someone defenceless.

PB: Is it true that, in conservative circles, communists are being identified as Jews?

AM: Yes, but this is artificial because sixty years ago there were many Jews among the Bolsheviks, but my generation does not remember this. I remember the communist authorities being comprised of people of Russian, Ukrainian and Caucasian descent. Kaganovich was the only Jew.

PB: Then the real problem is that the people don't want to admit their responsibility for what took place in this country?

AM: Make a comparative analysis of de-nazification in Germany and de-stalinization here and you'll understand.

PB: What about you personally? How do you view your work in this sense?

AM: I don't. All I do is carry on working. There are people who write history and people who simply live and work in it. I belong to the second category.

PB: Yes, but when you preach, you do put forward certain ideas.

AM: All my ideas can be found in [this book] here!

PB: In the Bible . . .

AM: Yes, of course. The gospel is the foundation of life.

Part III

Epilogue

10

The Christian Hope: 'Karabakh' or 'Bethlehem'?

This Christmas meditation was written in 1989 when the hostilities between Armenians and Azerbaijanis in Nagorno-Karabakh had flared up. The conflict had been preceded by a quite unwarranted and savage massacre of Armenians in Sumgait in Azerbaijan. And in April of that year Russian troops had violently attacked a peaceful demonstration in the streets of Tbilisi in Georgia. With all these events in mind, and the prospect of more national conflicts within the Soviet Union, Fr Alexander ponders the presence of evil and violence in the world. Today, with the experience of Chechnya and Bosnia, his words are still relevant. This meditation was first published in the popular newspaper Sovershenno Sekretno, *No. 7, 1989, and reprinted in* Kul'tura i dukhovnoe vozrozhdenie. *It has been very slightly abbreviated in translation.*

Karabakh stands in my mind as a collective symbol for the innumerable tragedies which seem to be erupting one after another in so many parts of the world.

Though the causes for these outbreaks of hatred and violence may be different in each place, the overall picture is one of disaster. Remember the squares of Beijing and Tbilisi, think of Ulster and Jerusalem, Sumgait and Kabul, think of Africa and Latin America . . . India too, traditionally a land of peace, has witnessed bloodshed. One can't help feeling that peoples and tribes, countries and governments, leaders and crowds – the whole human race is on the path to self-destruction.

Ideologies, traditions, political and national slogans, cults and languages – all have been used as weapons against human beings.

If the most unnatural war is civil war [. . .] then shouldn't we finally admit that we are witnessing a world-wide civil war between all the 'children of Adam', a war that is tearing the body of humanity apart?

This warfare is ceaseless. Terrorism and hatred know no truce. They are fuelled by lawlessness, crime and drug addiction. It seems as if in our age a barrier has been broken, and the floods of anger let loose. This is happening now, before our eyes, but the symptoms have been here for a long time.

Have we forgotten the awesome words of the *Dies Irae*? Do we need to be reminded of the Nazis, the Stalinists, the Khmer Rouge? Should we forget and bury our heads in the sand? But that won't stop the growth of evil!

Yet now today the Christmas star, the star of Bethlehem, shines once again, as it did two thousand years ago, over a world in turmoil. It calls us and reminds us of eternity.

That is why Christmas is more than just the 'children's festival', or a family get-together, more than just a holiday. For some people, the Christmas star is just a decoration on the Christmas tree, but those who think like that are missing the real significance of this holy day.

The star of Christ reminds people of their higher calling. It reminds us of the sacred spark which the Creator has placed in us, the spark which ignites in us love and freedom, faith and creativity, compassion and fellow-feeling.

Someone once asked the philosopher Nicolas Berdyaev the paradoxical question: 'Can God create a stone that he himself could not move?' And Berdyaev promptly answered: 'Yes, that stone is man.'

The church has always taught that people cannot be delivered from evil, nor the natural world either, without their active participation. We are made in the image and likeness of the animals, but as regards our essential being, we are made in the image and likeness of our Creator. Therefore freedom, which is our inalienable attribute, gives us the possibility of transforming our animal nature, and of activating those wonderful potentialities which are within us. But is this possible if people take only themselves as the starting-point?

For several centuries now the world has been nurturing the illusion that it can. It has tried not to notice 'Bethelehem', and not to see the gentle shining of that gospel star.

Intoxicated with science, proud of our power over the elements, we human beings have put our trust in our knowledge of the laws of nature, expecting peace and happiness to come from them. But it hasn't happened. Knowledge, when in the grip of that animal nature of ours with its reasoning powers, has not saved civilization, but has become its *memento mori*, its sword of Damocles. And the fault for this lies not in knowledge itself, nor in reason which is God's gift to us, but in the eclipse of the spirit which has not been able to withstand the force of the beast.

We human beings have relied on the ideals of secular, this-worldly humanism, which our century has taken such pride in. We thought we could do without the star of Bethlehem, since we had found our own tablets of the law. However, these tablets proved to be as fragile as glass, and the first blows of the World War smashed them to smithereens. Humanism was pitilessly crushed under the boots of the dictators whom the crowds followed blindly. So the beast had only lain low for a while, and with new strength once again swept over the planet, crushing everything in its path. And yet, the fault lies not in humanism as such, but in forgetting the higher, divine sources of the good.

We human beings thought that technology, comfort and a life which would guarantee the best possible conditions of work and rest, would solve all problems. But the example of the highly-developed countries has shown this to be an illusion. The example of these countries shows us vividly what moral, cultural and ecological dangers technical civilization is fraught with, and where satiety, 'ethical materialism', and 'consumerism' will lead. Of course, it's a good thing that people should be well fed and clothed, should have adequate housing, and be able to use modern technology in their daily lives. But to make of these things the only ideal is to diminish the purpose of life, and to lead people into the dead-end of materialism.

We human beings have for centuries dreamed of a transformation of society bringing prosperity and well-being to all, where liberty, equality and fraternity would reign. But the experience of the terror in the days of the French Revolution was already a warning and a prototype of everything that has come to pass in our own times. When the social order is taken as sacred, rather than people and their lives, their rights and dignity, then in the name of that social order thousands and perhaps millions may be destroyed as if they were nothing but worthless scum. Of course the idea of improving the social order is a noble and valuable one. But when that aim becomes sufficient unto itself and claims to be a religion and destroys individuals, then it leads to the opposite result.

I would remind you that prescriptions for general happiness have been around since very early times. Was it not in classical times that the cult of science was born, when the Epicureans preached hedonism and the cult of pleasure (though incidentally Epicurus himself was not to blame for this)? Was it not Plato who created his system of a police state, from which poets, free-thinkers and dissidents were expelled for the sake of the 'good of the citizens'?

The past has also left us the dread idea of a forcibly imposed religion. This is not to be wondered at, for if people turned the ideals of liberty, equality and fraternity into terror and new forms of slavery, why should not the same happen with religion?

But, you may object, religion, unlike the cult of science, hedonism, secular ethics or political utopias has to do with the spirit and the higher Being. That's certainly true. But when religion becomes an instrument in the hands of those in power, when its adherents use force, then faith loses its true nature and becomes the servant of political passions and the 'interests' of a particular social group. In many ways, our present spiritual crisis bears traces of that counterfeit, that metamorphosis of religion, when religion is darkened by fanaticism and violence and becomes merged with interests of the state (which is by definition imperfect).

'Karabakh' (understood symbolically) did not spring out of bare soil. Today we are beginning to understand that, however much the world has gained, it has lost even more. Now the time of decision and choice has come.

This is what the star of Christ, Christmas Day, reminds us of, the day when the shepherds of Bethlehem heard the song: 'Glory to God in the highest, on earth peace and goodwill towards men'. When the Son of Man – the Son of God – was born, a new power entered the stream of history, the power of love and spiritual transformation. To all who follow it, this star is not only a beacon in a dark world; it pours into them the mysterious energy of the spirit revealing the image and likeness of God.

Christ comes to people not in a halo of earthly wisdom, not on the shoulders of legionaries, and not with a social charter. The word of the gospel speaks to our hearts and minds, not just to change our 'ideology', but to make us into 'a new creation'.

The world stands at a crossroads. Perhaps we have reached the end of civilization.

The Pharisees, proud of their ancient heritage said: 'We are the sons of Abraham.' But John the Baptist rebuked them, saying that if they did not repent, God could raise up new children of Abraham from stones [Luke 3.8].

In exactly the same way, we now have to understand that unless we find the right path, our century may be the last in history. Isn't the Creator free to begin again from the beginning, perhaps with the little islets which will survive a nuclear catastrophe? Or with another planet, with another humanity? But I don't want to believe that.

When I look at Rublev's icon of the Trinity, it brings to my mind the Bible story from which Rublev took his subject [Gen. 18]. The Lord appeared on earth in the form of the three travellers in order to test, for the last time, the impious and sinful cities [of Sodom and Gomorrah]. And Abraham, the 'father of the faithful' prayed that the cities should be spared for the sake of a handful of the righteous. Alas, there were so few that God chose to lead them out of the doomed Sodom and Gomorrah.

But in us Christians, the hope lives that our common home, our earth, all the fair things made by mankind, will escape the fate of Sodom. We think of the self-sacrifice and heroism of the ascetics, of all the prayer and struggle, of all the service to one's neighbour, of all the compassion which shine in the darkness of the twentieth century. We remember the faithfulness to Christ, even to the death, of the new Russian martyrs,[1] and Martin Luther King; we remember Mother Maria and the heroes of the Resistance, those who kept their hearts pure during the reign of madness and hate. We remember the holiness of the Russian *starets* Siluan[2] living on Mount Athos, of Mother Teresa and her fellow-workers in India; we remember the sublime and noble thoughts of Berdyaev and Teilhard de Chardin, and the self-giving of Mahatma Gandhi, Dietrich Bonhoeffer and Bishop Helder Câmara. We remember the doctors and teachers, writers and philosophers, creative artists, politicians and countless others among our contemporaries who challenge the kingdom of materialism, greed, consumerism, evil and violence. They showed the world what it means to be faithful to Christ, even though some of them were not consciously Christians. Did not Christ himself say, 'Not every one who says to me "Lord! Lord!" will enter the kingdom of Heaven, but he who does the will of my heavenly Father?' [Matt. 7.21].

We also believe that this invincible power of good is rooted in human nature, in our divided and contradictory selves, and is nourished from the same source which created, sustains and gives life to the universe. That power for good is waiting for us. It has revealed itself to us. Now it's our turn to respond.

11

Christianity for the
Twenty-First Century

*This lecture was given on the evening of 8 September 1990,
the night before Fr Alexander was murdered. It was the
conclusion to a series of lectures on the world religions
which were thematically leading up to the revelation of God
in Christ. In it Fr Alexander reiterates his note of optimism:
that the victory has already been won, the new life has come
and Christianity is only in its infancy, only at the beginning.
In view of what was to happen the following day this lecture
has assumed enormous significance among his followers.
Many of them recall that on this occasion they had the
impression that Fr Alexander knew that his life was ap-
proaching its end: they noted that his voice was different,
that he seemed to speak straight from the heart. In the
words of Anastasia Andreeva, secretary of 'Cultural Renaissance', 'this lecture was his requiem, his testament to us who
are left behind'.*

*The text was published in A. Men', Byt' khristianinom,
Moscow 1992, pp. 19–32. The conversational style has been
retained in this translation.*

And so together we have reached the end of our journey which
has taken us through the ages, around the world philosophies,
and we have come to the summit, to that sparkling mountain
spring wherein the sun is reflected, which is called Christianity.

Though Christianity has of course thrown down a challenge
to many philosophical and religious systems, it is at the same
time an answer to the hopes present in the majority of them.

The strongest impulse in Christian spirituality is not to deny, but to affirm, to include and to complete.

We saw how Buddhism is permeated with a passionate longing for deliverance from evil, a striving for salvation – Buddha said that as the waters of the seas are saturated with salt, so his teaching, dharma, is drenched with the idea of salvation: so too is that same longing for salvation, the promise of salvation, inherent to Christianity, to the New Testament.

We saw how Islam teaches the absolute devotion of man to God, the God who is sovereign lord of the cosmos and judge of mankind: and we find the same in Christianity.

We saw how in the Chinese world view heaven – *tyan* – is a reference point for people on their life's journey (even in small things): so it is also in Christianity.

Brahmanism, contemporary Hinduism, speaks of the many forms in which the divine is manifest: so does Christianity.

Finally, pantheism declares that God is in everything, that he is a mysterious force permeating every drop, every atom of the universe: and Christianity is in agreement with this, though it teaches that the activity of God is not limited only to a pantheistic omnipresence.

But we would be mistaken to assume that Christianity is an eclectic doctrine which simply gathers to itself all the elements of previous belief systems. Something new and tremendously powerful is manifest in Christianity. The newness is not just a doctrine, but the inrush of a different life into this, our daily lives.

The great teachers of humanity, the authors of the *Upanishads*, Lao-Zi, Confucius, Buddha, Muhammad, Socrates, Plato and others perceived the truth to be like the summit of a high mountain which they ascended with the greatest difficulty. They were right because the truth is not something easily grasped. Truth is indeed like a high mountain that has to be climbed: we gasp for breath, clambering from ledge to ledge, at times looking back at the path behind, aware that yet another steep slope still lies ahead.

I shall never forget the remarkable words about truth spoken by the simple Himalayan mountaineer Tensing, the Sherpa who climbed Everest with [the New Zealander] Hillary. He said that we must approach mountains with reverence, and God in the same way. Indeed mountains demand a certain mind-set in order to grasp their magnificence and their beauty. Truth lies hidden from people who rush at it without reverence, who set out unprepared, disregarding the dangers, precipices and crevasses.

It is the mark of human history to strive upwards. You may well object: think how many steps there have been leading downwards. Yes, of course; at first glance there are more steps leading downwards; more people who have fallen and rolled down into the abyss. But the important thing is that human beings have all the same kept attempting to climb to this summit above the clouds, and the greatness of humanity lies in the fact that people have the capacity to reach the peaks of intellectual and spiritual contemplation, to reach what Pushkin called 'the neighbourhood of God'.

Human beings have two countries, two homelands. One is our own country, that place where each of us was born and grew up. But the other is that hidden world of the spirit which the eye may not see and the ear may not hear but where, by our nature, we belong. We are children of the earth and at the same time visitors to it.

In their spiritual searchings, people give rein to their higher nature far more than when they are making war, ploughing, sowing, or building. Termites also build, ants sow (there are such species of ant), and monkeys fight, in their own way, though not as cruelly as people, it is true. No living being, however, except humans, has ever pondered on the meaning of life, has ever risen above the physical needs of nature.

No living creature, except human beings, has the capacity to take a risk, even the risk of death, in the name of truth, for the sake of something which cannot be held in the hand. Thousands of martyrs of all times and nations exemplify this phenomenon, unique in the history of our entire solar system.

When we turn to the Gospels we find ourselves in another world; not the world of thrilling searches, and assaults on heaven, which I have been describing. With the Gospels we face the mystery of an answer. For twenty-five years, Prince Siddhartha Gautama, the future Buddha, undertook ascetic exercises in order to attain contemplation. In the same way, yogis, philosophers and ascetics have all laboured mentally, spiritually and psycho-physically.

But Jesus Christ came from a simple village, where he lived the life of an ordinary person. In him everything was already prepared. He did not clamber up anywhere; on the contrary he came down to people's level.

All the great sages have been conscious of their ignorance. Socrates said 'I know that I know nothing'. The great saints of all ages and all peoples have been much more acutely aware of their sinfulness than you or I because they were closer to the light and every stain on their life and conscience was much more apparent to them than ours are to us in our grey lives.

Jesus Christ had no consciousness of his own sinfulness, nor any sense that he had achieved anything. He came to people bringing to them what was in him from the beginning, by nature.

At this point I must stress the fact that Jesus did not begin to preach Christianity as some kind of intellectual system. What he proclaimed to the people, he called [in Hebrew] *besorah*, in Greek, *evangelion*, which means 'glad tidings', 'good news'. So what was this good news?

Human beings have the right not to trust the created world. Human beings have the right to feel themselves to be in an alien and hostile world. Such contemporary writers as Albert Camus, Jean-Paul Sartre and others often spoke about the terrible absurdity of existence: we are surrounded by something menacing, inhuman, meaningless, absurd, something which cannot be trusted – a cold, dead or lifeless world. True, I must point out that these writers, novelists, playwrights and philosophers were writing from an atheistic point of view. These atheistic existentialists somehow failed to notice one thing. When they said that the world is absurd, that it is meaningless, they thought like this only because the contrary idea, the idea of meaning, is inherent to human beings. Someone who does not know what meaning is, has not experienced it, can never understand what absurdity is, will never object to it, never rebel against it; that person will live in it like a fish in water. And it is precisely because a person can rise up against the absurd, against the meaninglessness of existence, which shows that meaning does exist.

To come back to the point: the ancient biblical prophets tell us that we can make an internal change and say 'yes' to existence and trust what seemed terrible and menacing. And then through the chaos, the absurdity, through the monstrousness of life, will peer the eye of God, like the sun shining through the storm clouds, the eye of a God whose person is reflected in each human person.

And contact with God is possible, like an alliance between similar beings. The point of all this is the amazing analogy between humanity and the one who created the cosmos. Once Charles Darwin said that although he interpreted the world mechanically, as a process, yet all the same, when he thought about the complexity of it, he could never accept that blind chance could have caused it all; shouldn't one then see some kind of reason behind it all, a reason that in some way is analogous to our own? We must add that this reason is not simply analogous to ours, but immensely surpasses it.

In the religion of the Old Testament, which we have discussed [in a previous lecture], there developed the notion of faith as trust. Not faith as a conviction, whether theoretical, philosophical or religious, but faith as the act of breaking through the absurdity of lifeless reality, the moment when a person says to God 'Yes, I accept, I am listening.' So the ancient covenant between God and humanity was born, the ancient alliance.

Naturally, the alliance between the primitive people of ancient times and the divine could not be final and complete: this was the period of human nurturing, the childhood of the human race, followed by its adolescence. In the seventh century before our era, the prophet Jeremiah said, 'Thus says the Lord, I will make with my people a New Covenant, ([Hebrew] *berit hadas* – a new testament, a new alliance), not like the old one, the former one. I will write it on their hearts' [Jer. 31. 31–33 paraphrased].

And then one night the sacrifice was celebrated. Seven hundred years after the prophet Jeremiah, in a small room, twelve men gathered together for the sacrifice. Usually the sacrifice was made with blood, for blood is the symbol of life, and life belongs to God alone; and the members of the group, gathered together, would be sprinkled with the blood of the sacrificial animal. This is how it was done among all peoples since distant primordial times, since the palaeolithic age. Moses, when he concluded the covenant of the people with God, sprinkled everyone with the blood of the sacrificial lamb.

That night I was speaking of, in the spring of the thirtieth year of the first century of our era, Jesus of Nazareth, surrounded by the twelve, celebrated the ritual – the memorial of the freedom which God bestows. There was no blood, but a chalice of wine and bread. And he broke this bread and gave it to them all and said, 'This is my body.' And he passed the chalice round the disciples and said, 'This is my blood, which is shed for you, this is the new covenant of my blood.'

And so, at this holy table God and humanity were joined together, no longer with real physical blood but with the symbolic blood of the earth, for grape juice, wine, is the blood of the earth, and bread is the flesh of the earth, is nature who feeds us, is God who sacrifices himself for people.

Jesus of Nazareth celebrated this sacrifice, and from that moment, from that holy night the chalice has not ceased to be raised up and the eucharist celebrated. In all branches of Christianity, in all churches, even in the sects, this sign is everywhere present.

People sometimes say that Christ proclaimed a new moral code. He said 'A new commandment I give you – love one another as I have loved you.' There had been an earlier commandment about love. The words 'Love your neighbour as yourself' come from Moses. But Christ gave the commandment a quite special note by adding 'as I have loved you', because through his love for humanity he stayed with us on this dirty, bloodstained and sinful earth, just to be beside us. His love, in fact, became self-giving love, and that's why he said 'Whoever wants to follow me, let them deny themselves.' Deny, that is, our individualism, not our personality; certainly not our personality, which is sacred, but our false identity, our individualism. 'Let each one of you,' he says, 'sacrifice yourselves, take up your cross, that is, your service in suffering and in joy, and then follow me.'

Christ calls people to bring the divine ideal to reality. Only short-sighted people imagine that Christianity has already happened, that it took place, say, in the thirteenth century, or the fourth, or some other time. I would say that it has only made the first hesitant steps in the history of the human race.

Many words of Christ are still incomprehensible to us even now, because we are still Neanderthals in spirit and morals; because the arrow of the Gospels is aimed at eternity; because the history of Christianity is only beginning. What has happened already, what we now call the history of Christianity, are the first half-clumsy, unsuccessful attempts to make it a reality.

You may object: then how is it that in Russia we have had such great artists, such profound icon painters, as Andrei Rublev. Yes of course, there have been great saints too; they were the forerunners. They lived against a background of a dark sea of mud, blood and tears. Obviously, that was what Tarkovsky wanted to emphasize in his film *Andrei Rublev*[1] (or maybe he didn't want to and it just turned out like that involuntarily). Think for a moment about the historical circumstances in which the icon painter produced his tender, magical, divinely-inspired vision of the Trinity; in what conditions? What the film showed is true: wars, tortures, betrayals, violence, conflagrations, destruction. In such circumstances someone who is not enlightened by God could create only pictures like Goya's *Los Caprichios*.[2] But Rublev created a divine vision. So he must have derived it not from the reality around him, but from the spiritual world.

Christianity is not a new ethical system, but a new life which leads us into direct contact with God. It is a new alliance, a New Testament. And what does the mystery consist of? How are we to understand it? Why are people drawn to the person of Jesus Christ, as if to a magnet, although he came to a disparaged world, and he had nothing in him of the mysteriousness either of the Indian sages or of the exotic poetry of Eastern philosophy?

Everything that he said was simple, clear, and even the examples in his parables were taken from daily life. This is the mystery which he revealed in a few short words. We heard them in St John's Gospel when Philip said, 'Show us the Father, the Father of all.' He, whom the Greeks called *Arche*, the first cause, where is he? Jesus replied as no other philosopher on earth had ever replied: 'How long have I been with you, and you do not know me, Philip? He who has seen me has seen the Father.' He said this more than once, and many people turned their backs on him and went away indignantly, because these words have always been a challenge. People had to grasp this special mystery.

Christ never formulated the mystery in plain words. He only asked 'What do people take me for? A prophet? The risen John the Baptist? But you?' – 'You are the Christ, the Anointed One, the King, the Messiah, the Son of the Living God.' To express this there has to be some inner experience, and Christ still puts the question to each one of us, because he is God speaking with human lips.

Jesus Christ is the human face of the infinite, the ineffable, the inscrutable, the unbounded, the nameless. And Lao Zi was right when he said that the name we pronounce is not the eternal name. Yes, God is nameless and incomprehensible. But Christ who bears the burdens of life with us is named with a personal name, a human name – this is the centre and the core of Christianity.

When we pass from the Gospels to the Acts of the Apostles and the Epistles we must look at another personality of the New Testament. One French scholar has said that the New Testament consists of two biographies, that of Jesus Christ and that of his follower, Paul of Tarsus, the apostle Paul. Of course any of us passing from the Gospels to Paul's Epistles will feel they have fallen from heaven to earth, though in many respects Paul outshone the evangelists.

He was a man of enormous talent, spiritual energy, learning, his writings are very personal. The Epistles are written with his heart's blood. To compare them with the Gospels is anyway difficult because the Gospels reflect not so much the literary gifts of the evangelists as the model person which they had before their eyes. And if the apostle Paul stood before us, we would see merely a man, whereas Christ is the revelation of God.

But why is Paul important to us? Why did the church put him next to Christ in the New Testament? Why are most of the Epistles – fourteen of them – written in his name? Why, in the Acts of the Apostles, does his biography take up the lion's share?

The whole point is that in actual fact Paul never saw Jesus face to face during his earthly life, though there are some historical conjectures that their paths may have crossed in Jerusalem.

Paul himself was born in the first years of our era in Asia Minor, but he studied in Jerusalem and might have seen Jesus there. But still we can confidently assume that he didn't ever see him. I think this is why the church is drawn to the personality of the apostle for we too have never seen that face. But Christ appeared to Paul with a vividness that far surpasses any outward encounter.

Christ's enemies too saw him from the outside; the scribes, the Pharisees and Pilate, but they were not saved. Paul was an enemy as well, but Christ stopped him on the road to Damascus and called him to be an apostle. This event changed not only his destiny, but also the destiny of the early church, because Paul became one of those who brought the gospel out of Syria and Palestine to the wide world. He was called the apostle to the nations or the apostle to the Gentiles.

Schooled in Judaism, Paul perfectly knew that truth that it was impossible to be merged with God. Someone from the East, who thinks that in ecstasy they have experienced a mystical union with the absolute is mistaken: they can only have just brushed against the absolute because in the divine depths burns the eternal fire which consumes everything in itself. Between the Creator and the created lies an abyss, like the abyss between the absolute and the contingent: we can never leap over, neither logically nor existentially.

Yet there is a bridge thrown over this abyss, and Paul experienced this bridge himself because he saw Christ and was inwardly united to him. Eternal love bound him to Christ so that it seemed to him that he bore on himself the wounds of Christ, that he died with him on the cross and was resurrected with him. He said: 'I no longer live, but Christ lives in me. Together with him, I died, and together with him I have risen to life' [Gal. 2.20].

We cannot merge with God, but we can with the God-man, for he belongs simultaneously to two worlds, ours and the world beyond. The entire path of the Christian mystics from Paul to the present day is based on this – the way to the Father is only through the Son. 'I am the door,' says Christ, 'I am the gateway to heaven.'

In their repetition of various set phrases, Christian ascetics may be compared to the ascetics of the East, of India, who repeat their mantras. There is a similarity and a parallel. But one of the chief prayers of Christian devotion is called the 'Jesus Prayer'[3] in which is repeated the name of the one who was born and lived on earth, who was crucified and rose again.

The Christ-centredness of this important Christian prayer radically distinguishes it from all other meditations and mantras, because during this prayer a meeting takes place. The prayer is not simply a means of focussing one's thoughts, not simply a way of concentrating, not simply immersion in some ocean or depths of spirituality, but a meeting face to face between the person praying and Jesus Christ who stands above the world and in the world.

A prose-poem by Turgenev comes to mind.[4] He was in a village church and suddenly felt that Christ was standing by him. Turning round, he saw an ordinary man. And then, when he turned back, he again felt that Christ was there. This is true, this is how it is, because the reason that the church of Christ exists and evolves is that he stands within it.

Notice that Christ did not leave Christianity with a single line of writing, as Plato left us his Dialogues. He did not leave us tablets, with the law inscribed on them, like the tablets that Moses left. He did not dictate the Koran like Muhammad. He did not organize an order like Buddha. But he said to us, 'I will be with you always, until the close of the age' [Matt. 28.20].

When his disciples felt he was leaving them, he spoke some prophetic and eternal words: 'I do not leave you orphaned but I will come back to you,' and this continues and is happening today. All the deepest Christian experience is founded only on this; all the rest, as it were, are superficial layers. In all the rest, Christianity looks like the other religions.

World religions are a part of culture. They grow up along with the urge of the human spirit towards eternity, towards values that are unchanging. But with Christianity the stream flows from on high, from heaven, and that's why one of the theologians of our century was right to say, 'Christianity is not one among other religions – it is the crisis of all religions.' It rises above all others because, as the apostle Paul said, 'No one is saved by works of the law, but only through faith in Jesus Christ' [Rom. 3.20–22].

In conclusion, I must explain this key phrase. What are these works of the law? They are a system of religious rites and regulations. Are they necessary? Yes they are. They were instituted by people as a means of education, sometimes with great insights, sometimes simply on the strength of tradition, sometimes in error. The works of the law . . . sometimes these laws come from divine revelation, as in the Old Testament; but at a particular phase of intellectual and spiritual development.

But what does it mean to be saved? It means uniting one's ephemeral temporal life with the immortal, with God – that's what salvation is.

Communion with the divine life. The thirst for this communion lives in us, in everyone. It is a hidden, secret thirst. We may drive it somewhere inside, but it still exists in people. To come back to the point: the apostle said that the law is sacred, the Old Testament law is sacred and good and God gave it, but communion with the divine life is only possible through faith in Jesus Christ.

And again, what does faith in Jesus Christ mean? Faith in the fact that this man lived on earth? That is not faith but knowledge. His contemporaries remembered that he lived. The evangelists have left us reliable evidence. A historian of today will tell you, yes, that's how it was. Attempts by various propagandists to assert that Christ was a myth have long since been demolished. Only in our country, that museum of all kinds of eccentricities, is this theory preserved. And what does it imply to believe in Christ? Belief in the fact that he came from other worlds? That's also true, but it's just theory.

At this point we must recall the faith that was announced in the Old Testament: trust in existence. When Abraham said 'yes' to God, or more correctly, didn't say anything, but quietly obeyed God's call, that was when faith was born.

In ancient Hebrew faith sounds like *omuna*, from the word *omen* – steadfast. 'Faith' is a concept very close to the concept of 'faithfulness'. God was faithful to his own promise; the people were faithful to God. Weak and sinful they may have been, but still they were faithful to God. But to what kind of God? To a God who was hidden and terrible, a God, like the universe, a God who at times was distant from people, like the ocean.

But Christ revealed another face of God in himself. He never addresses God other than as Father. Jesus Christ hardly ever uses the word God, he always calls him Father. And in his earthly life, he used a tender and affectionate word [*abba*], which children use in the East when speaking to their father. It is untranslatable, but that's how it is.

Christ reveals God to us as our heavenly Father, and by this revelation we are made brothers and sisters to one another, for brothers and sisters are those who have a common father.

And now we know that our common spiritual Father is God, and our hearts are opened to the good news of Jesus; that is the mystery of the Gospels.

Anyone of you knows perfectly well how confused people are, how weak, how many complications and sins have taken root in us. But there is a power which Christ left on earth, which is given to us for free: it is called grace. In Russian the word is *blagodat'* – 'the good' [*blago*] which is 'given' [*dat'*] for free. You don't have to work for it, it's a gift.

Yes, we must make an effort, yes, we must struggle against sin, yes, we must work for self-perfection; but we have to remember that we can't pull ourselves up by our own boot laces. And these efforts are only preparatory. This is the basic difference between Christianity and yoga: for yoga believes that we can reach to God and break in on him by our own volition.

Christianity, on the other hand, says: you may work to perfect yourself, but you can't reach God until he comes to you. Thus grace surpasses the law.

The law is the first stage of religion which begins with the child: you can't do this, you may do that, here are some rules and some norms. Do we need all this? Yes, of course, we do. But then comes grace – through the inner experience of a meeting with God. It is like love, like exultation, it is like a victory, like the music of the spheres. Grace is new life.

The apostle Paul said, 'People are arguing among themselves. Some are supporters of the old rites of the Old Testament, others are against them, but neither the one nor the other is of consequence. The only important thing is the new creation, and faith active in love.' This is true Christianity, all the rest is a historical shell, a framework, something circumstantial, to do with culture.

I am talking about the very essence of the Christian faith. The eternal value of the human personality, the victory of light over death and corruption, the New Testament, which grows, like a tree, out of a little acorn. The New Testament which permeates history, as the leaven does dough, so even today the kingdom of God is coming secretly among the people.

When you do good, when you love, when you contemplate beauty, when you feel the fullness of life, the kingdom of God is already touching you. The kingdom is not something only in the distant future, in a futurological conjecture, but it exists here and now. So Jesus Christ taught us. The kingdom will come but is already here. The judgment of the world is to come but has already started. 'Now is the judgment of this world,' said Jesus. Now, that is, meaning the moment when he first proclaimed the gospel.

And he also said that the judgment is seen in the fact that the light has come into the world, but the people have preferred darkness. This judgment began at the time of his preaching in Galilee, at Jerusalem, at Golgotha, in the Roman empire, in mediaeval Europe, in Russia, today in the twentieth century and in the twenty-fifth century, and throughout all human history the judgment will continue because it is Christian history, it is history in which the world walks with the Son of Man.

So if we once again ask ourselves the question, what is the essence of Christianity, then we must answer: it is God-manhood, the joining of the finite and temporal human spirit with the eternal Divinity, it is the sanctification of the flesh, for from that moment when the Son of Man took on our joys and our sufferings, our love, our labours, from that moment, nature, the world, everything in which he was, in which he rejoiced, as a man and as God-man, no longer is rejected, no longer is degraded but is raised up to a new level, and is sanctified.

Christianity is the sanctification of the world, the victory over evil, over darkness, over sin. But it is the victory of God. It began on the night of the resurrection, and it will continue as long as the world exists.

Afterword

This article by Cardinal Lustiger was written as an introduction to the French biography by Yves Hamant, Alexandre Men: Un Témoin pour la Russie de Ce Temps, *Editions Mame, Paris 1993. The translation, by Fr Steven Bigham, was made for the English language edition published in 1995 under the title* Alexander Men: a Witness for Contemporary Russia *by Oakwood Publications, Torrance, California. Its inclusion here is by kind permission of the publishers.*

When I found myself face to face with Fr Alexander Men, I felt I had known him all my life. He seemed like a brother, a friend who would always be close to me, despite the fact that we only spoke for perhaps ten minutes. Let me first tell you about the circumstances of our meeting.

It was during a trip to the USSR at the beginning of May, 1989. I had been invited by the Patriarch of Moscow, and at that time the Soviet government's religious policy was still uncertain. The law on freedom of conscience was then only under study.

Fr Alexander Men was one of those mystical figures whose light and influence was felt to be a menace by the Communist authority and its police. He was under suspicion by both the KGB and the antisemites, and in order to silence him, one or the other group, or both together, had him killed with an axe as he was going to his church.

From that moment on, his words have the ring of authority; they are sanctioned by his martyrdom. No human being can now silence the living words of his assassinated voice. Russia turned its ear to those words when Boris Yeltsin, then president of the Supreme Soviet, called the assembly to a moment of silence for the murdered Fr Men.

On Saturday, 6 May, 1989, my travelling companions and I

were on our way from Moscow to the Zagorsk monastery. The night before, I had asked our hosts at the Moscow patriarchate to stop at Novaya Derevnia, the village where Fr Alexander had his parish; more precisely, he was still the second priest and not yet the pastor. It had been impossible to inform him of our visit. We only knew that he would be happy to receive us and that he would be in church on that day. It was the week after Easter, called Bright Week in the Orthodox Church, and the liturgy would be celebrated in all the churches that were open.

We arrived at the end of the liturgy, during the pastor's sermon; it is customary to preach after the eucharist. My companions and I stayed in the back of the church. Fr Alexander saw us. The pastor's sermon went on and on, and there was no way to stop him. Fr Alexander came up to me, and we had a brief conversation in English at the back of the church, just the two of us. The pastor finally finished his sermon and invited me to say a few words and to bless the faithful. Then, because we were pressed for time, we said goodbye and left.

Without ever having met before, we felt we had many things to say to each other but not time to say them. My memory of the event has taken the form of a strong, beautiful vision of a meeting in the mystery of the suffering and raised Messiah, a mystery that we both contemplated together. We exchanged what was essential, and we comforted one another much more than words could say.

From then on, I have tried to explore the wealth of meaning contained in our encounter but have not been able to completely grasp its significance. It was obvious to us, first of all, that our fraternity of faith, that our communion in Christ was like a sign, a foretaste of the full communion in the mutual love and respect of the Patriarch of Moscow and the Church of Rome. When he was speaking of the gifts of the Spirit, St Paul called such a sign a 'guarantee', a 'pledge' (II Cor. 5.5). I say 'It was obvious *to us*' without any other certitude of being able to speak for Fr Men than the intuition of that moment which has always remained with me. Both he and I, in fact, by becoming Christian, were loving and serving the one Bride of Christ, his Church.

It was also obvious, however, that his disciples could only live this communion by sharing the mystery of the Cross.

Yet, the joy of that Easter Week, as it illuminated the poor assembly in which Fr Alexander and I exchanged a few words, was bathed in the mystery of the Cross and coloured by the threat of a powerless yet imminent death. The resurrected Christ gives us a freedom that is stronger than all the world's tyrannies. The victory of faith is a victory of deliverance, forgiveness, and love. The weakness of Christ, who was handed over to the power of men, makes God's power appear because it is he who frees us from the power of sin.

Fr Alexander and I knew all this, and yet, nearly without words, we gave thanks for having found one another, witnesses for one another of mercy after great trials, witnesses of hope in a closed horizon. We had to interrupt our brief dialogue with the feeling that we would not be able to finish it.

I do not know which one of us ended the conversation, but I had the last word. When Fr Alexander proposed that we meet again, I said something like this to him, 'Oh, we will see each other again in heaven.' I had such a strong impression that the Word we both announced dwelled in his life, more so than in mine, and that his life was inevitably to become the sign of that Word.

When I heard of Fr Alexander's death, I had buried this final sentence in my memory. Fr Men brought it to my mind, after his death. Here is how.

Thanks to Andrei Eriomin, the details of our conversation were reported. Eriomin, a Russian intellectual, had been an acolyte at Novaya Derevnia for some ten years, and for a certain time had functioned as Fr Alexander's secretary. After our departure from Novaya Derevnia, Fr Alexander spoke to Andrei Eriomin in more or less the following words:

I just had a striking conversation with Cardinal Lustiger. He told me that we could not talk very much because we were surrounded by people listening to us. The Cardinal said that he was very happy to have met me and added, 'We no doubt will not have the occasion to meet again, and we will only see each other in the Beyond.'

After Fr Alexander's death, Andrei Eriomin came to see me on 1 February 1992, to ask me what I had meant and why I had made that statement. In truth, I made it because I saw Fr Alexander's life as an offering and as an abandonment to the love of Christ, the source of all his courage. I did not prophesy his death. I said out loud only what Fr Alexander already knew through Jesus' words to Peter: ' . . .and another will gird you and carry you where you do not wish to go' (John 21.18).

I consider my short meeting with Fr Alexander to have been a grace from God; it was an anticipation of the fullness to come, a fullness that, though it is a future reality, is nonetheless partially present here and now.

Cardinal Jean-Marie Lustiger

Notes

Introduction

1. V.Ya. Vasilevskaya, 'Vospominaniya. Fragmenty iz knigi "Katakomby XX veka"', in *I bylo utro. Vospominaniya ob otse Aleksandre Mene*, pp. 65–117. The same volume contains Fr Alexander's brief historical account of the catacomb church and its leading figures ('O knige "Katakomby XX veka"'), pp. 118–124; also Elena Men's account of her spiritual search with memoirs of Fr Serafim ('Moi put"), pp. 125–146.

For this account of Fr Alexander's life I have followed closely Yves Hamant, *Alexander Men: A Witness for Contemporary Russia (A Man for our Times)*, Oakwood Publications, Torrance, California 1995. (English translation of Yves Hamant, *Alexandre Men: Un Témoin pour la Russie de Ce Temps*, Editions Mame, Paris 1993).

2. Hamant, p. 40, quoting A. Men, 'Letter to E. N.' in *Aequinox*, Moscow 1991, pp. 184–85. Few biographical details are known about Mother Mariya, the abbess of this little community, except that she lived on until she was 81 and is buried at Zagorsk.

3. On the monastery of Optina Pustyn see John Dunlop, *Staretz Amvrosy*, Mowbrays 1972. See also chapter 8 below.

4. Hamant, p. 40, quoting Men, 'Letter'.

5. Hamant, p. 49, quoting Z. Maslennikova, 'Fenomen o. Aleksandra Menya' in *Perspektivy*, No. 4, p. 46 and A. Belavin, 'Svyashchennik Aleksandr Men", *Pamyati protoiereya Aleksandra Menya*, Moscow 1991, p. 29.

6. On the Moscow period, see Hamant, pp. 47–53.

7. V. Levi, 'Ya ved' tol'ko instrument', in *I bylo utro*, p. 229.

8. Hamant, pp. 53–4.

9. Hamant, pp. 73–4.

10. S. S. Averintsev, 'Missioner dlya plemeni intelligentov', in *I bylo utro*, p. 327.

11. Hamant, p. 81; Fr Alexander's memoirs of the Yakunin-Eshliman episode and of church life in the 1960s have recently been published in English in *Religion, State & Society*, Vol. 23, No. 2, June 1995, pp. 125–158.

12. A. Bessmertny-Anzimirov, 'Pastyr Sergieva kraya', in *I bylo utro*, p. 333.

13. Hamant, p. 162.

14. Galich (Aleksandr Arkadyevich Ginzburg, 1919–1977) was baptized

in 1972 at a time when he had already been expelled from the Writers Union and was living a hand-to-mouth existence before leaving the Soviet Union in 1974.

15. Hamant, p. 116, quoting L. L. Vasilenko, 'Kul'tura, tserkovnoe sluzhenie i svyatost'', in *Aequinox*, p. 166.

16. Hamant, p. 119.

17. Hamant, p. 124.

18. Hamant, p. 190, quoting Belavin, op. cit.

19. Belavin, op. cit.

20. Hamant, pp. 193–4, quoting V. Fainberg, 'Otets Aleksandr, Aleksandr Vladimirovich, Sasha' in *I bylo utro*.

21. Personal experience of the writer in 1991.

22. Hamant, pp. 125, 128.

23. Fazil Iskander, 'On byl svetom', in *I bylo utro*, p. 321.

24. The Black Hundreds were the extreme nationalist and antisemitic gangs responsible for the anti-Jewish pogroms in tsarist times.

25. Hamant, pp. 203–4, quoting V. Levi, 'Prikhodilo zhivoe schastie', *Stolitsa*, Nos. 31–32, 1991.

26. Quoted in Hamant, p. 163, from *Na poroge Novogo Zaveta*, Brussels 1983, pp. 665–66.

27. Evgeniya Zavadskaya, 'Pobeditel'nyi svet ubiennogo' in *I bylo utro*, pp. 245–47.

28. Alexander Men to Vladimir Levi, in *I bylo utro*, p. 222.

29. V. Fainberg, *I bylo utro*, p. 176.

30. *A Solovyov Anthology*, arranged by S. L. Frank, translated by Natalie Duddington, SCM Press 1950, pp. 15–16.

31. The text of a lecture by Fr Alexander on Berdyaev was published in the Russian language newspaper, *Russkaya mysl'*, Nos 4050–4051, Paris 1994.

32. A. Andreeva, 'V nem zhilo bessmertie' in *I bylo utro*, p. 216.

33. A. Bessmertny-Anzimirov, op. cit., p. 337.

1 Why be a Christian?

1. [Bar-Cochba, leader of the second Jewish revolt against the Romans, by whom he was defeated in AD 135.]

2. [Andrei Rublev (*c*.1360–1430), one of the greatest of Russian icon-painters, canonized in 1988. Among his masterpieces is the famous icon of the Trinity which depicts three figures seated round the eucharistic table. The reference is to the story in Genesis 18, when three divine visitors (understood as prefigurements of the Trinity) come to visit Abraham. The icon was painted for the Trinity St Sergius monastery at Sergiev Posad (formerly Zagorsk) and now hangs in the Tretyakov gallery in Moscow.]

3. [The reference is to Dostoevsky's novel *The Brothers Karamazov* where Ivan Karamazov declares he is 'returning his ticket to God' on account

of the unbearable cruelty in the world. The story of the landowner setting his dogs on the child is part of the evidence Ivan produces to make his point (Fyodor Dostoevsky, *The Brothers Karamazov*, translated and annotated by Richard Pevear and Larissa Volokhonskaya, Vintage 1992, pp. 242–430)].

4. [Fr Sergei Zheludkov (d. 1984), Orthodox priest from Pskov of the older generation with whom Fr Alexander became friends. He was a notable supporter of the dissidents in the seventies. He stood for an open Christianity which welcomed all people of good will, whether nominal believers or not, on the lines of Karl Rahner's 'anonymous Christians'.]

5. [Elsewhere Fr Alexander made the point that the biblical seven days are symbolic and not chronological and that 'the question of when the universe came into being has to be studied rationally and scientifically, not by revelation which only opens things to people which they cannot understand by their own natural reasoning powers' (Conversation with Vladimir Levi, in *I bylo utro*, p. 186; see also chapter 5, 'Creation, evolution and human beings', of *Istoki religii).]*

2 Religion, Knowledge of God, and the Problem of Evil

1. [Otto Pfleiderer, *Religion and Historic Faiths*, translated from the German by Daniel A. Huebsch, Fisher and Unwin, London 1907, p. 121. A.M. refers to the Russian translation, *O religii i religiyakh*, St Petersburg 1908.]

2. Dietrich Bonhoeffer, *Letters and Papers from Prison*, The Enlarged Edition, SCM Press 1971, p. 282.

3. [On Mother Maria Skobtsova, see Sergei Hackel, *Pearl of Great Price. The Life of Mother Maria Skobtsova* (1891–1945), London 1982; David Wilkerson's experiences among the gangs of New York are recounted in *The Cross and the Switchblade*, 1967]

4. Utilitarians derive their ethics from the laws of society as a whole. Their standpoint is that moral principles stem from the needs of the social unit and serve that unit. [The Russian biologist and Darwinist] Kliment Timiryazev wrote: 'A society of egoists will never defeat a society guided by a sense of moral duty. In open physical struggle this moral sentiment acts even as a direct material force' (K. A. Timiryazev, *Charlz Darvin ego i uchenie*, Moscow 1940, p. 43 [*Charles Darwin and his Teaching* was first published in 1865].) While acknowledging the relative truth of this standpoint we must not forget that ethics contains a good deal that does not serve the 'social unit' or the 'whole'. From the point of view of social expediency, for instance, the Nazis were right to kill the incurably ill and insane; but individual morality strongly objects to such 'artificial selection'. On this point social and individual ethics part company: and this divergence indicates that there are other sources of morality than the laws of society. Albert Schweitzer rightly made the point:

The great mistake of ethical thought down to the present time is that it fails to admit the essential difference between the morality of ethical personality and that which is established from the standpoint of society, and always thinks that it ought, and is able, to cast them in one piece. The result is that the ethic of personality is sacrificed to the ethic of society.

[Albert Schweitzer, *Civilization and Ethics*, 3rd English edition, revised by Mrs Charles E. B. Russell, A & C. Black 1946, p. 225; A. M. refers to the Russian translation of 1973.]

5. [Goethe, *Faust*, Part One, translated with an introduction by David Luke, The World's Classics, OUP 1987, p. 109.]

6. [Rudolf Bultmann, in *Kerygma and Myth* ed. H. W. Bartsch, 1953, volume 1, p. 3. A. M. refers to the German edition]. Bultmann's method is extremely fruitful in the interpretation of the Old Testament and, as he himself recognizes, is one used by early church commentators. Bultmann's ideas were popularized by John Robinson in his book *Honest to God* which is a highly dubious attempt to rethink Christianity 'in the spirit of the times'. Both Bultmann and Robinson unintentionally impoverish contemporary thinking by representing science as it was in the last century. (See for example, John Robinson, *Honest to God*, SCM Press, London, and Westminster Press, Philadelphia, 1963, p. 27.) In accommodating Christianity to this false image, they distort both the spirit of contemporary science and the spirit of Christianity. See the critical work. E. Mascall, *The Secularization of Christianity*, London 1967, pp. 190 ff.

7. Paul Tillich, *The Shaking of the Foundations*, SCM Press 1949, p. 57 ['The name of this infinite and inexhaustible depth and ground of all being is *God*. That depth is what the word *God* means.']

8. [Mascall] is right to point this out. See Mascall, op. cit. pp. 175–77 [A. M. refers erroneously to Cogley, op. cit.]

9. The most valuable thing in what is called 'death of God' theology is its protest against the treatment of God as an 'object' akin to other objects in being. But this idea is perfectly well known in the Christian tradition. (See the collection, *Orthodoxy and the Death of God* ed. A. M. Allchin, Fellowship of St Alban and St Sergius, London 1971). And in this century it has been studied in great depth by Nicolas Berdyaev.

10. Bishop Vasily Rodzianko of the Orthodox Church points out that there are practically no references in Robinson's book to patristic literature where plenty of arguments against anthropomorphism and crude images of God can be found. See, V. Rodzianko, '*Honest to God* under the Fathers' Judgement', *Orthodoxy and the Death of God*, pp. 55 ff.

11. Brhadāranyaka, *Upanishadā* 3, 9, 26; 4, 4, 22; [Pseudo-Dionysius, *The Complete Works*, translated by Colin Luibheid, SPCK 1987, p. 109 ('The Divine Names', 7, 3); Maximus the Confessor, *Selected Writings*, translated by George C. Berthold, SPCK 1985, p. 130; Nicolas Cusanus, *Of Learned Ignorance*, translated by Fr Germain Heron, Routledge and Kegan

Paul 1954 ('Sacred ignorance has taught us that God is ineffable, because He is infinitely greater than anything that words can express. So true is this that by process of elimination and the use of negative propositions we come nearer to the truth about Him', p. 60).] Extensive material on apophatic theology is to be found in Sergei Bulgakov, *Svet nevechernyi* [The Uncreated Light] Moscow 1917, pp. 103–146.

12. [S. Radhakrishnan, *Indian Philosophy*, George Allen and Unwin 1923, vol. 1, pp. 178–79.]

13. [Jean Daniélou, *God and Us*, translated from the French by Walter Roberts, Mowbray 1957, p. 54.]

14. Fr Pavel Florensky writes extensively about this in his book, *Stolp I utverzhdenie istiny* [*The Pillar and Affirmation of Truth*], Moscow 1914, in the chapter on 'contradiction', pp. 143 ff.

15. [Lines from the poem 'God' (1883) by Dmitri Merezhkovsky. D. S. Merezhkovsky, Z. N. Gippius, *Stikhotvoreniya*, Tallinn: Aleksandra 1992, p. 11.]

16. ['God-man', i.e. Christ – a key term in Russian religious philosophy.]

17. [Quotation translated from the Russian. A. M. refers to Norbert Wiener, *Kibernetika i obshchestvo* (Cybernetics and Society).]

We should recall that Clausius and Kelvin had derived from the idea of entropy the theory of the 'heat death' of the universe, that is of the time when the possibilities for energy to change from one form into another are exhausted. But . . . there is a contrary tendency in the universe. See, Ya.A. Vin'kovetsky, *Geologiya i obshchaya evolyutsiya prirody* [Geology and the General Evolution of Nature], Leningrad 1971, pp.10 ff.

18. [Jacob Boehme, *The Aurora*, translated by John Sparrow, London, John M. Watkins 1914, p. 8. A. M. refers to the Russian translation of 1914.] These ideas of Boehme's were developed by Vladimir Solovyev.

19. In this connection we can understand the tendency of William James and Norbert Wiener to regard divine omnipotence on a non-absolute level. This point of view is fully justified in the light of *kenosis* and the freedom of created beings. [See William James, *A Pluralistic Universe, Hibbert Lectures*, New York 1909. A. M. refers to Russian translation of 1911; Norbert Wiener, *God and Golem, Inc.: A comment on certain points where cybernetics impinges on religion*, MIT Press, 1964 (Russian translation, *Tvorets i robot*, Moscow 1966).]

20. Nikolai Berdyaev, *Filosofiya svobody* [The Philosophy of Freedom], Moscow 1911, p. 148.

3 Faith and its Enemies

1. [Cf. Nicolas de Cusa, 'No nation ever existed which did not worship God', *Of Learned Ignorance*, p. 17.]

2. Arnold Toynbee, 'Introduction' to John Cogley, *Religion in a Secular*

Age, Pall Mall Press, London 1968. See also, Mircea Eliade, 'The Sacred in a Secular World', *Cultural Hermeneutics*, 1973, No. 1, p. 104. This is even discussed by such a 'free-thinking' author as Ashley Montagu (*Man: His First Million Years*, New York 1957, p. 181). The terms 'religion' and 'faith' are so close in meaning that as a rule they are regarded as synonymous. The psychoanalyst Erich Fromm writes: 'I understand by religion any system of thought and action shared by a group which gives the individual a frame of orientation and an object of devotion' (Erich Fromm, *Psychoanalysis and Religion*, Victor Gollancz, London 1951, p. 29). However we are concerned with 'faith' in the widest sense of the word, whereas 'religious faith' is reverence for God directed towards the highest principle (as distinct from neo-pagan beliefs which deify earthly objects).

3. Albert Camus, *Essais*, introduced by R. Quilliot, Bibliotèque de la Pleiade, Paris 1965, p. 240 [The quotation is from the fourth of the 'Lettres à un ami allemand' of July 1944.]

4. Erich Fromm, op. cit., p. 34.

5. This episode is described in E. Voronitsyn, *Istoriya ateizma [History of Atheism]*, Moscow 1930, p. 233.

6. On Huxley's creed, see *Religion without Revelation*, Max Parrish, London 1957, pp. 188 ff.

7. [The movement 'to the people', or Narodnik movement, gripped the younger members of the intelligentsia in the 1870s when hundreds of students went into the country to propagandize the peasants.]

8. Sergi Bulgakov, *Dva grada [Two Cities]*, Moscow 1911, vol. 2, p. 176.

9. A. V. Lunacharsky, 'Pis'mo v redakstiyu', *Obrazovanie*, 1908, No. 1, p. 163. [Lunacharsky became Lenin's Commissar for Education.]

10. Nikolai Berdyaev, *Marksizm I religiya (Marxism and Religion]*, Prague 1929, p. 7.

11. [Another key term in Russian religious philosophy. If the 'God-man' referred to Christ and uniting of the divine with the created order, the 'Man-god' referred to those humanistic and atheistic thinkers whose philosophies eliminated God and proposed man to be the measure of all things.]

12. The goddess of Reason in these rites was played by a French actress.

13. William Hocking. *The Meaning of God in Human Experience*, New Haven 1924, pp. ix-x.

14. Similar sentiments are expressed in the works of a number of contemporary western theologians (William Hamilton, Harvey Cox, John Robinson).

15. Contemporary theologians are justified in talking of the advantages to the church of being 'in diaspora' (that is being able to witness freely to Christ in the world) rather than clinging to the outward 'triumphalism'

which drew Christians to it in the past. See, Cogley, op. cit., pp. 93–95 [quoting Karl Rahner.]

16. Cogley, p. 111. [' . . . the inner life of the individual is superior to any value incorporated in the state . . . religion validates and nurtures the primacy of the person.'] A German scholar of the psychology of religion, Trillhaas remarks that 'religion is not only the innermost realm of human nature, but the most individual one too' (Wolfgang Trillhaas, *Die innere Welt*, Munich, 1953, p. 5).

17. A. Donini, *Lyudi, idoly i bogi [People, idols and gods]*, M. 1962, p. 8. More recent data do not alter the picture.

18. For the story of the conversion of leading intellectuals to faith in our century, see F. Lelotte (ed.), *Convertis du XXe siècle*, vols 1–3, Casterman, Tournai-Paris 1953–55.

19. Charles Townes, 'The fusion of science and religion', in *Dialogi: polemicheskie stati o vozmozhnykh posledstviyakh razvitiya sovremennoi nauki [Dialogues: Polemical articles on the possible consequences of the development of modern science]*, Moscow 1979, p. 61 [Translation of quotation from the Russian.]

20. V. V. Zenkovsky, *A History of Russian Philosophy*, translated by G. L. Kline, 2 vols, London & New York 1953; N. Zernov, *The Russian Religious Renaissance of the Twentieth Century*, London 1963; W. Nicholls, *The Pelican Guide to Modern Theology*, London 1971, vols. 1–3; J. B. Agus, *Guideposts in Modern Judaism: an Analysis of Current Trends in Jewish Thought*, Bloch 1954; P. S. Sarma, *Hinduism through the Ages*, Bombay 1956.

21. See Michael Novak, *The Open Church*, London 1964; A. Kloosterman, *Contemporary Catholicism: Thoughts since Vatican II*, Fontana, London 1972.

22. John Robinson, *Honest to God*, SCM Press, London and Westminster Press, Philadelphia, 1963, pp. 138–139. [Robinson writes there (p. 138): *I am not greatly excited by the current signs of the survival of religiousness in Russia . . . It may even confirm, as Daniel Jenkins has suggested*, 'Oswald Spengler's remarkable prophecy of a generation ago, in *The Decline of the West*, when he spoke of the appearance of "a second religiousness" which is, according to him, the sign that a culture is drawing to the end of the cycle of its life'.]

23. Max Born, *My Life and Views*, New York 1968, p. 112.

4 A Credo for Today's Christian

1. [In order to become a bishop an Orthodox priest must become first a monk, whereas the parish clergy are married.]

5 Christianity: The Universal Vision

1. [Karl Jaspers, *The Origin and Goal of History*, translated from the German by Michael Bullock, Routledge & Kegan Paul 1953. A. M. refers to the Russian translation, K. Yaspers, *Istoki istorii i ee tsel'*, translated by M. I. Levina, Moscow 1978; on Jaspers, see P. Schlipp (ed.), *The Philosophy of Karl Jaspers*, New York, 1952.]

2. [In this passage, Men is referring to his own study of magic beliefs, *Magizm i edinobozhie [Magism and Monotheism]*, Moscow, 1991.]

3. [Sir James] Frazer believed that magic was the precursor of religion, but this view finds few supporters nowadays. Magism as a type of thinking merely gave primitive and ancient religion a certain colour and intention. See my book, *Magizm i edinobozhie*.

4. The fullest account of apophatic teachings is to be found in S. Bulgakov, *Svet nevechernyi [The Uncreated Light]*, Moscow 1917. But even there pre-Christian apophaticism is restricted only to the classical period and does not include Indian or Chinese versions of it. As far as I am aware, there are no non-Russian studies of the world-wide apophatic tradition. [On apophaticism, see also above in chapter 2.]

5. Jaspers, *Origin*, p. 2.

6. Ibid., p. 58.

7. Ibid., p. 2.

8. Ibid., p. 75.

9. I. Veinberg, *Chelovek v kul'ture Drevnego Blizhnego Vostoka [Man in the Culture of the ancient Near East]*, Moscow 1986, p. 4. Designs inspired by ancient oriental motifs started to appear in Europe soon after the first archaeological discoveries in the East.

10. [Afanasy Nikitin, a merchant from the Russian city of Tver', travelled in India, Persia and Turkey in the years 1467–72 and recorded his thoughts and impressions in diary form.]

11. Afanasy Nikitin, 'Khozhdenie za tri morya' ['Journey over three seas'] in *Pamyatniki literatury drevnei Rusi. Vtoraya polovina XV veka*, Moscow 1982, p. 473. We have to bear in mind that Afanasy was in India at a time when Islam was widely spread as well as Hinduism.

12. See A. Cronin, *A Pearl of India: the Life of Roberto di Nobili*, New York 1959; Stephen Neill, *A History of Christian Missons*, New York 1979, pp. 163–65, 183–87.

13. The first translation of the *Avesta* into French was made by Anquetil Duperron in 1771; the first Russian translation of the *Bhagavadgita* (from the English) was published by Nikolai Novikov in Moscow in 1788; the first English translation of the *Laws of Manu* was published by William Jones in 1790.

14. [Friedrich Max Müller (1823–1900), orientalist and philologist, professor at Oxford, editor of *The Sacred Books of the East*, which came out in 50 volumes between 1879 and 1910; Paul Deussen (1845–1919), author

of a general history of philosophy and religions which did much to make Indian philosophy known in the West.]

15. [Iakinf Bichurin (1777–1853), Russian monk and sinologist, archimandrite of the monastery of the Ascension in Irkutsk and from 1807–22 head of the church mission to Beijing. Published nine books on China and other Asian countries; Aleksi (Aleksandr Nikolaevich) Vinogradov (1845–1919), scholar and orientalist.]

16. [A. M. refers to those edited by Helmolt and von Pflügk-Harttung.]

17. [Ram Mohan Roy (1772–1833), Indian religious reformer who promoted the idea of monotheism in Hinduism and founded the Bramo Samaj movement; Ramakrishna (1834–1886), Hindu mystic who propounded an inclusive view of all varieties of Hinduism and other religions; Devi Vivekananda (1863–1902), disciple of Ramakrishna, who developed the idea of a world-wide religion based on Hinduism; Aurobindo Ghose (1872–1950), Sanskrit scholar and yoga, translator of the *Rig-Veda*. One of the founders of the Indian cultural renaissance.]

18. This process incidentally is not yet exhausted. Think of the influence of Dostoevsky on Japanese writers.

19. [Slavophilism is the name given to an intellectual movement in nineteenth-century Russia which turned away from western influences and looked to the Slavonic roots of Russian culture for future cultural and social development. Its leaders included Aleksei Khomyakov, theologian and thinker, Ivan Kireevsky, and the Aksakov brothers, Ivan and Konstantin.]

20. Nikolai Danilevsky, *Rossiya i evropa [Russia and Europe]*, St Petersburg 1889, p. 82 (quoted from the fourth edition).

21. Only the first volume of Spengler's *The Decline of the West* was translated into Russian (an incomplete version in 1922 and a complete one in 1923); the final chapter of the second volume 'Money and machine' was published in Petrograd in 1922.

22. [Nestor the Chronicler (*c.* 1056–1112), monk of the monastery of the Caves at Kiev, who is traditionally credited with the authorship of the *Primary Chronicle*, the earliest source for Russian history.]

23. *Osval'd Shpengler i Zakat Evropy [Oswald Spengler and the Decline of the West]*, Moscow 1922. Includes articles by Berdyaev and S. L. Frank.

24. *Os'vald Shpengler*, op. cit., pp. 42–43.

25. Jaspers, *Origin*, p. 58.

26. [Asvaghosha, Brahmin convert to Buddhism (*c.* AD 80–150); Shankara (788–820), founder of Advaita Vedanta; Tsongkhapa (1357–1419), Tibetan lama and monastic reformer.]

27. Tatian, *Oratio ad Graecos*; Tertullian, 'Letter to Scapula, proconsul of Africa'.

28. Acts 17. 22–31. On the 'holy pagans' of the Old Testament, see Jean Danielou, *Les saints paiens de l'Ancient Testament*, Paris 1956.

29. Plato had a particularly important place in patristics and Byzantine Orthodox thought, while Aristotle was more important for the western

scholastic tradition. But Byzantium did not ignore Aristotle: his ideas were used by John of Damascus. It is interesting that images of pre-Christian thinkers are found in mediaeval church paintings (in Byzantium, early Russia and in the West). As regards the Buddhist connection of the 'Tale of Varlaam and Jehoshaphat', which was widely known in Byzantium, early Russia and Georgia, the question is an open one. Many scholars have no doubt that the legend of the young Buddha was the prototype for the 'Tale', but there is another theory according to which the Indian story is a reflection of a plot which was widely used throughout the East.

30. [Vladimir Sergeevich Solovyev (1853–1900); see Introduction.]

31. Vl. Solovyev, *Mifologicheskii protsess v drevnem yazychestve [The Mythological Process in Ancient Paganism]*, in *Collected Works*, 2nd edn, vol. 1, St Petersburg 1911.

32. Ibid., p. 151.

33. *Pis'ma Vladimira Sergeevicha Solovyeva [The Letters of V. S. Solovyev]*, St Petersburg, vol. 3, p. 105.

34. Vl. Solovyev, *Collected Works*, vol. 3, p. 86.

35. Ibid., p. 37.

36. Ibid., p. 45. Solovyev accepted Schelling's theory that the beginning of all religious-historical development was a primitive monotheism. But he regarded this monotheism not so much as a stage in religious history as a prelude to it. Subsequently A. Lang, in *The Making of Religion*, London 1898, and P. W. Schmidt in *Der Ursprung der Gottesidee*, Munster, 1912–15, vols 1–12, sought to confirm the theory of pre-monotheism with ethnographical data. But empirically it was possible only to confirm the existence among 'primitive' people of an understanding of a supreme Being.

37. Solovyev, op. cit., vol. 4, p. 363.

38. Idem, vol. 3, p. 80.

39. Idem, vol. 3, p. 167.

40. [Petr Yakovlevich Chaadaev (1793–1856), philosopher and writer. His philosophic letter published in 1836 argued that Russia had no past or present and her future could only lie in rejoining European civilization. He was declared insane by the authorities.]

41. [Sergi Nikolaevich Bulgakov (1871–1944), priest and theologian. Expelled from Russia in 1922 and became professor at the St Sergius Theological Institute in Paris; Pavel Florensky (1882–1937), priest, professor of electron physics, mathematician, musicologist, theologian; prince Evgeny Nikolaevich Trubetskoi (1863–1920), philosopher and historian of ideas; Semen Lyudvigovich Frank (1877–1950), religious philosopher, lived in London; Dmitri Sergeevich Merezhkovsky (1865–1941), literary critic and poet, leader of the older Symbolists; Vyacheslav Ivanov (1886–1949), writer and philosopher, emigrated to Italy.]

Notes

42. [Nicolas (Nikolai) Berdyaev (1874–1948); see Introduction.]

43. [Nicolas Berdyaev, *Freedom and the Spirit*, Geoffrey Bles 1935, p. 88. (English translation by O. F. Clarke of *Filosofiya svobodnogo dukha*, Paris 1928).]

44. Idem. 'Nauka o religii i khristianskaya apologetika' ['The science of religion and Christian apologetics'], *Put'*,1927, no. 6, pp. 57–58.

45. Berdyaev, *Freedom*, p. 271.

46. [Berdyaev, *The Meaning of History*, translated by George Reavey, London 1936, p. 29.]

47. Ibid., p. 29.

48. Berdyaev, *Filosofiya svobody [The Philosophy of Freedom]*, Moscow 1911, p. 169.

49. Berdyaev, *Opyt eskhatologicheskoi metafiziki [Attempt at an eschatological metaphysics]*, Paris 1947, p. 213.

50. Bultmann is concerned that the biblical idea of a three-storied universe is old-fashioned. 'It is impossible,' he writes, 'to use electric light and the wireless and to avail ourselves of modern medicine and surgical discoveries, and at the same time to believe in the New Testament world of demons and spirits' (R. Bultmann in *Kerygma and Myth: A Theological debate* ed. H. W. Bartsch, trans. R. H. Fuller, SPCK 1960, pp. 4–5. Berdyaev on the other hand is concerned with quite another aspect of demythologization: he believes that myth as such is inseparable from religion and is its natural symbolic language. The problem then is to overcome the 'objectivization' of the myth when people begin to perceive it as wholly corresponding to reality, when it becomes full of socially formed elements (violence, cruelty, domination, etc.). 'The conceptions which have been worked out for the phenomenal world and are applicable to it alone are not transferrable to God' [(Berdyaev, *The Divine and the Human*, translated by R. M. French, London, 1949, p. 8.)] Berdyaev wrote a book specially on this theme [*Truth and Revelation*, translated by R. M. French, London 1952.]

51. Berdyaev, 'Nauka', p. 57.

52. Charles Dawson, *Progress and Religion: An Historical Enquiry*, Sheed and Ward 1929. [Page numbers below are to this edition; A. M. quotes from the New York edition of 1960.] Dawson [1889–1970] was born into a military family, and studied at Oxford. In 1914 he converted to Catholicism. He was lecturer and professor at the universities of Exeter, Liverpool, Edinburgh and Harvard. He was one of the pioneers of the ecumenical movement. His chief works include: *The Age of the Gods*, 1928; *The Making of Europe*, 1932; *Religion and the Modern State* 1935; *Christian Freedom*, 1943; *Religion and Culture*, 1948; *The Understanding of Europe*, 1952; *The Revolt of Asia*, 1957.

53. Dawson, *Religion and Culture*, p. 217.

54. Dawson, *Progress*, pp. 75–76.

55. Ibid., p. 119.

56. Ibid., p. 89.

57. Dawson himself did not use the term 'axial period' and we use it here for convenience.

58. Dawson, *Progress*, p. 154.

59. Ibid., p. 155.

60. Ibid., p. 157.

61. Ibid., p. 246. Dawson refers to the possibility of a second world war whose advent he often foretold.

62. Ibid., p. 247.

63. Berdyaev, *Freedom and the Spirit*, pp. 88–9.

6 Religion, the 'Cult of Personality' and the Secular State

1. [Conversation with V. Fainberg, in *I bylo utro*, p. 178.]

2. [Conversation with A. Andreeva, ibid., pp. 216–7.]

3. ['Konets spora?' ['Is it the end of the argument?'], an interview with the editors of the journal *Yunost' [Youth]*, held in August 1989. Text reprinted in *Kul'tura i dukhovnoe vozrozhdenie*, Moscow 1992, pp. 117–138.]

4. [Batu Khan (d. 1255), grandson of Genghis Khan, conquered Russia in 1236–40.]

5. [Count Aleksandr Vasilevich Suvorov (1730–1800), one of the greatest of Russian generals.]

6. [The fourth chapter of the official Stalinist *Short History of the Communist Party of the Soviet Union (Bolsheviks)* contained Stalin's contribution 'On dialectical and historical materialism'.]

7. [Reference to the story 'Kleine Zaches' (1819) by E. T. A. Hoffmann.]

8. [Pol Pot, leader of the Khmer Rouge in Cambodia.]

9. [The film 'Ordinary Fascism' by the well-known Soviet film director Mikhail Ilyich Romm (1901–1971) came out in 1966.]

10. L. Radzikhovsky, 'S tochki zreniya psikhologa' ['From a psychologist's point of view'] in *Znanie – sila*, No. 10, 1988.

11. [Evgeny Evtushenko, poet, born 1933, became famous for his outspoken lyrics at the time of the Khrushchev thaw in the early sixties.]

12. Sigmund Freud, *Izbrannoe [Selected Works]*, ed. E. Ziglevic, vol. 1, London 1969, p. 125 [quotation translated from the Russian.]

13. [Fustel de Coulanges (1830–89), author of *La cité antique* (1864), a study of the part played by religion in the political and social development of Greece and Rome.]

14. Quoted from V. Vasilevsky, *Politicheskie reformy i sotsial'nye dvizheniya v Drevnei Gretsii v periode ee upadka [Political Reforms and Social Movements in Ancient Greece in the Period of its Decline]*, St Petersburg 1869, p. 35.

15. [Epistles 2. 1. 15–17, in *The Complete Works of Horace (Quintus Horatius Flaccus)*, translated by Charles E. Passage, Frederick Ungar Publishing Co., New York 1983, p. 341.]

16. [St Ambrose (*c.* 339–97) excommunicated the emperor Theodosius; St John Chrysostom (*c.* 347–407) antagonized the empress Eudoxia and was condemned at the Synod of Oak in 403; Pope Martin (d. 655) refused to sign the *Typos* of the emperor Constans II and was banished to the Crimea; St Maximus the Confessor (*c.* 508–662) also refused to sign the *Typos* and was banished; the defenders of icons in the Byzantine iconoclast controversy (*c.* 725–842) opposed the edicts of the emperor Leo III; the *nestyazhateli* (non-possessors) in sixteenth-century Russia were the group of learned churchmen who stood for an independent church and were not afraid to criticize the sovereign. Their leader was St Maxim the Greek who was imprisoned by Tsar Vasily III; Girolamo Savonarola, religious reformer, burnt as a heretic in Florence in 1498; Jan Huss, Bohemian religious reformer, burnt as heretic in 1415; St Filipp, metropolitan of Moscow, who dared to stand up to Ivan the Terrible. He was strangled on Ivan's orders in 1568.]

17. [F. R. de Lamennais (1782–1854), French liberal religious and political writer.]

18. [Emelyan Pugachev, Cossack leader of a widespread popular revolt. Executed in 1775. The Russian poet Aleksandr Sergeevich Pushkin wrote a *History of the Pugachev Revolt* (1834) and his novel, *The Captain's Daughter* (1836) is set in the same period.]

19. [*Cathedral Folk* (1872) by Nikolai Leskov, was an immensely popular fictional 'chronicle' of church life in sleepy Stargorod.]

20. V. I. Lenin, *Polnoe sobranie sochinenii [Complete Works]*, Vol. 7, p. 173.

21. [Reference to the Karlovci Synod, later the Russian Orthodox Church Abroad.]

22. [The government ordered the church to release its valuables in order to pay for relief to the victims of the famine. Many local churches resisted. The patriarch agreed to the confiscations provided the churches could retain their eucharistic vessels. The situation led to many acts of violence and misunderstandings. The saintly metropolitan Venyamin of Petrograd who appealed to all for non-violence was tried and shot for allegedly resisting the confiscations in 1922.]

23. [See Introduction.]

24. [Andrei Platonov, author of the powerful anti-Utopias, *Chevengur* (1929) and *The Foundation Pit [Kotlovan]* (1930).]

25. [The popular poet Sergei Esenin (1895–1925), famed for his lyrics about the Russian countryside, showed his darker 'hooligan' side at the time of the revolution. 'Inoniya', the name of an imaginary city, was written in 1918.]

26. [Konstantin Kharchev, Party functionary who headed the Council for Religious Affairs from 1985, is thought to have contributed to the change in government attitude towards religion.]

27. [Church of Christ the Saviour, an enormous church in the centre of

Moscow which was built to commemorate the Russian victory in the Napoleonic wars, was blown up in 1931. Rebuilding is now under way.]

28.]Lion Feuchtwanger (1884–1958), German author, visited the Soviet Union in 1937 and wrote a eulogy of Stalin in *Moscow 1937*.]

29. Memorial, society founded in 1988 with Andrei Sakharov as its first president, to record the memory of those persecuted for political offences in the Soviet Union and to offer practical help to the survivors of the Gulag and the families of the victims.

7 Russia in Crisis

1. [Marquis de Condorcet (1743–94) proclaimed the idea of progress and the perfectability of the human race.]

2. [Gaius Suetonius Tranquillus, Roman historian (75–160 AD), author of *De vita Caesarum*.]

3. [St Sergius of Radonezh (*c*. 1315–1392), great Russian saint, known for his asceticism and gentleness. He inspired prince Dmitri Donskoi and his allies to victory over the Tatars at Kulikovo in 1380.]

4. [Reference to the verse fable by Ivan Krylov (1769–1844) in which four animals are given musical instruments: they think that all they need do to be able to play them is to change their seating positions.]

5. [Pitirim Sorokin served as minister in Kerensky's Provisional Government in 1917. He then emigrated to America where he became professor of sociology at Harvard.]

6. [Pico della Mirandola (1463–94), philosopher and writer; Savonarola, see above, ch. 6, no. 16; Desiderius Erasmus (1466–1536), Dutch scholar and Christian humanist.]

7. [Mikhail Tareev (1866–1934), Russian moral theologian.]

8. [Mikhail Bulgakov's comic masterpiece *The Master and Margarita* intersperses wildly fantastical scenes of contemporary Moscow life with an account of the last days of Jesus of Nazareth, named Yeshua, and his confrontation with Pilate. The novel written in the late 1930s was published in Moscow in 1966 and has been immensely popular ever since.]

8 Two Understandings of Christianity

1. [On the term *starets*, and on Optina Pustyn, see Introduction.]

2. [A. S. Khomyakov (1804–60), lay theologian and Slavophile; I. V. Kireevsky (1806–56), Slavophile philosopher; K. N. Leontyev (1831–91), critic and anti-liberal writer.]

3. [Nadezhda A. Pavlovich (b. 1895), poet, spent ten years close to the last Optino *starets* Nektary. She kept a diary of this time and has written memoirs of him. Thanks to her efforts a museum was re-opened in Optino in 1974 and restoration work begun. The monastery reopened in 1988.]

4. [Vladimir Solovyev, *Lectures on God-manhood*, translated by Peter Zouboff, Dennis Dobson Ltd 1948. The *Lectures* were published in Russian in 1878.]

5. [When the writer Nikolai Gogol published his conservative and pietistic *Selected Passages from a Correspondence with Friends* in 1847 the critic Vissarion Belinsky responded with a vitriolic letter, accusing Gogol of betraying progressive ideals and distorting Christianity.]

6. [*Philokalia*, anthology of spiritual writings, collected by St Nicodemus of the Holy Mountain and first published in Venice in 1782. A Russian translation came out in 1876–90.]

9 The Russian Orthodox Church Today

1. [Reference to Fr Gleb Yakunin, Fr Nikolai Eshliman, among others. See Introduction.]

2. ['Karlovci synod', now Russian Orthodox Church Abroad, formed after the revolution, and so named after the Yugoslav town where it first met.]

3. [Reference to Stalin's deportation of the Chechen and Ingush peoples in 1943.]

4. ['Pamyat' is the extreme right-wing nationalist movement.]

5. [Nikolai Gogol wrote a story entitled 'Taras Bulba' (1835), eulogizing the free life of the Cossacks and their campaigns against the Catholic Poles.]

6. [For an English translation of this interview, see Fr Alexander Men', 'The Jews and Christianity', *Religion, State and Society*, Vol. 23, No. 1, 1995, pp. 25–29.]

7. [Lazar Moiseevich Kaganovich (1893–1987), one of Stalin's chief lieutenants.]

10 The Christian Hope: 'Karabakh' or Bethlehem?

1. [The 'new Russian martyrs' refers to those who died for their faith during the Soviet persecutions.]

2. [St Siluan (1866–1938) was a Russian peasant who became an ascetic on Mount Athos. On his remarkable teachings, see *Wisdom from Mount Athos: the Writings of Staretz Silouan*, by Archimandrite Sophrony, translated from the Russian by Rosemary Edmonds. St Vladimir's Seminary Press, Crestwood, New York 1974; Archimandrite Sophrony, *The Monk of Mount Athos: Staretz Silouan*, translated from the Russian by Rosemary Edmonds, Mowbrays 1973.]

11   *Christianity for the Twenty-First Century*

1. [Tarkovsky's film *Andrei Rublev* (1969) depicts the violence of late fourteenth century Russia rather than the spiritual significance of the icon-painter.]

2. [Francisco Goya's series of satirical etchings, *Los Caprichios*.]

3. [In its simplest form the Jesus Prayer runs 'Lord Jesus Christ, have mercy on me a sinner'.]

4. [Reference to I. S. Turgenev's prose-poem 'Christ'. See *Poems in Prose in Russian and English*, edited by André Mazon, English translations by Constance Garnett and Roger Rees, Basil Blackwell 1951, pp. 139, 141.]

Select Bibliography

I Works by Alexander Men [Pseudonyms in square brackets]

1. [A. Bogolyubov], *Syn chelovecheskii [The Son of Man]*, Brussels: La Vie avec Dieu 1968.
2. [E. Svetlov], *Istoki religii [The Sources of Religion]*, Brussels: La Vie avec Dieu 1970.
3. [E. Svetlov], *Magizm i edinobozhie [Magism and Monotheism]*, Brussels: La Vie avec Dieu 1971.
4. [E. Svetlov), *U vrat molchaniya [At the Gates of Silence]*, Brussels: La Vie avec Dieu 1971.
5. [E. Svetlov], *Dionisi, Logos, sud'ba [Dionysius, Logos, Fate]*, Brussels: La Vie avec Dieu 1972.
6. (E. Svetlov), *Vestniki tsarstva Bozhiya [Messengers of the Kingdom of God]*, Brussels: La Vie avec Dieu 1972.
7. [E. Svetlov]. *Na poroge Novogo Zaveta [On the Threshold of the New Testament]*, Brussels: La Vie avec Dieu 1983.
   (Nos. 2–7 make up the series *V poiskakh puti, istiny i zhizni [In Search of the Way, the Truth and the Life]*. A new edition, under A. Men's name is being published by Slovo, Moscow 1991 in progress. It includes No. 1 as volume 7.)
8. *Pravoslavnoe bogosluzhenie: tainstvo, slovo, i obraz [Orthodox Worship: Sacrament, Word and Icon]*, Brussels: La Vie avec Dieu, 1980. 2nd edn Moscow: Slovo 1991.
9. *Kak chitat' bibliyu [How to read the Bible]*, Brussels: La Vie avec Dieu 1981.
10. *Radostnaya vest' [Glad Tidings]*, collected papers, Moscow: Vita-tsentr 1991.
11. *Propovedi [Sermons]*, Moscow: Kul'turnoe vozrozhdenie 1991.
12. *Propovedi: Paskhal'nyi tsikl [Sermons: the Easter Cycle]*, Moscow: Kul'turnoe vozrozhdenie 1990.
13. *Prakticheskoe rukovodstvo k molitve [Practical guide to prayer]*, Riga 1991.
14. *Kul'turnoe vozrozhdenie [Cultural Renaissance]*, collected papers, Moscow: Iskusstvo 1992.
15. *Trudnyi put' k dialogu [The Difficult Path to Dialogue]*,

collected papers, Moscow: Raduga 1992. Introduction by Metropolitan Antony of Sourozh.

II Translations

16. Fr Alexander Men, *Awake to Life! The Easter Cycle*, translated by Marite Sapiets, London: The Bowerdean Press 1992. Translation of 12.
17. A. Men, *Les Sources de la Religion*, Paris: Desclée 1991. Translation of 2.
18. Fr Aleksandr Men', 'The 1960s Remembered', *Religion, State & Society*, Vol. 23, No. 2, June 1995, pp. 125–158.

III Works about Fr Alexander Men

19. Yves Hamant, *Alexandre Men: Un Temoin pour la Russie de ce Temps*, Paris: Mame 1993.
20. [English translation of 19] Yves Hamant, *Alexander Men: A Witness for Contemporary Russia (A Man for our Times)*, translated by Fr Steven Bigham, Introduction by Fr Maxym Lysack, Oakwood Publications, Torrance, California 1995.
21. *Pamyati protoiereya Aleksandr Menya [In Memory of Archpriest Alexander Men]*, collected memoirs, Moscow: Rudomino 1991.
22. *I bylo utro [And Morning Came]*, collected memoirs, Moscow: Vita-tsentr 1992.
23. A. I. Zorin, *Angel-chernorabochiy*, Moscow: Progress-Kultura 1993.
24. *Aequinox*. Collection of articles in memory of Fr Alexander Men, Moscow: Carte Blanche 1991. Contains bibliography of 129 titles of Fr Alexander's writings compiled by Ya. G. Krotov.
25. *Vokrug imeni o. Aleksandra Menya*, eds. A. I. Zorin, V. I. Ilyushenko, Moscow: Kul'turnoe vozrozhdenie 1993.

Index

Abraham, call of, 162, 177, 189
Akbar, Mogul emperor
  (1542–1605), 85, 89
Aksakov, Ivan Sergeevich,
  Slavophile (1823–86), 205n
Aksakov, Konstantin Sergeevich,
  Slavophile (1817–60), 205n
Albigensian heresy, 51
Alexi I (Sergei Simansky), patriarch
  (1877–1970), 7, 12
Alexi II (Ridiger), present patriarch,
  169
Alexander the Great (356–23 BC),
  110, 117
Ambrose, St, bishop of Milan
  (c.334–97), 122, 209n
Amvrosy, St, *starets* of Optina
  Pustyn (1812–91), 152
Andropov, Yuri, Soviet leader
  (1914–84) 12, 15
Antichrist, 94
Antiochus IV of Syria, 117
antisemitism, 9, 15, 17, 18, 169–70
apophatic tradition, 39, 45–8, 79,
  93, 200–201n, 204n
Aristotle (384–22 BC), 90,
  205–206n
Armenians, 173
asceticism, 72–3, 103, 154–5, 188
Asvaghosha, Brahmin Buddhist
  (c.AD 80–150), 88, 205n
atheism, 33, 34, 52, 55, 56–61, 63,
  67, 107, 108, 131–2, 135, 143,
  182

Augustine St, of Hippo (354–430),
  86, 145, 159
Augustus, Roman emperor (63
  BC–AD 14),118, 119
avant-garde art, 148–9
Avesta, 78, 204n
Averintsev, S.S., 11
'axial period', 21, 75, 77–82, 88, 90,
  95, 98, 99
Ayatollah Khomeini, 136

Bach, J.S., 54, 80
Barbusse, Henri, author of book on
  Christ (1874–1935),148
Bar-Cochba (2nd c. Jewish leader),
  32, 198n
Barth, Karl, Protestant theologian
  (1886–1968), 64, 102
Basil, St, 'the Great' (c.330–79) 46,
  159
Batu Khan (conqueror of Russia, d.
  1255), 109, 208n
Belinsky, Vissarion Grigorevich,
  radical Westernizer (1811–48),
  158, 211n
Berdyaev, Nicolas (Nikolai) Aleksandrovich, Russian religious
  philosopher (1874–1948), 3, 24,
  35, 52, 59, 64, 75, 76, 90, 94–8,
  103, 145, 157–8, 160, 174, 178,
  198n, 200n, 207n
Bergson, Henri, French philosopher
  (1859–1941), 23, 38, 64
Beria, Lavrentiy Pavlovich, head of

Soviet secret police (1899–1953), 112

Besant, Annie, theosophist (1847–1933), 96

Bhaghvadgita, 30, 89, 204n

Bible, 32, 61, 66, 69, 70, 93, 141, 153

Bible Society in Russia, 17

Bichurin, Iakinf, Russian orientalist (1777–1853), 84, 205n

birth control, 168

Black Hundreds, 18, 198n

Blok, Aleksandr Aleksandrovich, Russian poet (1880–1921), 131, 152

Bloy, Leon, French writer, 63

Boehme, Jacob, German mystic (1575–1624), 52, 201n

Böll, Heinrich, German writer, 63

Bohr, Niels, physicist (1885–1962), 64

Bolshevik government, 3, 128–9, 164

Bolshevik (October) revolution, 130, 132

Bonhoeffer, Dietrich, Lutheran pastor (1905–45), 40–1, 178

Born, Max, physicist (1882–1970), 67

Bradbury, Ray, American writer (b. 1920), 63

Brahmanism, 50, 100, 180

Brahmo Samaj movement, 85, 205n

Breuil, Henri, abbé, palaeontologist (1877–1961), 64

Brezhnev, Leonid Ilyich, Soviet leader (1906–82), 12, 15

Brezhnev period, 13, 15

Britten, Benjamin, composer (1913–76), 54

Buber, Martin, philosopher (1878–1965), 64

Buddha, Siddhartha Gautama (c.563–c.483 BC), 31, 77, 117, 120, 180, 181–2, 188, 206n

Buddhism, 21, 30, 55, 65, 79, 84, 88, 128, 180

Bukharev, Fedor, archimandrite, 19th c. Orthodox writer, 155–6

Bulgakov, Mikhail Afanasyevich, Russian writer (1891–1940), 63, 147–8 *The Master and Margarita*, 147–8, 210n

Bulgakov, Sergi (Sergei Nikolaevich) (1871–1944), priest and theologian, 3, 64, 94, 152, 206n

Bultmann, Rudolf, theologian (1884–1976), 43, 97, 200n, 207n

Byzantium, 61, 103, 126, 127, 209n

Calvin, Jean, reformer (1509–64), 136

Câmara, Helder, archbishop, 178

Camus, Albert, existentialist writer (1913–60), 49, 56, 182

Cantor, Georg, mathematician (1845–1918), 64

Castro, Fidel, Cuban leader, 66

'catacomb' church, 4–5, 7, 8, 197n. *See also* Mariya, Mother; Serafim, Fr; Vasilev, V.A.

Catherine II, the Great, empress of Russia (1729–96), 127

Chaadaev, Petr Yakovlevich, Russian philosopher (1793–1856), 94, 206n

Chagall, Marc, artist (1889–1985), 63

Champollion, Jean François, French Egyptologist (1790–1832), 83

Chechen and Ingush peoples, 211n

Chechnya, war in, 173

Chernyshevsky, Nikolai Gavrilovich, radical thinker (1828–89), 41

Chesterton, G.K., 63, 148

Christ, Jesus, 24, 31, 32, 33, 37, 38, 44, 61, 68, 69, 70, 71, 72, 73, 80, 82, 84, 88, 93, 97, 98, 100, 103,

120, 121, 122, 145, 147, 178,
182, 184–6, 188, 190
Christian art, 30, 71, 76, 103, 137,
143, 149, 161. *See also* icons
Christian church, 70, 71
diversity within, 151–63
historical schisms of, 153
'in diaspora', 202–3n
persecutions of, 60–1, 118, 119
Christian doctrine, 47. *See also*
Trinity, doctrine of; personhood
of God
Christian ethics, 30, 31, 128, 137–8,
143
Christian missionaries, 82–3
Christian Way, 69
Christian world-view, 68, 102
Christianity and world faiths, 20–1,
29, 75–103, 137, 179–81
Christianity as state religion, 121–3
Christianity, uniqueness of, 31, 32,
179–92
Christmas, meaning of, 173–8
Church Fathers, 8, 22, 45, 63, 70,
71, 86, 90, 102, 125, 159, 160
Church of Christ the Saviour,
Moscow, 170, 209n
Claudel, Paul, French writer
(1968–1955), 63
Clausius, R., physicist (1812–88),
201n
Clement, St, of Alexandria
(*c.*150–*c.*215), 90
Communism, causes of, in Russia,
107–8
Comte, Auguste, positivist
(1798–1857), 34, 58, 76, 92
Condorcet, marquis de, philosopher
(1743–94), 140, 210n
confiscation of church property
(1922), *see* Russian Orthodox
Church
Confucius, Chinese philosopher
(551–479 BC), 77, 180
Confucianism, 21

Congar, Yves, French theologian,
64
Constantine, first Christian Roman
emperor (d. 337), 121
consumerism, 175, 178
Coulange, Fustel de, French classi-
cist (1830–89), 116, 208n
Council for Religious Affairs, 7, 15,
132, 209n
Cox, Harvey, theologian, 202n
'cult of personality', 113, 107–38.
See also Stalinism
'Cultural Renaissance' society, 17,
138, 179

Dali, Salvador, artist (1904–89), 63
Danielou, Jean, theologian, 47
Danilevsky, Nikolai Yakovlevich,
Slavophile (1822–85), 86
Dante, 121, 144
The Divine Comedy, 54
Daoism, 48, 79, 88
Darwin, Charles (1809–82), 183
Dawson, Christopher (1889–1970),
75, 90, 98–101, 124, 207n, 208n
'death of God' theology, 200n
Deism, 89, 101, 124
Demetrius Poliorcetes, of
Macedonia (*c.*339–283 BC), 117
democracy, 111, 117–7, 124, 125
in Athens, 116–7
'demythologizers', 39, 43–4, 97,
207n. *See also* Bultmann, Rudolf
Desert Fathers, 160
Deussen, Paul, orientalist
(1845–1919), 84, 204–5n
d'Holbach, baron, French
philosopher, 57
Diderot, Denis, French philosopher
(1713–84), 57, 127
Dobrolyubov, Nikolai Aleksandrovich, radical (1836–61), 41
Dostoevsky, Fedor Mikhailovich
(1822–81), 6, 24, 37, 49, 54, 152,
153, 155, 205n

The Brothers Karamazov, 37, 151, 152, 153, 198–99n

Douroff, Assia, 13

Dudko, Dmitri, priest, 11

dualism, doctrine of, 50–1, 97

ecumenism, 17, 24, 29, 65, 71, 75, 102, 168

Eddington, Sir Arthur, astronomer (1882–1944), 64

Einstein, Albert, physicist (1879–1955), 34, 64

Eliot, T.S., poet (1888–1965), 63

emperor-worship, 114–119. *See also* idolatry

Encyclopaedists, French, 57, 127

Enlightenment, 57, 59, 76, 81, 108

entropy, 50, 201n

Epictetus, Stoic philosopher (*c*.AD 55–135), 31

Epicureans, 176

Epicurus, philosopher (314–270 BC), 31, 176

Erasmus, Desiderius, Christian humanist (1466–1536), 144, 210n

Ermogen, metropolitan, 12

Eremin, Aleksei, secretary to A.M., 195–6

Esenin, Sergei Aleksandrovich (1895–1925), poet, 131, 209n

Eshliman, Nikolai, priest (d. 1985), 11, 211n

eucharist, significance of, 183–4

Eurocentrism, 75, 82–5, 86, 88

evil, problem of, 29, 35, 36, 37, 39, 49–53, 69, 157, 173–8

evolution, theory of, 38, 146, 199n

Evtushenko, Evgeny Aleksandrovich, poet (b. 1933), 112–3, 208n

faith, nature of, 33, 39–41, 69, 73, 113, 183, 189–90, 191, 202n, 203n

fascism in contemporary Russia, 168–9. *See also* 'Pamyat'

Feuchtwanger, Lion, German writer (1884–1958),134, 210n

Filipp, St, metropolitan of Moscow (1507–69), 122, 126, 146, 209n

Florensky, Pavel Aleksandrovich (1882–1937), priest and theologian, 9, 64, 94, 156, 162, 201n, 206n

Foyer Oriental Chrétien, Brussels, 13

Francis of Assisi, St,122, 142

Frank, Semen Lyudvigovich (1877–1950), philosopher, 3, 23, 87, 94, 198n, 206n

Frazer, Sir James, social anthropologist (1854–1941),115, 204n

freedom. *See* human beings

Freud, Sigmund, founder of psychoanalysis (1856–1939), 57, 115

Fromm, Erich, American psychoanalyst (1900–80), 57, 112, 202n

Gagarin, Yury, astronaut, 10

Galich (Aleksandr Arkadyevich Ginzburg), songwriter (1919–77), 14, 197–8n

Gandhi, Mahatma (1869–1949), 65, 110, 178

Genghis Khan, Mongol conqueror (1162–1277), 109, 208n

Ghose, Aurobindo, Indian scholar (1872–1950), 64, 85, 205n

Gnedich, Petr Petrovich, art historian (1855–1925), 76

Gnostics, 51, 90

'God-man', 23–4, 49, 69, 93, 154, 187, 192

'Godmanhood', 23–4, 47, 94, 157, 191–2

Goethe, J.W. v.on, 81
Faust, 42, 62

Gogol, Nikolai Vasilevich
(1809–52), 155, 158, 211n
Taras Bulba, 168, 211n
Golubtsov, Nikolai, priest, 9, 10
Gorbachev, Mikhail Sergeevich,
Soviet leader (b.1931),15, 16,
136, 164, 169
Goya, Francisco, Spanish artist
(1746–1828), 185, 212n
grace, divine, 190
Graham, Billy, American evangelist,
65
Green, Julian, French writer, 63
Greene, Graham, novelist
(1904–91), 63
Gregory, St, theologian, 160
Guardini, Romano, Catholic
theologian, 64
Gulag (Soviet labour camps), 3,
210n
Solovki labour camp, 131

Haeckel, Ernst, naturalist
(1834–1919), 58
Hamant, Yves, biographer of A. M.,
17, 197n
Hamilton, William, theologian, 43,
202n
Hare Krishna, 32
Hegel, G.W.F., philosopher, 47,
82–3, 85
Heisenberg, Werner, physicist
(1901–76), 64
Helmolt, Hans, historian of
religion, 205n
Herder, Johann von, German writer
(1744–1803), 83
Hesse, Hermann, German writer
(1877–1962), 63, 81
Hillary, Edmund, mountaineer, 180
Hinduism, 64, 85
history, Christian attitude towards,
20, 73, 84, 86, 96–8, 100, 146.
See also kingdom of God
Hitler, Adolf, 112

Hobbes, Thomas, (1585–1879),
124
Hocking, William, American
philosopher, 60
Hoffmann, E.T.A., German writer
(1776–1822), 110–1, 208n
Horace, Roman writer, 118
human beings,
need for God, 29–30, 32, 34, 48,
57, 59, 61, 62, 112, 175–8,
181, 188–9
place in nature, 35, 49, 51–2, 57,
78, 79, 80, 92–3, 94, 112, 141,
175, 181
freedom as essential quality of,
24, 35–6, 40, 52, 53, 62, 72,
96, 111–12, 120, 144, 147,
174
humanism, 59–60, 61, 143, 144,
175
Huss, Jan, Bohemian reformer
(d.1415), 122, 209n
Huxley, Julian, biologist
(1887–1975), 58

iconoclast controversy, 209n
icons, Russian, 33, 54, 76. *See also*
Christian art
idolatry, 30, 24, 57, 107–38. *See
also* 'cult of personality'
Indian philosophy, 39, 45, 78, 84,
85, 93
Islam, 55, 59, 65, 78, 82, 85, 126,
128, 180
Ivan IV, the Terrible (1530–84),
126, 146
Ivanov, Vyacheslav, Russian poet
and philosopher (1886–1949),
94, 206n

Jainism, 78
James, William, American
philosopher (1842–1910), 201n
Jaspers, Karl, existentialist
(1883–1969), 21, 64, 77–82, 88,

90, 91, 98, 101, 102, 204n

Jeans, Sir James, astrophysicist (1877–1946), 64

'Jesus Prayer', 188, 212n

Jews, 96, 107, 121, 128, 141, 170

Job, book of, 49

John XXIII, pope (1881–1963), 65

John the Baptist, 177

John Chrysostom, St (347–407), 122, 159, 209n

John of Damascus, St (675–c.749), 46, 206n

John Paul II, pope, 168

Jordan, Pascual, scientist, 64

Journal of the Moscow Patriarchate, 9, 19

Judaism, 64, 82, 187

Julius Caesar, 110, 118

Jung, Carl, psychologist (1875–1961), 64

Justin Martyr, Christian apologist (c.100–c.165), 90

Kafka, Franz, writer (1883–1924), 63

Kaganovich, Lazar Moiseevich, Soviet leader (1895–1987), 170, 211n

Kalinin, M.I., Soviet leader (1875–1946), 134

Kant, Immanuel, philosopher (1724–1804), 8, 81

Karabakh. *See* Nagorno-Karabakh

Karlovci synod. *See* Russian Orthodox Church Abroad

Kelvin, W.T., physicist (1824–1907), 201n

kenosis, 52, 201n

Kepler, Johannes, astronomer (1571–1630), 63

KGB, Soviet secret police, 11, 12, 15, 165

Kharchev, Konstantin, head of Council for Religious Affairs, 132, 209n

Khmer Rouge, 208n

Khomyakov, Aleksei Stepanovich, Slavophile (1804–60), 152, 205n, 210n

Khrushchev, Nikita Sergeevich, Soviet leader (1894–1971), 10, 136

anti-religious campaign, 10, 11–12, 54, 136

Kierkegaard, Sören, philosopher (1813–55), 54

King, Martin Luther, civil rights leader (1929–68), 65, 146, 178

kingdom of God, 73, 74, 98, 125, 146, 181. *See also* history, Christian attitude to

Kireevsky, Ivan Vasilevich, Slavophile (1806–56), 152, 205n, 210n

Kolbe, Fr Maximilian, Polish priest (1894–1941), 41

Krishnamurti, Jiddu, Indian theosophist (1895–1986), 43, 44

Krylov, Ivan, Russian fabulist (1769–1844), 'The Quartet', 142, 210n

Lamennais, F.R. de, French writer (1782–1854), 125, 209n

Lao Zi, Chinese philosopher (4th c. BC), 79, 117, 180, 186

Laws of Manu, 204n

Lenin, Vladimir Ilyich, Bolshevik leader (1870–1924), 107, 110, 128, 129, 134

Leonardo da Vinci, 80

Leontyev, Konstantin Nikolaevich, Russian thinker (1831–91), 152, 210n

Leskov, Nikolai Semenovich, Russian writer (1831–95), 155, 158
Cathedral Folk, 127, 209n

Lessing, Gotthold, German writer (1729–81), 51

Levitin-Krasnov, Anatoly, writer on church affairs, 11, 12

Lévy-Bruhl, Lucien, ethnographer (1857–1939), 114

Lewis, C.S. (1898–1963), 62, 63

Logos, 49, 53, 90

Lossky, Vladimir, Russian theologian (1903–58), 64

Machiavelli, Niccolo (1469–1525), 123–4

magism (magic beliefs), 78–9, 80, 115, 204n

Mahabharata, 30, 78, 79

Mandelshtam, Nadezhda Yakovlevna (1899–1980), 14

'Man-god', 202n

Manichaean heresy, 51, 90

Mann, Thomas, German novelist (1875–1955), 63

Mao Tse-tung, Chinese communist leader (1893–1976), 34, 111

Maoism, 30

Marchais, Georges, French communist, 66

Maria, Mother, Skobtsova, (1891–1945), 41, 199n

Maritain, Jacques, French Thomist philosopher (1882–1973), 64

Mariya, Mother, abbess of clandestine community, 5–6, 7, 8–9, 197n

'Maroseikans' (parishioners of St Nicholas on Maroseika street), 5, 8, 9, 10

marriage, Christian, 72

Martin, pope, (d. 655), 122, 209n

Marx, Karl, 54

materialism, 36, 58, 78, 156, 175, 178

Mauriac, François, French novelist (1885–1970), 63

Maxim the Greek, Russian church leader (c.1470–c.1556), 122, 209n

Maximus, the Confessor, St, (580–662), 45, 122, 209n

Mechev, Aleksei, priest, 8

Mechev, Sergei Alekseevich, priest, 8

'Memorial' society, 138, 210n

Men, Aleksandr Vladimirovich (1935–1990), priest
childhood and youth, 3–9
baptism, 5
education, 7–10
student at Institute of Fur, 9–10
marriage, 10
ordination, 10
deacon at Akulovo, 10
parish priest at Alabino, 10–12
parish priest at Tarasovka, 12–13
parish priest at Novaya Derevnya, 14–19
work with intelligentsia, 11, 12, 13, 14, 19, 76
public lectures, 16–17
attitude to *perestroika*, 16
attitude to work, 17–18, 22
prayer life, 18
antagonism towards, 22, 38
death, 19, 195
influences on, 23–4
work on dictionary of the Bible, 22
Publications: *The Son of Man*, 13, 19–20
   In Search of the Way, the Truth and the Life, 13, 20
   Sources of Religion, 21, 39, 54
   Magic and Monotheism, 21, 204n
   At the Gates of Silence, 21–22
   Dionysius, Logos and Fate, 22
   Messengers of the Kingdom of God, 22
   On the Threshhold of the New Testament, 13, 22
   How to read the Bible, 13
   Heaven on Earth, 13

Men, Elena Semenova (née Zupersein) (mother), 4, 197n
Men, Irina Aleksandrovna (daughter), 10
Men, Natalya Fedorovna (née Grigorenko) (wife), 2, 10
Men, Pavel Aleksandrovich (son), 4, 5
Men, Vladimir Grigorevich (father) (1908–69), 4
Merezhkovsky, Dmitri Sergeevich, Russian writer (1865–1941), 94, 206n
Michelangelo, 80
Millas, O., Chilean communist, 66
millennium of Christianity in Russia (1988), 15–16, 137, 166
Mirandola, Pico della (1463–94), 144, 210n
Mithridates VI of Pontus, 117
monasticism, 72, 160, 203n
Moses, 36, 141–42, 184, 188
Mozart, Wolfgang Amadeus, 81
Müller, Max, orientalist (1823–1900), 81, 84, 204n
    Sacred Books of the East, 84
Müntzer, Thomas, Anabaptist leader of Peasants' revolt (1490–1525), 54
Muhammad, 31, 32, 120, 180, 188

Nagorno-Karabakh, war in, 173
Napoleon, 110, 132
Naram-Suene (Mesopotamian ruler), 114
'Narodnik' movement, in Russia in 1870s, 202n
nature, human place in. *See* human beings
Nektary, *starets* of Optina Pustyn (d. 1928), 6, 210n
Nestor the Chronicler, Kievan monk (c.1056–1112), 86, 205n
'new Russian martyrs', 178, 211n
Newton, Isaac, 63

Nicolas de Cusa (Cusanus) (1401–64), 45
Niebuhr, Reinhold, American theologian (1892–1971), 64
Nietzsche, Friedrich, 55–6, 115
Nikitin, Afanasy, 15th c. Russian traveller, 82, 204n
Nikon, patriarch (1605–81), 126
Nobili, Roberto di, missionary (1577–1656), 83
'non-possessors', 122, 209n
Novalis, German poet (1772–1801), 35
Novgorod, republic of, 61

October revolution. *See* Bolshevik revolution
Old Believers, 127, 128
Old Testament, 30, 45, 51, 69, 71, 82, 90, 93, 95, 96, 97, 115, 116, 119, 162, 183
Optina Pustyn (Optino), monastery, 6, 151, 152–53, 197n, 210n
Origen (c.185–254), 45

paganism, 75, 82, 83, 89, 90, 92, 95, 96, 121, 146
'Pamyat' (neo-Fascist organization), 168, 211n. *See also* Fascism in Russia
pantheism, 48, 180
Papini, Giovanni, Italian writer, 63
Pasternak, Boris Leonidovich, Russian writer (1890–1960), 63
Pasteur, Louis, French scientist (1822–95), 63
patriarchate, Moscow, abolished, 126; restored, 3
Paul, St, 35, 44, 46, 51, 67, 72, 73, 90, 119, 120, 121, 141, 147, 186–7, 189, 191
Pavlovich, Nadezhda Aleksandrovna, poet and theologian (1895–1980), 152, 210n

Péguy, Charles, French writer
(1873–1914), 63
perestroika, 16, 18, 136, 139
personhood of God, 48–9, 96, 103.
  See also Christian doctrines
Pestov, Nikolai Evgrafovich
(1892–1978), 8
Peter the Great, emperor of Russia,
108, 167
  church reforms of, *see* Russian
  Orthodox Church
Peter, St, 119
Pfleiderer, Otto, German theolog-
ian, 40, 199n
Pflügk-Hartung, Julius von, histo-
rian of religions, 205n
Pharisees, 31, 161, 177, 187
Phariseeism, 145
Philo of Alexandria, (*c.* 20 BC–*c.*
AD 50), 22
Philokalia, 160, 211n
Pimen, patriarch (Izvekov)
(1917–90), 16, 136
Pinochet, dictator of Chile, 112
Plank, Max, scientist (1858–1947),
64
Plato, 21, 45, 54, 79, 90, 176, 180,
188, 205n
Platonism, 45
Platonov, Andrei, Russian writer
(1899–1951), 131, 209n
Plutarch, Roman writer, 89
Pol Pot, leader of Khmer Rouge,
111, 208n
positivism, 91, 156
Posnoff, Irene, 13
Progress, belief in, 101, 125, 140
proofs of the existence of God, 35,
40
prophets, Israelite, 77, 79, 80, 93,
96, 100, 117, 120, 122, 141, 146,
183
Protestantism, 65, 153, 162
Pseudo-Dionysius, the Areopagite,
45

Ptolemy I of Egypt, 117
Pugachev, Emelyan Ivanovich,
leader of popular revolt
(1726–75), 127, 209n
Pushkin, Aleksandr Sergeevich,
poet, (1799–1837), 25, 127, 155,
181, 209n

racism, 58. *See also* antisemitism
Radhakrishnan, Sarvepali, Indian
philosopher and statesman
(1888–1975), 46, 81, 102
Radzhikovsky, Leonid, psychologist, 112
Rahner, Karl, theologian, 64, 199n
Ramakrishna, Hindu teacher
(1834–86), 85, 205n
Raphael, 80
Renovationist schism. *See* Russian
Orthodox church
reason, human, 46–7, 57, 100, 124
Reformation, 55, 123
religion and science, 63–4, 73, 76,
101, 125
religion, objections to, 32, 33–4, 42,
55. *See also* atheism; evil, problem of
religious language, 41–4, 46, 47
religious symbolism, 41–4, 47
Rembrandt, 80
Renaissance, 59, 61, 80, 81, 123,
143, 144
repentance, 141, 142
Ricci, Matteo, missionary
(1552–1610), 83
Rig-Veda, 205n
Rilke, Rainer Maria, poet
(1875–1926), 63
Robespierre, Maximilien, French
revolutionary leader, 132
Robinson, John, Anglican bishop,
65, 200n, 202n, 203n
Rodzianko, Vasily, bishop, 200n
Roerich, Nikolai, Russian painter
(1874–1947), 63

Roman Catholicism in Russia, 128, 130, 167, 168

Romm, Mikhail Ilyich, Soviet film director (1901–71)
Ordinary Fascism, 111, 208n

Rose, Serafim, monk of ROCA (d. 1979), 102

Rosenberg, Albert, Nazi ideologist, 58

Rouault, Georges, French artist (1871–1958), 63

Roy, Ram Mohan, Indian religious reformer (1772–1833), 85, 205n

Rublev, Andrei, icon-painter (c.1360–1430), 33, 122, 177, 185, 198n
The Trinity, 177, 185, 198n

Rus, baptism of, 16

Russian culture, 139–50, 158

Russian history, 126–32

Russian Orthodox Church, 3, 65, 68, 126–28, 136, 151, 158, 164–70
in Russian history, 126
reforms of Peter the Great, 108, 126
'synodal period' of, 3, 108, 126, 127,
restoration of patriarchate (1917), 3
Renovationist schism in, 3, 130
confiscation of church valuables, 3, 130, 209n
persecution of, under communism, 3, 4, 101, 130–1, 132–3, 165
restored by Stalin (1943), 7, 130
two traditions within, 151–163
conservatism in, 164–65, 167, 168
liberals in, 165
nationalism in, 166, 167, 168
See also catacomb church; 'new Russian martyrs'; Khrushchev campaign

Russian Orthodox Church Abroad (Karlovci synod), 3, 102, 129, 166, 167, 211n

Russian religious philosophers, 8, 147

Russian religious renaissance (early 20th c.), 3, 108

Russo-Japanese war (1905), 128

sacraments, 70. *See also* eucharist

Saint Exupéry, Antoine de, French writer (1900–44), 63

Sakharov, Andrei, physicist and human rights leader (1921–89), 12, 15, 210n

Salinger, J.D., American novelist, 63, 81

Sartre, Jean Paul, existentialist (1905–80), 182

Satan, 51

Savanarola, Girolamo, religious reformer (d.1498), 54, 122, 144, 209n

Schelling, Friedrich, German philosopher (1775–1854), 84, 91, 206n

Schleiermacher, Friedrich, German theologian (1768–1834), 103

Schmidt, P.W., ethnographer, 64, 206n

Schrödinger, Erwin, physicist (1887–1961), 64

Schopenhauer, Arthur, German philosopher (1788–1860), 81, 84, 91

Schwann, Theodor, German physiologist (1810–82), 64

Schweitzer, Albert, physician and theologian (1875–1965), 81, 199–200n

Science and Religion (atheist journal), 10

Second Vatican Council (1962–65), 65

secularism, 61, 63, 100, 144

secular state, advantages of,
123–26, 128–29, 136–38
Seneca, Roman philosopher (*c.*4
BC–AD 65), 31, 40
Serafim, Fr (Sergei Batyukov), cata-
comb priest (1880–1942), 4–5,
6, 8, 9, 197n
Serafim, S., of Sarov (1759–1833),
5
Sergi, metropolitan, later patriarch
(Sergei Stragorodsky) (d. 1945),
4, 5, 7, 130
declaration of loyalty to Soviet
state (1927), 4
Sergius, St, of Radonezh
(*c.*1315–92), 5, 142, 210n
Shakespeare, William, 80, 210n
Shankara, Vedantist (AD
788–820), 88, 205n
Shaumyan, L.S., philosopher, 114
Siluan, St, Russian Athonite monk
(1866–1938), 178, 211n
Slavophilism, 86, 205n
Socrates, 97, 180, 182
Solovyev, Vladimir Sergeevich,
Russian philosopher and
theologian (1853–1900), 6, 8,
20, 23–4, 51–2, 75, 90–4, 145,
152, 156–57, 201n, 206n
Publications: *Crisis of Western
Philosophy,* 91
Lectures on Godmanhood, 92,
156
*Russia and the Universal
Church,* 92
Three Conversations, 94
A Solovyov Anthology, 198n
See also God-man; Godmanhood
Solzhenitsyn, Aleksandr Isaevich,
Russian writer (b.1918), 12, 13,
63
Sorokin, Pitirim, sociologist
(1889–1968), 88, 143, 210n
Spengler, Oswald, German writer
(1880–1936), 86–7

The Decline of the West, 86–7,
203n, 205n
Spinoza, philosopher (1632–77),
81
Stalin, Joseph Vissarionovich
(Dzhugashvili) (1879–1953), 7,
9, 107, 109, 110–11, 132–4, 135
persecution of the church by, 3,
4, 130–31, 132–33
recreates the church in 1943, 7,
133
Stalinism, 30, 108, 109–11, 113
Stalin-worship, 132–36
starets/startsy (spiritual guide/s), 6,
15, 152–53
Stefany, metropolitan, 10
Steiner, Rudolf, anthroposophist
(1861–1928), 96
Stoic philosophers, 30, 31, 97
Suetonius, Roman writer (AD
75–160)
Lives of the Twelve Caesars, 141
Suvorov, Aleksandr Vasilevich,
Russian general (1730–1800),
110
Synod of Oak (AD 403), 209n
'synodal period'. *See* Russian
Orthodox Church

Taizé community, 66
Tareev, Mikhail, Russian theolog-
ian (1866–1934), 145
Tarkovsky, Andrei, film director
(1932–86)
Andrei Rublev, 185, 212n
Tatar yoke (period of Mongol
domination of Russia), 126
Tatian, Christian apologist (b.
*c.*120), 90
Teilhard de Chardin, Pierre,
theologian and scientist
(1881–1955), 64, 178
Tensing, Sherpa, mountaineer,
180–81
Teresa, Mother, of Calcutta, 178

Tertullian, theologian (*c.*160–
  *c.*225), 90
theosophy, 89, 96, 98
Tiberius, Roman emperor, 118, 119
Tikhon, patriarch (Vasily Ivanovich
  Belavin) (1866–1925), 3, 4, 129,
  130
Tillich, Paul, theologian
  (1886–1965), 43, 64, 200n
Timiryazev, K.A., Russian Darwin-
  ist (1843–1920), 199n
Tolstoy, Lev Nikolaevich, novelist
  (1828–1910), 6, 81, 152, 155,
  156
Tolstoyans, 130
Townes, Charles, American physicist, 64
Toynbee, Arnold, British historian
  (1899–1975), 55, 64, 87, 89,
  101, 102, 144
Trinity, doctrine of, 44, 47, 69
Trubetzkoi, Evgeny Nikolaevich,
  prince, philosopher (1863–
  1920), 94, 206n
Trud (Labour), journal, 15
Tsongkhapa, Tibetan lama
  (1357–1419), 88, 205n
Turgenev, Ivan Sergeevich, Russian
  novelist (1818–83), 188, 212n
Twentieth Party Congress (1956),
  10
Tyutchev, Fedor Ivanovich, poet
  (1803–73), 43

Upanishads, 45, 48, 50, 78, 79,
  180
Updike, John, American writer, 63
utilitarian ethics, 199n

Vasiliev, Boris Aleksandrovich,
  catacomb priest, historian
  (1899–1976), 8
Vasilevskaya, Vera Yakovlevna,

cousin of A.M.'s mother, 4, 5,
  197n
Vedantic teaching, 88, 89
Vedernikov, Anatoly V., editor of
  Journal of Moscow Patriarchate,
  9
Venyamin, metropolitan of Petro-
  grad (d. 1922), 209n
Vinogradov, Aleksi (Aleksandr
  Nikolaevich) (1845–1919), Rus-
  sian orientalist, 84, 205n
Virgil, Roman poet, 118
Vivekananda, Devi, Hindu thinker
  (1863–1902), 85, 205n
Vladimir, prince of Kiev, 'the
  baptizer' (956–1015), 16

Waugh, Evelyn, British writer, 63
Wells, H.G., British writer, 87
Whitehead, A.N., philosopher
  (1861–1947), 64
Wiener, Norbert, founder of
  cybernetics (1894–1964), 50,
  201n
Wilkerson, David, American evan-
  gelist, 199n
World Council of Churches, 65

Yeltsin, Boris, 193
Yakunin, Gleb, priest, 9, 11, 12, 15,
  211n
Yakunin-Eshliman letter (1966), 12,
  197n
Zarathustra (Zoroaster), founder of
  Zoroastrianism, 21, 51, 77, 117
Zavadskaya, Evgeniya, orientalist,
  11–12
Zen, 65
Zheludkov, Sergei, priest (d.1984),
  37, 199n
Zhuang Zi, Chinese philosopher (*c.*
  400–300 BC), 79
Zoroastrianism, 85, 96